FILM LANGUAGE

FILM LANGUAGE

A Semiotics of the Cinema

Christian Metz

Translated by Michael Taylor

The University of Chicago Press

Published by arrangement with Oxford University Press, Inc.

The University of Chicago Press, Chicago 60637
© 1974 by Oxford University Press, Inc.
All rights reserved. English translation. Originally published 1974
Note on Translation © 1991 by the University of Chicago
University of Chicago Press edition 1991
Printed in the United States of America

09 08 07   6 7 8 9 10

Library of Congress Cataloging-in-Publication Data

Metz, Christian.
    [Essais sur la signification au cinéma. English]
    Film language : a semiotics of the cinema / Christian Metz :
    translated by Michael Taylor.
        p.   cm.
    Translation of: Essais sur la signification au cinéma, tome 1.
    Reprint. Originally published: New York : Oxford University
    Press, 1974.
    Includes bibliographical references.
    ISBN 0-226-52130-3 (pbk.)
    1. Motion pictures—Semiotics.   2. Motion pictures—
    Philosophy. I. Title.
PN1995.M4513   1991
791.43'014—dc20   90-46965
                                                  CIP

The French edition of Christian Metz's *Essais sur la signification
au cinéma,* volume 1, was published by Editions Klincksieck in
1971, © Editions Klincksieck, 1968.

∞ The paper used in this publication meets the minimum
requirements of the American National Standard for Information
Sciences–Permanence of Paper for Printed Library Materials,
ANSI Z39.48–1992.

To Georges Blin, Professor at the Collège de France, without whom none of these pages would have been started.

CONTENTS

A Note on the Translation
by Bertrand Augst

When *Film Language* was translated, nearly twenty years ago, very few texts about semiotics and especially film semiotics were available in English. Michael Taylor's translation represents a serious effort to make Metz's complicated prose, filled with specialized vocabularies, accessible to a public unfamiliar with the concepts and terms of semiotics. Excepting the inadequate translation of a few words which either cannot be translated into English or only approximately translated, few semantic and stylistic improvements are needed and the translation does justice to Metz's text. In some instances, usage did not adopt Michael Taylor's solution. The most glaring example of his innovative translation is the word "significate" —now usually translated by "signified" (*signifié* in French)—which is used throughout the text. *Langue* and *parole* have increasingly been translated by "language" and "speech," although this is not an ideal solution. *Découper*, translated by Taylor in a number of ways ("break up," "break down analysis," etc.), would more easily be translated by "segmenting" when used in the linguistic sense, and by *découpage* when used to describe the final stage of a shooting script. Michael Taylor also coined the expression "mirror construction" to translate *construction en abîme*, to describe embedded narrative structures like a film within a film. This is not really very accurate but I have not found any solution better than "embedded structure"; see his explanation on page 230. "Single shot sequence" is usually used to translate *plan sequence* rather than "shot sequence." Similarly "dolly in" and "dolly out" are used rather than "forward" and "rear." *Mise en scène* is also retained in its filmic use, while "staging" is used to describe a stage production. The term *constantif*, which Metz borrowed from Austin, should be rendered by "constative" and not by "ascertaining" (p. 25). Finally, "actor" to translate Greimas's concept of *actant* is misleading and *actant* is usually kept (see Ducrôt and Todorov, *Encyclopedic Dictionary of the Sciences of Language*, Johns Hopkins University Press, 1979, p. 224), and *discours image* when translated as "image discourse" is not very clear, since it is referring to film, which is made up of images.

The following rough spots occur only once each: "Unusual" (p. 5) translates weakly *insolite*, which has also the connotation of strange, disquieting, surprising, unexpected, and uncanny. A "slice of cinema" (p. 14) would be preferable to a "piece of cinema." "Narrative agency" rather than "instance"; "de-realization" or "de-realizing" rather than "unrealizing." "A seminal concept" (p. 58) doesn't really render *une notion gigogne* (again the idea of embedded concepts). The title of Lang's film which is translated by *The Damned* is actually *M*. "Signifying statements" should be "semenes" (p. 26). I have not found an English equivalent for *mise en grilles*, which refers to a gridlike breakdown of linguistic units and which Taylor translates by "pigeon-holing" (p. 35).

1990

Preface

This book is divided into four sections, and it groups ten chapters corresponding to twelve previously published articles. The disparity between ten and twelve is caused by the fact that Chapter 5 was condensed out of three separate articles. As the title indicates, the articles included in this volume have been selected exclusively from the author's writings on cinematographic problems.*

Since this is, therefore, a collection, I have not tried to eliminate or disguise the few inevitable repetitions. Similarly, I have not allowed myself to excise or replace passages that, as a result of the lapse in time between their original publication and the printing of this volume, have become obsolete and no longer correspond to the present state of my investigations.** Thus, in the case of partial changes in my orientation, or simply of new developments, or even when recent contributions to the field by other authors had to be accounted for, I have preferred to "update" merely by adding notes (rather long ones when necessary) instead of modifying the original texts.†

* Originally published in French under the title *Essais sur la signification au cinema*—TRANSLATOR.

** Except in one case, where the repetitive passage was too long and was removed, the reader being informed of this deletion in a footnote.

† It is principally in Chapters 3, 4, and 6 that the reader will encounter these rather exhaustive notes. This is especially true of Chapter 3, "The Cinema: Language or Language System?" which is the earliest of the articles reprinted

On the other hand, I have allowed myself to make various minor corrections and adjustments in wording, for the purpose of clarification.

The exception is Chapter 5, "Problems of Denotation in the Fiction Film." I have taken this opportunity to bring together (and to add to considerably) three earlier articles bearing on related topics, but each one giving only a partial treatment (furthermore, there were certain discrepancies among the articles). This chapter has, therefore, not heretofore been published in its present form, although many of the passages in it have been published.

In attempting to improve the phrasing of the original articles, in adding notes wherever necessary to account for more recent developments, and, finally, in striving, in Chapter 5, to give a general and current description of the main problems at issue, my goal has been, in the still new and developing field of film semiotics, to present the reader with a work as coherent and up-to-date as its nature permits.

I wish to express my thanks to the five publications in which the texts that make up this volume originally appeared: *Revue d'esthetique, La Linguistique, Cahiers du cinéma, Image et son,* and *Communications,* as well as to the Centre d'Étude des Communications de Masse (École Pratique des Hautes Études, Paris) which publishes *Communications,* the Polish Academy of Sciences, which organized the international symposium where one of the papers that constitute Chapter 5 was first read, and the Festival of the New Cinema (Pesaro, Italy), which organized the round-table discussion during which the last chapter in this volume was originally presented.

The idea of bringing together a number of my essays in a single volume, thus making them more easily available, originated with Mikel Dufrenne, Professor at the University of Paris-Nanterre and editor of the series in which this work was published in French. He has my very warm gratitude.

C.M.

Cannes
August 1967

---

here. On two or three definite and important points, this text no longer corresponds to the present state of the problems it confronts. I have taken this opportunity to clarify it and place it in perspective by means of footnotes, for the method and the structure of this program text will perhaps let it reveal, in a more sensitive and less technical way than elsewhere, the nature of the semiological enterprise as it confronts a new field.

A Note on Terminology

The special terminology of European semiotics and structural linguistics may be unfamiliar to many American readers. It is impossible to give full definitions of all the terms that occur in this book without discussing the theories behind them at considerable length. It is hoped, simply, that the following explanations will give the reader a basic orientation. To accomplish this, references are provided to the key theoretical passages in the fundamental writings of linguistics and semiotics from which the author has drawn, and to which he refers frequently.

A fountainhead of semiotics and structural linguistics is Ferdinand de Saussure's *Course in General Linguistics* (Translated by Wade Baskin. Philosophical Library: New York, 1959). The terms *language* and *language system* (see especially Chapter 3 of this volume) translate de Saussure's crucial distinction between *langage* and *langue*. Language (*langage*) indicates language in general, that is, the human linguistic capacity. It is the universal category that contains the myriad specific instances of language system (*langue*): French, English, Urdu, but in addition, those other "languages" of chess, of heraldry, of computers, etc. *Speech* (parole) is the antithesis, or, rather, correlative, of language system: language system is the social aspect of language, whereas speech is the utterance, the actual practice, of a language system. (See de Saussure, *Course*, pp. 7–17.) De Saussure saw the linguistic sign as a unit of relation between a signifier (*signifiant*) and what it "signifies," or conveys, the significate (*signifié*).* Signs (or units of relation) are related to other signs *syntagmatically* or *paradigmatically*: Syntagmatic relations are those which exist among the actual (or "present") elements of a statement, and paradigmatic (or associative) relations are those which occur among the potential (or "absent") elements of a statement (those elements which might have been but were not actually selected). A *syntagma* is, consequently, a unit of actual relationship, while a *paradigm* is a unit of potential relationship. The *large syntagmatic category* (*la grande syntagmatique*—Metz's own term) is the organization of the major actual relationships among units of relation in a given semiological system (these relations may be potential ones, but they are not paradigmatic, because they are actualized in analysis).

The work of the contemporary French linguist André Martinet provides the author with more methodological concepts (see *Elements of General Linguistics*, translated by Elizabeth Palmer. London: Faber & Faber, 1960; also, *A Functional View of Language*, Oxford University Press, New York, 1962). Especially important is Martinet's theory of *double articulation*, according to which the potentially unlimited number of linguistic statements a language system may express is derived from a "few thousand . . . freely combinable" minimal lexicogrammatical units called *monemes* (first articulation), which, in turn, derive from a very small number of "units of a different type," the phonemes (second articulation; see *Elements*, Chapter 1, Sections 8–14). The first articulation involves both the signifier (or expression) and the significate (or content) of the linguistic unit, but the second articulation can affect only the signifier of its corresponding unit. Monemes may be "lexical" or "grammatical." The sentence "We are working" contains four monemes; the word "working" is constituted of the "lexical" moneme (or *semanteme*, or, as Mar-

---

* De Saussure's translator used the terms "signifier/signified." The translator of André Martinet's *Éléments de linguistique générale* prefers "significans/significatum." My justification for introducing yet another variation is that *significate*, with the exact meaning of "that which is signified," already exists in English (see the OED), and it possesses the advantage that its ending emphasizes its inherent difference from the other term of the dichotomy, *signifier*.

tinet prefers to call it, *lexeme*) "work" and the "grammatical" moneme "-ing" (Chapter 1, Section 9).

Commutation, a concept the author borrows from the Danish linguist Louis Hjelmslev (*Prolegomena to a Theory of Language*, translated by Francis J. Whitfield. Madison: University of Wisconsin
Press, 1961, pp. 73–75), is a relation between "a correlation in one
plane . . . and a correlation in the other plane of language" (73).
More specifically it is "mutation between the members (i.e., components) of a paradigm" (p. 135), where mutation is the "function existing between first-degree derivates (components) of one and the
same class, a function that has relation to a function between other
first-degree derivates of . . . the same class" (p. 134).*

Other Terms

HAPAX: A unique determination.

DIEGESIS: Not in the vocabulary of linguistics or semiotics, the term
was coined by the French writer Étienne Souriau to indicate the denotative material of a film. (See Chapter 4 in this volume, pp. 97 ff.)

SEME: A basic semiological concept variously defined in the writings
of the French semanticists Bernard Pottier, Émile Beneveniste, and
Algirdas Greimas. Greimas sees it as a "property" of a lexeme, where
the meaning of that lexeme is a function of the lexeme's "semic integrity" (ensemble semique), i.e., the totality of its constituent semes.
For example, the lexical sense of the English word "girl" derives from
at least two semes: *young* and *female person*. (See Greimas, *Semantique structurale*, Paris, 1966, especially p. 27.)

In different contexts, the lexeme "girl" will have different meanings (a "little girl," a "young girl," etc.), or, to put it in Greimas's
terms, various "contextual semes" accrete around a "semic nucleus"

---

* For Christian Metz, establishing a correlation (which appears to be what
he means when he uses the term "commutation") is methodologically related to
the identification of a *relevant feature* (*trait pertinent*), i.e., the concrete feature, or quality, of a given linguistic or semiological component distinguishing
that component from the set of components identical to it in all respects save one:
they do not possess the revelant feature. Consequently, identification of the
relevant feature results in the establishment of a new, unique, objective category.

xvi A NOTE ON TERMINOLOGY

(noyeau semique) and are, therefore, semantic variables (compare with Émile Beneveniste's "extrinsic" semes). The new integrity of semic nucleus plus contextual seme(s) constitutes a *sememe*. (Note that in the terminology of the American linguist Leonard Bloomfield, a sememe is the significate of a morpheme. Metz, however, is clearly referring to Greimas, not to Bloomfield.)

SEMEME: *See* Seme.

TAXEME: In the terminology of Louis Hjelmslev, a taxeme is the last determination made on the basis of selection. In other words, it is a minimal unit.

WRITING: The term (*écriture* in French) is borrowed from the French critic and semiologist Roland Barthe (*Writing Degree Zero*, translated by A. Lavers, London, 1967), who uses it to indicate the presence of the interaction between an author and the society he writes in and for, and which is neither literary idiom nor literary style. "Within any literary form there is a general choice of tone, of ethos . . . and there is precisely where the writer shows himself clearly as an individual because this is where he commits himself" (p. 19). Thus, writing is the "tone, delivery, purpose, ethos and naturalness" of a writer's "expression" (p. 21); it is "essentially the morality of form, the choice of that social area within which the writer elects to situate the Nature of his language" (p. 21).

M.T.

FILM LANGUAGE

I PHENOMENOLOGICAL
APPROACHES TO FILM

1 On the Impression of Reality in the Cinema

In the days when the cinema was a novel and astonishing thing and its very existence seemed problematical, the literature of cinematography tended to be theoretical and fundamental. It was the age of Delluc, Epstein, Balázs, Eisenstein . . . Every film critic was something of a theoretician, a "filmologist." Today, we tend to smile at this attitude; at any rate we believe, more or less surely, that the criticism of individual films states all there is to be said about film in general. And certainly the criticism of films—or, better yet, their analysis—is an enterprise of utmost importance: it is the film-makers who create the art of the cinema; it is through reflection on those individual films we have liked (or those we have disliked) that we have gained insights into the art of the film in general. Still, there are other approaches. Cinema is a vast subject, and there are more ways than one to enter it. Taken as a whole, it is first of all a *fact*, and as such it raises problems of aesthetics, of sociology, and of semiotics, as well as of the psychologies of perception and intellection. Whether good or bad, each film is, first of all, a *piece of cinema* (in the way that one speaks of a piece of music). As an anthropological fact, the cinema has a certain configuration, certain fixed structures and figures, which deserve to be studied directly. In its broadest sense, the fact of film is too often taken for granted—yet there is so much that remains to be said about it. As Edgar Morin has written, the sense of wonder at the cinema has given us some of the most meaningful works devoted to the seventh art.

One of the most important of the many problems in film theory is that of the *impression of reality* experienced by the spectator. Films give us the feeling that we are witnessing an almost real spectacle—to a much greater extent, as Albert Laffay has noted, than does a novel, a play, or a figurative painting.[1]* Films release a mechanism of affective and perceptual *participation* in the spectator (one is almost never totally bored by a movie). They spontaneously appeal to his sense of belief—never, of course, entirely, but more intensely than do the other arts, and occasionally films are, even in the absolute, very convincing. They speak to us with the accents of true evidence, using the argument that "It is so." With ease they make the kind of statements a linguist would call fully assertive and which, moreover, are usually taken at face value. There is a filmic mode, which is the mode of presence, and to a great extent it is *believable*. More than the latest play or novel, a film, with its "impression of reality," its very direct hold on perception, has the power to draw crowds. We know that André Bazin attached great importance to this popularity of the art of motion pictures.[2] Although it is by no means rare for an excellent film to be a commercial failure, by and large the cinema—even in its "advanced" or experimental forms—commands a large audience. Can as much be said for the other arts of our time? Can one really speak of an audience, in the full sense of the word, when referring to the narrow circles of the initiates of abstract painting, serial music, modern jazz, or the French *nouveau roman*—small groups of the enlightened which have little in common with even the cultivated layer of society (not to mention the mass) and which, furthermore, consist mostly of the creative artist's "accomplices," whether known or unknown to him, his peers, and his real or potential colleagues? A following does not become an audience until there

---

* Superscript numerals refer to the References, which follow the text.

is at least a minimum numerical and sociocultural difference between the creators and the spectators.

The reason why cinema can bridge the gap between true art and the general public, in large part anyway, and why film-makers are able to speak for others, and not just for their friends (or for those who might be their friends), is that films have the *appeal* of a presence and of a proximity that strikes the masses and fills the movie theaters. This phenomenon, which is related to the impression of reality, is naturally of great aesthetic significance, but its basis is first of all psychological. The feeling of credibility, which is so direct, operates on us in films of the unusual and of the marvelous, as well as in those that are "realistic." Fantastic art is fantastic only as it convinces (otherwise it is merely ridiculous), and the power of unreality in film derives from the fact that the unreal seems to have been realized, unfolding before our eyes as if it were the flow of common occurrence—not the plausible illustration of some extraordinary process only conceived in the mind. The *subjects* of films can be divided into the "realistic" and the "nonrealistic," if one wishes, but the filmic vehicle's power to make real, to *realize,* is common to both genres, imparting to the first an impression of familiarity which flatters the emotions and to the second an ability to uproot, which is so nourishing for the imagination. The fantastic creatures of *King Kong* were drawn, but the drawings were then filmed, and that is where, for us, the problem begins.

In his article on the rhetoric of the image,[3] Roland Barthes devotes some attention[4] to the question, but only in connection with still photography: What, he asks, is the impression of reality produced by the photograph? What, above all, are the limits of photography? These issues, we know, have been raised frequently enough with respect to cinema (indeed, they constitute one of the classic topics of filmology and of the theory of film), but to a much lesser extent with respect to still photography. When we look at a photograph, says Roland Barthes, we do not see a presence "being there"—for this definition is too loose and can be applied to any copy—but a presence that "has been there." "We therefore have a new category of space-time: place present but time past—so that in still photography there is an illogical conjunction of *here* and *then.*" This explains the photograph's quality of "real unreality." The portion of reality is to be found in an earlier temporal position, for the image existed at one time in front of the camera lens; photography—a mechanical means of reproduction—had simply to record the image to give us that "rare miracle: a reality from which we are sheltered." As for the unreality, it is produced by the "deliberation of time" (things have been thus, but no longer are), and also by our awareness of what is "here"—for, "we must insist upon the magical aspect of the photographic image," which is never experienced as a total illusion. We always know that what the photograph shows us is not really *here.* For this reason, Barthes continues, photography has little projective power (projective tests are based, preferably, on drawings) and gives rise to a purely spectatorial awareness, an attitude of externalized contemplation, rather than an awareness of magical or fictional possibilities. *"This has been"* overpowers *"Here I am"* (Barthes's italics). There is thus a great difference between photography and the cinema, which is an art of fiction and narration and has considerable projective power. The movie spectator is absorbed, not by a "has been there," but by a sense of "There it is."

Taking this too briefly summarized analysis as a starting point, I would like to extend it with some observations more directly related to the cinema. The impression of reality—varying as it does in intensity, for it has many degrees—yielded by each of the different techniques of representation existing today (still and motion-picture photography, the theater, figurative sculpture and painting, representational drawing, and so on) is always a two-sided phenomenon. One may seek to explain it by examining either the object perceived or the perception of that object. On the one hand, the reproduction resembles the original more or less closely; it contains a number, more or less great, of *clues* to reality. On the other hand, the vital, organizing faculty of perception is more or less able to *realize* (to make real) the object it grasps. Between the two factors, there is a constant interaction. A fairly convincing reproduction causes the phenomena of affective and perceptual participation to be awakened in the spectator, which, in turn, give reality to the copy. With this in mind, we may ask ourselves why the impression of reality is so much more vivid in a film than it is in a photograph—as so many writers have observed, and as each of us may verify in his own experience.

An answer immediately suggests itself: It is *movement* (one of the greatest differences, doubtless the greatest, between still photography and the movies) that produces the strong impression of reality. This, of course, has often been pointed out, but the observation has perhaps never been pushed far enough. "The combination of the *reality* of motion and the *appearance* of forms* gives us the feeling of concrete life and the perception of objective reality. Forms lend their objective structure to movement and movement gives body to the forms," observes Edgar Morin in *Le Cinéma ou L'homme imaginaire*.[5] Compared to still photography, motion-picture photography possesses a higher degree of reality (because the spectacles of real life have motion). But, as Edgar Morin further notes,[6] drawing on Albert Michotte van den Berck's famous analysis,[7] there is more to it than that: Motion imparts corporality to objects and gives them an autonomy their still representations could not have; it draws them from the flat surfaces to which they were confined, allowing them to stand out better as figures against a background. Freed from its setting, the object is "substantiated." Movement brings us volume,** and volume suggests life.[8]

Two things, then, are entailed by motion: a higher degree of reality, and the corporality of objects. These are not all, however. Indeed, it is reasonable to think that the importance of motion in the cinema depends essentially on a third factor, which has never been sufficiently analyzed as such—although Edgar Morin does mention it in passing (when he contrasts the appearance of forms to the reality of movement in film) and Albert Michotte van den Berck does grant it separate treatment.[9] Here is what the latter says: Motion

* The italics are Morin's.
** I mean, simply, an acceptable equivalent for volume. The problem of volume in the film is vast and complex.

contributes *indirectly* to the impression of reality by giving objects dimension, but it also contributes *directly* to that impression in as much as it appears to be real. It is, in fact, a general law of psychology that movement is always perceived as real—unlike many other visual structures, such as volume, which is often very readily perceived as unreal (for example, in perspective drawings). Albert Michotte van den Berck examined the causal interpretations—the impression that something had been "pushed, pulled, thrown, etc." —advanced by test subjects to whom movement had been shown by means of a small device constructed in such a way that only movement, and not the mechanisms that produced it, would appear. In Michotte van den Berck's opinion, these spontaneous causal explanations derive from the fact that the subjects never doubt, even for an instant, that the motions they perceive are real.

Let us go further: Because still photography is in a way the *trace* of a past spectacle—as André Bazin has said[10]—one would expect animated photography (that is to say, the cinema) to be experienced similarly as the trace of a past motion. This, in fact, is not so; the spectator always sees movement as being present (even if it duplicates a past movement). Thus, Roland Barthes's "deliberation of time"—the impression of another time that makes the photograph's presence seem unreal—no longer functions when there is motion. The objects and the characters we see in a film are apparently only effigies, but their motion is not the effigy of motion—it seems real.*

Movement is insubstantial. We see it, but it cannot be touched, which is why it cannot encompass two degrees of phenomenal reality, the "real" and the copy. Very often we experience the representation of objects as *reproductions* by implicit reference to tactility, the supreme arbiter of "reality"—the "real" being ineluctably confused with the tangible: There, on the screen, is a large tree, faithfully reproduced on film, but, if we were to reach forward to grasp it, our hands would close on an empty play of light and shadow, not on the

---

* Of course, minus one of the three spatial dimensions in which it usually unfolds. I am talking about its phenomenal character of reality, not its richness or its diversity.

rough bark by which we usually recognize a tree. It is often the criterion of touch, that of "materiality," confusedly present in our mind, that divides the world into objects and copies.* It never allows the division to be seriously transgressed (except in certain cases, which are considered pathological). Roland Barthes is right to remind us that even the most intense photographic "participations" do not involve the illusion of the real. The strict distinction between object and copy, however, dissolves on the threshold of motion. Because movement is never material but is *always* visual, to reproduce its appearance is to duplicate its reality. In truth, one cannot even "reproduce" a movement; one can only re-produce it in a second production belonging to the same order of reality, for the spectator, as the first. It is not sufficient to say that film is more "living," more "animated" than still photography, or even that filmed objects are more "materialized." In the cinema the impression of reality is also the reality of the impression, the real presence of motion.

In his book *Le Cinéma et le temps*,[11] Jean Leirens develops a theory that, in the cinema, identification—closely linked to the impression of reality—may be in some ways a negative phenomenon. He supports this with Rosenkrantz's famous distinction[12] between the character in the theater, who is an object of "dissociation," and the film character, who is an object of identification.

For his part, the French dramatist Jean Giraudoux[13] writes that in the theater "one presents the spectator with inventions, but each one is disguised by a whole rigorously sexed body." According to Rosenkrantz, the spectator is summoned to take a position in relation to these very real actors, rather than to identify himself with the characters they embody. The actor's bodily presence contradicts the temptation one always experiences during the show to perceive him as a protagonist in a fictional universe, and the theater can only be

* The case of sculpture, where even the effigy possesses a high degree of materiality, raises different problems. And yet, imagine a statue whose visual resemblance to a human model would be so great as to deceive one's eyes (think of Mme. Tussaud's); it would still be the criterion of touch—wax against flesh—that would ultimately allow us to distinguish between the copy and the original model.

a freely accepted game played among accomplices. Because the theater is too real, theatrical fictions yield only a weak impression of reality. Conversely, according to Jean Leirens,[14] the impression of reality
we get from a film does not depend at all on the strong presence of
an actor but, rather, on the low degree of existence possessed by those
ghostly creatures moving on the screen, and they are, therefore, unable to resist our constant impulse to invest them with the "reality"
of fiction (the concept of diegesis*), a reality that comes only from
within us, from the projections and identifications that are mixed in
with our perception of the film. The film spectacle produces a strong
impression of reality because it corresponds to a "vacuum, which
dreams readily fill."[15] In his article, "L'Acte perceptif et le cinéma,"[16]
Henri Wallon develops an idea that partly confirms Jean Leirens's
theory. The theatrical spectacle, he says, cannot be a convincing
duplication of life, because it is itself a part of life, and too visibly so:
Consider the intermissions, the social ritual, the real space of the
stage, the real presence of the actor—their weight is too great for the
fiction the play elaborates to be experienced as real. The stage setting,
for example, does not have the effect of creating a *diegetic* universe;
it is only a convention within the real world. (One might add, in the
same vein, that what one calls "fiction" in the cinema is, in fact, the
diegesis, whereas in the theater the "fiction" exists only in the sense
of a "convention," in the same way that there are fictions in everyday life, for example, the conventions of politeness or of official
speeches.)

The cinematographic spectacle, on the other hand, is completely
unreal; it takes place in another world—which is what Albert Michotte van den Berck calls the "segregation of spaces":[17] The space
of the diegesis and that of the movie theater (surrounding the spectator) are incommensurable. Neither includes or influences the other,
and everything occurs as if an invisible but airtight partition were
keeping them totally isolated from each other. Thus, the sum of the
spectator's impressions, during a film's projection, is divided into two
entirely separate "series": according to Henri Wallon[18]—the "visual

* See A Note on Terminology, p. ix.

series" (that is to say, the film, the diegesis) and the "proprioceptive
series" (one's sense of one's own body) and, therefore, of the real
world, which continues to be a factor, though weakened, as when
one shifts around in one's seat for a more comfortable position). It is
because the world does not intrude upon the fiction and constantly
deny its claim to reality—as happens in the theater—that a film's diegesis can yield the peculiar and well-known impression of reality
that we are trying to understand here.

It can be argued that the negative explanations I have just summarized are, precisely, too negative. They account for the circumstances that render the impression of reality possible, but not for
those that actually produce it; they define the necessary, not the
sufficient, conditions. It is quite obvious that when a stage actor
sneezes or hesitates in his delivery the brutal interruption by "real"
reality disrupts the reality of the fiction; it is equally apparent that
such interferences exist not only in the caricatural and unusual form
of a sneeze, but that they have a thousand more insidious embodi-
ments, which the quality of even the most perfectly regulated performances cannot suppress—since one finds them arising from the
audience as well as from the stage, in the "man's pose of independence, in the woman's dress and make-up."[19] By hermetically isolating
fiction from reality, film instantly dismisses this set of resistances and
levels all obstacles to spectator participation. Participation, however,
must be engendered. A man may be freed from his bonds and still
not act. In still photography and figurative painting, the separation
of the real and the fictitious is as strict as it is in film (two incommen-
surate spaces, and no human interpreters), but neither of the first
two produces a strong impression of reality. Jean Mitry[20] rightly observes that the attempts to explain the "filmic state" by hypnosis,
mimicry, or other procedures wherein he is entirely passive, never
account for the spectator's participation in the film, but only for the
circumstances that render that participation not impossible. The
spectator is indeed "disconnected" from the real world, but he must
then connect to something else and accomplish a *"transference" of
reality*,[21] involving a whole affective, perceptual, and intellective

activity, which can be sparked only by a spectacle resembling at least slightly the spectacle of reality. If one wants to explain a powerful phenomenon like the impression of reality, one has, therefore, to fall back on the necessity of accounting for positive factors, and notably for the elements of reality contained within the film itself, the principal one then being of the reality of motion.

Rudolf Arnheim[22] recognizes that, lacking the dimensions of time and volume, still photography produces an impression of reality much weaker than that of the cinema, with its temporal aspect and its acceptable equivalent for depth (obtained mainly through the interplay of movement). But, he adds, the stage spectacle is more convincing than the cinematographic fiction. Arnheim's theory of "partial illusion" is well known:[23] Each of the representative arts is based on a partial illusion of reality, which defines the rules of the game for that art. In the theater, one laughs if a stage prop collapses but not at the sight of a "parlor" with only three sides. This statutory illusion is more or less great according to the art: Film is given a middle position between photography and theater. In each case, the nature and the degree of the partial illusion depend on the material and technical conditions of the representation; now, film gives us images only, whereas a play unfolds in real time and real space.[24] This analysis seems hardly acceptable; it is contradicted by common experience (one "believes" in the film's fiction much more than in the play's). Furthermore, if one follows the author, the element that is more powerful in the theater is not the "illusion" of reality but *reality itself* (precisely, the real space of the stage and the real presence of the actors)—to which Arnheim contrasts the simple images that are all the nourishment the film spectator gets. But if this is true, the spectator no longer has the illusion of reality; he has the perception of reality—he is a witness to real events.

All arguments of this kind show that a much clearer distinction is needed—even in terminology, where the word "real" is forever playing tricks on us—between two different problems: on the one hand, the impression of reality *produced by the diegesis,* the universe of fiction, what is *represented* by each art, and, on the other hand, the reality of the vehicle of the representation in each art. On the one hand, there is the impression of reality; on the other, the perception of reality, that is to say, the whole question of the degree of reality contained in the material available to each of the representative arts. It is indeed because the art of theater is based on means that are too real that the belief in the reality of the diegesis finds itself compromised. And it is the total unreality of the filmic means—here we return to the ideas of Jean Leirens and Henri Wallon—which allows the diegesis to assume reality.

However, it by no means follows that, as by some mechanical law, the impression of the diegetic reality becomes stronger as the vehicle of representation is removed further from reality. For if that were true, still photography—whose means have even less reality than those of film, because they lack motion—would have to involve the viewer's sense of belief even more powerfully than does the cinema. And figurative drawing even more so, being further from reality than photography is, since it cannot represent the literalness of graphic contours with the accuracy of a photographic image. It is easy to see how this concept of a continuous scale of inverse proportions would lead to countertruths. The truth is that there seems to be an optimal point, film, on either side of which the impression of reality produced by the fiction tends to decrease. On the one side, there is the theater, whose too real vehicle puts fiction to flight; on the other, photography and representational painting, whose means are too poor in their degree of reality to constitute and sustain a diegetic universe. If it is true that one does not believe in the reality of a dramatic intrigue because the theater is too real, it is also true that one does not believe in the reality of the photographed object—because the rectangle of paper (grayish, scant, and motionless) is *not real enough*. A representation bearing too few allusions to reality does not have sufficient *indicative* force to give body to its fictions; a representation constituting total reality, as in the case of the theater, thrusts itself on perception as something real trying to imitate something unreal, and not as a realization of the unreal. Between these two shoals, film sails a narrow course: It carries enough elements of reality—the literal translation of graphic contours and, mainly, the real presence of motion—to furnish us with rich and varied information about the diegetic sphere. Photography and painting cannot do this. Like both these arts, film is still composed of images, but the spectator perceives it as such and does not confuse it with a real spectacle (this is Albert Michotte's notion of the "segregation of spaces"). Being too weak to present itself as a *part* of *reality,* the *partial reality* integrated into the means of the spectacle is entirely discarded in favor of the diegesis: This is what makes the difference between film and theater. The total reality of the spectacle is greater in the theater than in motion pictures, but the portion of reality available to the fiction is greater in the cinema than in the theater.

In short, the secret of film is that it is able to leave a high degree of reality *in its images,* which are, nevertheless, still perceived as images. Poor images do not sustain the world of the imagination enough for it to assume reality. Conversely, the simulation of a fable by means that are as rich as reality itself—because they are real—always runs the danger of appearing to be merely the too real imitation of an unreal invention.

Before the cinema, there was photography. Of all the kinds of images, the photograph was the richest in clues to reality—the only kind, as André Bazin observes,[25] that can give us the absolute certainty that graphic outlines are faithfully respected (because their representation is obtained by a process of mechanical duplication) and where, in some way, the actual object has come to print itself on the virgin film. But, accurate as it was, this means was still not sufficiently lifelike: It lacked the dimension of time; it could not render volume acceptably; it lacked the sense of motion, that synonym for life. All these things were suddenly realized by the cinema, and—an unexpected bonus—what one saw was not just some plausible reproduction of motion but motion itself in all its reality. And it was the very images of still photography that this so real motion came to animate, thereby bestowing on them a novel power to convince—but, since they were, after all, only images, it was all to the advantage of the imagination.

In these few pages, I have attempted to outline one of the several*
aspects of that problem, the impression of reality in the cinema. To
inject the reality of motion into the unreality of the image and thus
to render the world of the imagination more real than it had ever
been—this is only part of the "secret" of motion pictures.

* There is also, of course, the fact that a film is composed of *many* photographs, which raises all the problems of montage and discourse, both of which
are very closely linked to the impression of reality but should be studied
separately.

2 Notes Toward a Phenomenology
of the Narrative

The study of narrative[1] is presently enjoying the interest of several scholars of the structuralist persuasion. Following Vladimir Propp's famous work on Russian folk tales and Claude Lévi-Strauss's writings on myths, various "models" for the analysis of the narrative—or, depending on the case, of specific narratives—have been suggested (Algirdas Julien Greimas, Roland Barthes, Claude Brémond, *Communications* no. 8, etc.).

It is my intention in the following paragraphs not to advance still another model, but rather, to invite the reader to reflect on what has brought about all the attempts already presented. It seems to me, indeed, that the narrative lends itself to structural analysis because it is primarily, in some way, a real object, which even the naïve listener clearly recognizes and never confuses with what it is not.

According to Algirdas Julien Greimas (*Semantique structurale*), the minimum structure any signification requires is the presence of two terms and the relationship linking them; thus, he notes, signification presupposes perception (of the terms and of their relation). Similarly, it might be said that the main interest of structural analysis is only in being able to find what was already there, of accounting with more precision for what a naïve consciousness had "picked up" without analysis. Let us also remember what Claude Lévi-Strauss wrote about myths in his *Structural Anthropology:* that a myth is always recognized as being such by those to whom it is recited, even when it has been translated from one idiom into another, even when its exact formulation has been somewhat modified.

Let us say, therefore—perhaps a little cavalierly—that structural analysis always assumes, by virtue of an implicit or explicit prior stage, something like a phenomenology of its subject, or, again, that *signification* (which is constructed and discontinuous) renders explicit what had first been experienced only as a perception (which is continuous and spontaneous). It is from this point of view that I would like to explore some answers to the question: How is a narrative recognized, prior to any analysis?

I

A narrative has *a beginning and an ending*, a fact that simultaneously distinguishes it from the rest of the world and opposes it to the "real" world. It is true that certain types of narrative, culturally highly elaborated, have the peculiarity of *cheating on the ending* (conclusions that are withheld or are evasive, "mirror" constructions* in which the end of the recited event establishes and explains the conditions that produced the instance of recitation, denouements in an endless spiral, etc.), but these are only secondary elaborations, which enrich the narrative without destroying it, and which are neither intended nor able to remove it from its basic requirement of *enclosure:* It is the reader's imagination, and not the substance of the narrative sequence, that these trick endings project into infinity. In a literary narrative that trails off in points of suspension (whether real or implied), the effect of being suspended does not apply to the narrative object, which, for its part, retains a perfectly clear ending—indicated, precisely, by the three dots. The British film *Dead of Night* con-

* See Chapter 7.—TRANSLATOR

cludes in a spiral,* but, as a suite of images, it has a definite ending
—the last image of the film.

Children are not fooled when being told stories. For them, the
question of knowing whether the story has ended is always relevant,
even when they have the maturity to glimpse possible extensions of
the *semantic substance* of the story (but not of the story itself). They
ask, "Is that the end? But *afterward* what does the prince do?"

II

A beginning and an ending—that is to say, the narrative is a *temporal sequence*. A doubly temporal sequence, one must hasten to
specify: There is the time of the thing told and the time of the telling (the time of the significate and the time of the signifier). This
duality not only renders possible all the temporal distortions that are
commonplace in narratives (three years of the hero's life summed
up in two sentences of a novel or in a few shots of a "frequentative"
montage in film, etc.). More basically, it invites us to consider that
one of the functions of narrative is to invent one time scheme in
terms of another time scheme—and that is what distinguishes narrative from simple *description* (which creates space in time), as well
as from the *image* (which creates one space in another space).

The example of the cinematographic narrative easily illustrates
these three possibilities: A motionless and isolated shot of a stretch
of desert is an image (space-significate—space-signifier); several partial and successive shots of this desert waste make up a description
(space-significate—time-signifier); several successive shots of a cara-
van moving across the desert constitute a narrative (time-significate
—time-signifier).

This example was purposely simplified (in film, indeed, space is

* It is morning. The hero, an architect, wakes up. He has had a bad night:
always that same recurring dream. The telephone rings. It is a neighboring
landowner who wishes to make some improvements on his property and invites the architect to spend the weekend at his manor. The hero accepts. Upon
his arrival, he gradually recognizes the manor of his dream. The party takes
place, and ends as the hero wakes up. He gets out of bed: So it was a dream
after all. The same recurring dream. The telephone rings. Etc. . . .

always present, even in the narrative, because the cinematic narrative is produced by images). But their simplification is of little importance here, and it was intended only to show that the narrative is, among other things, a system of temporal transformations. In any narrative, the narrative object is a more or less chronological sequence of events; in any narrative, the narrative instance takes the form of a sequence of signifiers that has a certain duration—for the literary narrative, the time it takes to read it; for the cinematographic narrative, the time it takes to see it, etc.

In still photography, by contrast, what is represented is a point in time that has been frozen; the viewer's intake is also supposed to be instantaneous; and, even when it is prolonged, it is not a reading of the signifiers in a single, controlled order of concatenations.

It is within the framework of this opposition between the narrative and the image that one can perhaps explain the awkward, hybrid position of description. We all assume that description differs from narration, and that is a classical distinction, but, on the other hand, a large number of narratives contain descriptions, and it is not even clear that descriptions exist other than as components of narratives. Thus, description appears simultaneously as the opposite of narration and as one of the great figures, or one of the important *moments,* of narration. This curious mixture of antinomy and kinship, which intuitively defines the relationship between narration and description, can be made a little clearer if one brings a third term into the system—the image. Narration and description are opposed in common to the image because their signifiers are temporalized, whereas the image's signifier is instantaneous; thus, the kinship. But within this "narrative-descriptive" category, which is defined by a feature of the signifier, narration and description are contrasted by a feature of their significates, for in the narrative the signified is temporalized, whereas it is instantaneous in description; thus, the antinomy.[2]

Within the narrative, the descriptive passage immediately reveals itself: It is the only one within which the temporal concatenation of the signifiers—though it is not interrupted—ceases to refer to the temporal relation (whether consecutive or not) among the corresponding significates, and the order it assigns to their signified elements is only one of spatial coexistence (that is to say, of relationships supposed to be constant whatever moment in time is chosen). From the narrative to the descriptive, we pass through a *change of intelligibility,* in the sense in which one speaks of a change of gears in automobiles.

III

A closed sequence, a temporal sequence: Every narrative is, therefore, a discourse (the converse is not true; many discourses are not narratives—the lyric poem, the educational film, etc.).

What distinguishes a discourse from the rest of the world, and by the same token contrasts it with the "real" world, is the fact that a discourse must necessarily be made by someone (for discourse is not language), whereas one of the characteristics of the world is that it is uttered by no one.

In Jakobsonian terms, one would say that a discourse, being a statement or sequence of statements, refers necessarily to a subject of the statement. But one should not hastily assume an author, for the notion of authorship is simply one of the forms, culturally bound and conditioned, of a far more universal process, which, for that reason, should be called the "narrative process." It is true that in certain highly elaborated narratives of modern Western society the subject of the statement is most often the author, but, aside from that, there are the myths, the folk tales, the many narrative films of everyday consumption, which are passed from hand to hand in the course of their industrial or "craft" manufacturing, the many radio and television shows put together by teams (whether as an organized group or in gleeful disorder), etc.—in short, all the *authorless* narratives, at least in the sense "author" has in the humanist tradition of "high culture."

Narratives without authors, but not without narrators. The impression that *someone is speaking* is bound not to the empirical presence of a definite, known, or knowable speaker but to the listener's spontaneous perception of the linguistic nature of the object to which he is listening; because it is speech, someone must be speaking.

Albert Laffay, in *Logique du cinéma,* has shown this to be true of film narrative. The spectator perceives images which have obviously been selected (they could have been other images) and arranged (their order could have been different). In a sense, he is leafing through an album of predetermined pictures, and it is not he who is turning the pages but some "master of ceremonies," some "grand image-maker" (*grand imagier*) who (before being recognized as the author, if it is an *auteur* film, or, if not, in the absence of an author) is first and foremost the film itself as a linguistic object (since the spectator always knows that what he is seeing is a film), or more precisely a sort of "potential linguistic focus" (*"foyer linguistique virtuel"*) situated somewhere behind the film, and representing the basis that makes the film possible.[3] That is the filmic form of the narrative instance, which is necessarily present, and is necessarily perceived, in any narrative.

IV

A closed sequence, a temporal sequence, discourse—therefore, the perception of the narrative as real, that is, as being really a narrative, must result in rendering the recited object *unreal.*

I will not linger over deliberately imaginary narratives (fantastic tales, legends, etc.); far from being convincing examples of the process of *unrealization* (*irréalization*), which is at the heart of every narrative act, they would divert our attention toward a second level of unrealization, which is unnecessary and is very different from the first. Whether the narrated event follows nonhuman logic (a pumpkin metamorphosed into a carriage, etc.) or the ordinary logic of everyday life ("realistic" tales of various kinds), it has, because it is perceived as narrated, already been unrealized. Realism is not reality. No one expects to meet in the street the hero of some scrupulously realistic contemporary novel. Realism affects the organization of the contents, not narration as a status. On one level of perception, Emma Bovary is no less imaginary than Cinderella's fairy godmother.

We must, however, go one step further, for, along with realistic stories (which nobody believes have really occurred), there are also *real stories:* accounts of historical occurrences (the assassination of Marat), accounts of daily life (I tell a friend what I have done the evening before), accounts to oneself (my memories as I recall them), and the news accounts of film, radio, the press, etc. Now, these "true" accounts are characterized, just as much as the imaginary accounts, by the form of unreality that we are examining here: The reader of a history book knows that Marat is not actually being assassinated now; the friend to whom I am talking understands that, although I am describing my activities, I am no longer living them (or, more precisely, that, because the narrative act is, in turn, another part of my life, that part of my life I am recounting to him ceases to be lived as it is being told); the viewer of television news does not consider himself a direct witness to the event the images bring to him.

Reality assumes *presence,* which has a privileged position along two parameters, space and time; only the *here* and *now* are completely real. By its very existence, the narrative suppresses the *now* (accounts of current life) or the *here* (live television coverage), and most frequently the two together (newsreels, historical accounts, etc.).

An account is perceived as such only as long as a margin, even an infinitesimal one, separates it from the fullness of *here* and *now.* Certain examples of minimum *unreality* are very enlightening: The paradoxical situation has occasionally been noted of participants in a political parade who, transistor radio in hand, were listening, while demonstrating, to the live coverage of their own demonstration. But, perhaps because the inordinate overvaluation of the specificity of the audiovisual media may occasionally blur more general truths, sufficient attention has not been given to the fact that, for the listening demonstrators, the radio report remained entirely an account; for, at the precise moment they were listening, they were no longer demonstrating (or at least it was not their listening self which was demonstrating), and the narrated parade they were hearing could only be confused with the demonstration they were taking part in from a positivistic point of view, introducing the notion of secondary information (whether or not the demonstrators had availed themselves of this intelligence). To be sure, between these two parades there is not the same difference as, say, between a parade held on May 15 and one held on May 16, but this order of difference is not the only possible one, and indeed one substantial parade can, as is the case here, correspond to two phenomenal parades. The first parade is the one the man with the radio knows he is participating in, and which he is experiencing instant after instant, at the precise point in the march where he finds himself each second—a parade that, like Fabrice at the battle of Waterloo, he will never dominate. The second is the one whose account he is listening to, and it is only the first parade made unreal—this unrealization being due to the presence of the newscaster, who is, however, notably absent from the first parade, as well as to a spatiotemporal displacement (reduced to a minimum in this example), which necessarily brings about the intrusion of the narrator. It is this second parade, and only this second parade, that the man with the radio can dominate, like the reader of Victor Hugo's "Waterloo." (A. J. Greimas would say that the man with the radio is actually two actors: the demonstrating actor and the listening actor).

We are approaching a concept that has been developed frequently since Jean-Paul Sartre made his studies of the world of the imagination: Reality does not tell stories, but memory, because it is an account, is entirely imaginative. Thus, an event must in some way have ended before its narration can begin. One might add that, in the case of the strictly simultaneous accounts that live television coverage offers, spatial displacement—that is, the fact of the image itself—can assume the role of temporal displacement (which is the predominant feature of traditional narratives), thereby alone ensuring the correct functioning of narrative unrealization (otherwise how could one explain the remarkable absence of traumatism in the television-viewer?): The event described by live news coverage is real, but it occurs elsewhere. On the screen, it is unreal.

V

A closed sequence, a temporal sequence, discourse, and the unrealizing instance—one term of the definition is still missing, one that is suggested both by the notion of sequence and by that of unrealization (a sequence of what? the unrealization of what?).

A narrative is a sum of *events;* it is these events which are ordered into a sequence; it is these events which the narrative act, in order to exist, begins by making unreal; it is these events, again, which provide the narrator with his necessary correlative: He is a narrator only in so far as the events are narrated by him. (On the other hand, it is not the set of events but the discourse which is closed. A narrative is not a sequence of closed events but a closed sequence of events. Traditional narratives, with their definite conclusions, are closed sequences of closed events; the trick-ending narratives which cultural modernism enjoys are closed sequences of unclosed events. The closing of the narrated matter is a variable, whereas the closing of the narrative is a constant; thus, the relationship of syntagmatic simultaneity of these two factors in the various narrative corpora is a *determination* in the Hjelmslevian sense: When there is a sequence of closed events, there is always a closed sequence, but, when there is a closed sequence, there is not always a sequence of closed events.)

Although several different methods have been proposed for structurally breaking down the narrated events (which do not initially constitute discrete units), the event is still and always the basic unit of the narrative. The notion of the predicate, in reference to the narrative, has been advanced explicitly by A. J. Greimas in his theory of actors and predicates, as well as by Claude Lévi-Strauss (according to his method, the unit of the mythical narrative, which is, as a first step, isolated on a filing card, is furnished by "the assigning of a predicate to a subject"). It is equally clear that Vladimir Propp's "functions," each one defined by an abstract substantive—that is to say, borrowing the words of the linguist W. Porzig (see References

Section, Chapter 3, reference 86), by the substantiation of a sentence predicate; Claude Brémond's "elementary sequences"; the concepts of performative or ascertaining statements, which Tzvetan Todorov borrowed from Austin and Benveniste in order to apply them to the literary narrative—these all correspond to successive predications (Propp) or to groups of successive predications (Brémond).

In every narrative whose vehicle is articulated language (written or oral), the properly narrative unit, as we know, is neither the phoneme nor the moneme—which are the units of idiom and not of narrative—but, rather, the sentence, or at least some segment similar in magnitude to the sentence (Émile Benveniste's "completed assertive statement"—*énoncé assertif fini*—or some other type of minimum complete statement). I said that the narrative is a discourse because it implies a subject of statement; we now see that it is also a discourse in another way. A linguistic syntagma greater than the sentence and composed of several sentences—a "transphrastic" entity—the narrative is "discourse" in the sense of American linguistics (see Zellig Harris's notion of *Discourse Analysis*), which is, in turn, partially covered by Émile Benveniste's definition of "discourse."*

---

* In several of the essays collected here, the term *discourse* is employed in what might be called a "broad" sense, corresponding to Zellig Harris's use of it: Discourse is that which is opposed to *langue* (language system); it is language being performed (*langage en acte*) in contrast to language as a potential but motionless structure. Thus, any *true* sequence of statements *in context* pertains to discourse (see p. 130 of Beneveniste's *Problèmes de linguistique générale,* Paris, 1966). However, in his article "Les Relations de temps dans le verbe Français" (*Bulletin de la Société de Linguistique de Paris,* vol. LIV, 1959; reprinted in *Problèmes . . . , op cit.* pp. 237–50), Benveniste extends his analysis, which leads him to a more restrictive view of discourse (pp. 238–42): discourse as opposed to *histoire*—story ("impersonal" narratives of all varieties). Thus, the term would designate only a present, living, and "personalized" exchange of statements, indicated by the oral or written presence of an "I" and a "you" (conversations, letters, dialogue in novels, etc.). To simplify matters, one might observe that (1) to Benveniste, story and discourse in the narrow sense are both aspects of discourse in the large sense; (2) Benveniste's "story" corresponds approximately to what I call the "narrative"; (3) consequently, the narrative, although it is by definition excluded from Benveniste's "discourse" in the "narrow" sense, is eminently a part of his "broad" use of discourse. That is why I have characterized the narrative as a discourse, while pointing out that this use corresponds only partially to Benveniste's definition.

In other narratives, the image is the vehicle; this is the case with the film narrative. Elsewhere[4] I have shown that each image, far from being equivalent to a moneme or even to a word, corresponds rather to a complete statement, of which it exhibits five fundamental characteristics: (1) Film images are, like statements and unlike words, infinite in number; they are not in themselves discrete units. (2) They are in principle the invention of the speaker (in this case, the film-maker), like statements but unlike words. (3) They yield to the receiver a quantity of indefinite information, like statements but unlike words. (4) They are actualized units, like statements, and unlike words, which are purely virtual units (lexical units). (5) Since these images are indefinite in number, only to a small degree do they assume their meanings in paradigmatic opposition to the other images that could have appeared at the same point along the filmic chain. In this last respect, again, they differ less from statements than from words, since words are always more or less embedded in paradigmatic networks of meaning (traditional lexicological networks, networks of semes—that is, signifying statements—in Greimas or Bernard Pottier, etc.).

A third type of narrative uses gesture as a vehicle (classical ballet, pantomime, etc.). Each gesture, as I have stated elsewhere,[5] constitutes a signifying statement—or a seme (this time as Éric Buyssens and Luis J. Prieto define the term)—and thus comes closer to the sentence than to the word (Joseph Vendryes had already noted this fact in his article on the language of gestures).

Thus, beyond the diversity of semiological vehicles that can carry the narrative, the essential division of the narrating sequence into actualized statements (successive predications)—and not into units that can be assimilated more or less to the moneme, word, or phoneme—seems to be a permanent characteristic of narrativity.

None of this is new: My intention is simply to remind the reader that if the narrative can be structurally analyzed into a series of predications it is because phenomenally it is a series of events.

Under the influence of Étienne Souriau and Mikel Dufrenne, contemporary aesthetics has turned its attention to the great "categories," such as the graceful, the sublime, the elegiac, etc., which, in the domain of art, of human relations, and of the emotions, define the affective-aesthetic equivalent of Kantian transcendentalism, itself reinterpreted into phenomenological terms and stripped of any trace of idealism.

The universal characteristics of the world as it appears, or of man as he apprehends the world—since one cannot break away from this constant shuttling implied by the statement *"there is,"* and since the affective universal features are simultaneously cosmological and existential—these *a priori* determinations at any rate inform the world that man is able to perceive (that is to say, the totality of the phenomena), thus making possible the contact between man and the world; they explain, moreover, why something like the impression of gracefulness, or of the sublime, can only be experienced.

Of course I have no intention of placing the narrative in the same category as the graceful or the sublime; a narrative, and any number of objects other than a narrative, may also be graceful or sublime. Furthermore, the impression of the graceful or of the sublime cannot, given the present state of structural methods, be broken down, whereas some narratives already have been analyzed. (This does not imply that the *impression of narrativity,* the certainty of being confronted with a narrative, which is different from any given narrative, is necessarily any more accessible to analysis—at least as it is being experienced—than the impression of the graceful or of the sublime.) Whatever the case, the graceful and the sublime appear more as tonalities, whereas the narrative appears more as a genre, so that the two orders of concepts cannot be arranged along the same axis of classification.

Nevertheless—aside from the fact that the distinction I am suggesting here is, in more than one case, extremely difficult to maintain, owing to the fact that certain tonalities become institutionalized in genres (for example, the elegiac)—it seems to me that the *narrative* (to give it its true name at last) bears this much in common with the affective—aesthetic categories: It represents one of the great anthropological forms of *perception* (for the "consumers" of narratives), as well as of *operation* (for the inventors of narratives).

It is that great form of the human imagination which, to conclude and to summarize, I should like to define in the following manner: *A closed discourse that proceeds by unrealizing a temporal sequence of events.*

II PROBLEMS OF FILM SEMIOTICS

3 The Cinema:
Language or Language System?

The Era of "Montage-or-Bust"*

In April 1959, in one of the famous interviews in the *Cahiers du cinema*[1] Roberto Rossellini—discussing, among other subjects, the problem of montage—expressed an opinion which was not new but to which, toward the end of the text, he gave a more personal twist. First, he made a commonplace observation: In the modern cinema, montage does not occupy the same place it did in the great period of 1925-30. Of course it remains an indispensable phase of film creation: One must select what one films, and what one has filmed must be combined. And, since one must edit and adjust, should one not do it in the best possible way and make the cut in the right place? However, continued the creator of *Paisà*, montage is no longer conceived of today as *all-powerful manipulation*. These are not the actual words of the Italian film-maker, but the formula does summarize Rossellini's most suggestive remarks.

Montage as supreme ordering—is that not the montage which, during its great period, lay claim to a persuasive power considered in some way absolute and which was "scientifically" guaranteed by Kuleshov's famous experiments? And is it not that montage whose effectiveness—overestimated perhaps, but nonetheless very real—made

---

* The French is: *montag roi.*—Editor.

such a vivid impression on the young Eisenstein? Startled at first by the almost dishonoset grossness of the efficacy* it gave him, Eisenstein soon let his own mind be conquered by the desire to conquer other minds, and he became the leading theoretician of the "montage or bust" approach.[2] What followed was like a fireworks display. With Pudovkin, Alexandrov, Dziga-Vertov, Kuleshov, Béla Balázs, Renato May, Rudolf Arnheim, Raymond J. Spottiswoode, André Levinson, Abel Gance, Jean Epstein—and how many others?—montage, through the enthusiastic and ingenious exploitation of all its combinations, through the pages and pages of panegyric in books and reviews, became practically synonymous with the cinema itself.

More direct than his fellows, Pudovkin was unwittingly close to the truth when he declared with aplomb[3] that the notion of montage, above and beyond all the specific meanings it is sometimes given (end-to-end joining, accelerated montage, purely rhythmic principle, etc.), is in reality the sum of filmic creation: The isolated shot is not even a small fragment of cinema; it is only raw material, a photograph of the real world. Only by montage can one pass from photography to cinema, from slavish copy to art. Broadly defined, montage is quite simply inseparable from the composition of the work itself.[4]

For the modern reader, a fanaticism, as it must indeed be called, of montage emerges from Eisenstein's great theoretical works, *Film Form* and *The Film Sense*. Micha rightly observes that, obsessed by that single idea, the Soviet film-maker saw montage everywhere and extended its boundaries disproportionately.[5] The histories of literature and painting, pressed en masse into the service of Eisenstein's theory, are used to furnish precursive examples of montage. It was enough that Dickens, Leonardo da Vinci, or any number of others combined two themes, two ideas, or two colors for Eisenstein to discover montage; the most obvious pictorial juxtaposition, the most properly literary effect of composition, were, to hear him, prophetically precinematographic. All is montage. There is something relent-

---

* The word is used as defined by G. Cohen-Séat (*efficience*): not as the effectiveness of a particular approach or specific act, but as the power peculiar to a means of expression.

less, almost embarrassing at times, in Eisenstein's refusal to admit even the smallest place for continuous flows of creation; all he can see anywhere are prefragmented pieces, which ingenious manipulation will then join together. Furthermore, the manner in which he describes the creative work of all those he enlists as his forerunners does not fail, in certain truly improbable passages, to contradict even the slightest likelihood of any psychogenesis of creation.[6]

In the same way Eisenstein categorically refused to admit any kind of descriptive realism into the cinema. He would not accept that one could film a scene continuously, and he was full of scorn for what he called, depending on the passage, "naturalism," "purely objective representation," or narrative that is simply "informative" (as distinguished from "pathetic" or "organic," that is, in the final analysis, edited into montage sequence). He would not even consider that the continuous recording of a short scene that was itself composed and acted out could be a choice among others. No, one must fragment, isolate the close-ups, and then reassemble everything. Could not the filmed spectacle have its own beauty? One dare not say so. As if forever to reassure himself, that great artist whose genius and glory could have encouraged him a thousand times, manages to have beauty, which has been pitilessly rejected from every "profilmic"* occasion, emerge without possible confusion from the filming, and only from the filming. Even more: from the montage, and only from the montage. For, on the level of each shot, there is filming, therefore composition. But Eisenstein never loses an opportunity to devalue, in favor of his concern for sequential arrangement, any element of art that might have intruded into the forming of the ordered segments.**

---

* As defined by Étienne Souriau. Whatever is placed in front of the camera, or whatever one shoots with the camera is "profilmic."

** We know that in his "last period" (*Alexander Nevsky* and *Ivan the Terrible*), Eisenstein was governed by a very different aesthetic, an aesthetic of the image much more than of montage. But this development has left only a faint trace in his theoretical writings, which concern us here. However, the unpublished manuscripts, which will be gradually published, will have to be seen.

THE SPIRIT OF MANIPULATION. A comparison suggests itself—and deserves more attention than the brief remarks that follow—between that obsession with breakdown analysis and montage and certain tendencies of the "modern" spirit and civilization. In its moments of excess, when inspiration would desert it, montage cinema (other than in Eisenstein's films) came at times very close to being a kind of mechanical toy—in a world, it is true, where erector sets are not the only syntagmatic toys to captivate our children, who acquire a taste for manipulation in their playing, which, if they later become engineers, specialists in cybernetics, even ethnographers and linguists, may be extended into a whole operational attitude, whose excellence of principle will be more evident here than in film. And, surely, we know anyway that an age is not defined by the state of mind of a few, just as "montage or bust" does not define all of the cinema. One man may be a cybernetics specialist, but another a farmer or a janitor; one film may be all montage, but another may unfold in large sections. A period, however, is shaped by all of its activities. If one chooses to emphasize one aspect of it, one is too often criticized for having at the same time neglected the others; the lack of ubiquity becomes a sin against intelligence. Nevertheless we must renounce discussing, along with our subject, all that is not our subject.

At the time of *Citizen Kane*, Orson Welles, whom the RKO producers had given an unusual freedom of means, would go into raptures, according to his biographer,[7] at all the apparatus he had been made master of: "That was the finest electric toy ever given to a boy." Erector set, electric train: both montage toys. Department stores sell electric trains in separate pieces: A new package of tracks acquired later on allows a small boy to reassemble his old switching in a new way; everything fits together. Catalogues list the different pieces one can buy (classifying them according to their functions in the over-all scheme): "right switch," "left switch," "ninety-degree angle crossing," "a twenty-two-degree angle crossing." You would think they were the parts of discourse according to Kuryglowicz, or a "text" spewed out by some American fanatic about distributional analysis. Still, toys are only an amusing example. There is also "pho-

tomontage," collage, paper cut-outs in the animated films of Boro-
wizyk and Lenica, or certain "experimental" shows by the research
teams of ORTF (French national television). Above all there are
cybernetics and the theory of information, which has outdone even
the most structuralist of linguistics: Human language is already
fairly organized, much more in any case than many other code systems, such as the rules of politeness, art, custom; verbal language is
enriched by a sufficiently rigorous paradigmatic category permitting
the most varied syntagmatic arrangements. But, in the eyes of certain modern tendencies, it still bears too much "substance" and is not
entirely organizable. Its double substantiality, phonemic and semantic (that is to say, twice human, through the body and the mind),
resists exhaustive pigeon-holing. Thus the language we speak has
become—very paradoxically if one thinks about it—what certain
American logicians call "natural" or "ordinary" language, whereas
no adjective is needed to describe the languages of their machines,
which are more perfectly binary then the best analyses of Roman
Jakobson. The machine has ground up human language and dis-
penses it in clean slices, to which no flesh clings. Those "binary
digits," perfect segments, have only to be assembled (programed) in
the requisite order. The code triumphs and attains its perfection
in the transmission of the *message*. It is a great feast for the syntagmatic mentality.

There are other examples. An artificial limb is to the leg as the
cybernetic message is to the human sentence. And why not mention
—for amusement and a change from erector sets—powdered milk and
instant coffee? And robots of all kinds? The linguistic machine, at
the forefront of so many modern preoccupations, remains nevertheless the privileged example.

The attitude that conceives and produces all these *products* is
broadly the same: The natural object (whether human language or
cow's milk) is considered as a simple point of departure. It is analyzed, literally and figuratively, and its constituent parts are isolated;
this is the moment of *breakdown analysis,* as in the cinema. Then
the parts are distributed into isofunctional categories:[8] straight tracks

to one side, curved to the other. This is the paradigmatic aspect—and it is only preparatory, as was the filming of individual scenes for Eisenstein. The grand moment, which one has been waiting for and thinking about since the beginning, is the syntagmatic moment. One reassembles a duplicate of the original object, a duplicate which is perfectly grasped by the mind, since it is a pure product of the mind. It is the intelligibility of the object that is itself made into an object.

And one never takes into account that the natural object has been used as a *model.* Quite the contrary, the assembled object is taken as the model object—and let the natural object keep still! Thus the linguist* will try to apply the conditions of the theory of information to human language, while the ethnographer will call "model" not the reality he has studied but the formalization he has derived from that reality. Claude Lévi-Strauss is especially clear on this point.[9] The difference between the natural object and its reconstructed model is insisted upon, but somehow it is neutralized; the optional or individual variations of articulation in phonemics, for example, are "nonrelevant." The goal of the reconstruction, as Roland Barthes emphasizes, is not to reproduce reality; the reconstruction is not a reproduction, it does not attempt to imitate the concrete aspect of the original object; it is neither *poiesis* nor *pseudo-physis,* but a simulation, a product of *techne.*[10] That is to say: the result of a manipulation. As the structural skeleton of the object made into a second object, it remains a kind of prosthesis.

What Eisenstein wanted to do, what he dreamed of perpetually, was to make the lesson of events visually apparent, and through breakdown analysis and montage to make it itself an appreciable event. From this comes his horror of "naturalism." To Rossellini, who said "Things are. Why manipulate them?" the Soviet film-maker might have replied, "Things are. They must be manipulated." Eisenstein never shows us the course of real events, but always, as he says, the course of real events refracted through an ideological point of

* Who is, incidentally, reticent at times and of two minds about these problems (consider André Martinet's attitude). Others, like P. Guiraud or Roman Jakobson, are more positive.

view, entirely thought out, *signifying* from beginning to end. Meaning is not sufficient; there must also be signification.

Let there be no misunderstanding; this is not a matter of politics. It is not a question of opposing Eisenstein's political options to some kind of objectivity; nor is it a question of opposing to his purely narrative (nonpolitical) "prejudices" the possibility of some other reading, direct and mysteriously faithful to the deeper meaning of things, as André Bazin, more subtle than those who find fault with Eisenstein for being a Communist, has done.[11] It is a question only of semiotics: What we call the "meaning" of the event narrated by the film-maker would in any case have a meaning *for someone* (since no others exist). But from the point of view of the means of expression, one can distinguish between the "natural" meaning of things and beings (which is continuous, total, and without distinct signifiers: the expression of joy on the face of a child) and determined signification. The latter would be inconceivable if we did not live in a world of meaning; it is conceivable only as a distinct organizational act by which meaning is reorganized: Signification tends to make precise slices of discontinuous *significates* corresponding to so many discrete signifiers. By definition it consists in informing an amorphous semanticism. In *Potemkin,* three different lion statues filmed separately become, when placed in sequence, a magnificent syntagma; the stone animal seems to be rising and is supposed to yield an *unequivocal* symbol of the workers' revolt. It was not enough for Eisenstein to have composed a splendid sequence; he meant it to be, in addition, a fact of language (*fait de langue*).

How far can the taste for manipulation, one of the three forms of what Roland Barthes calls "sign imagination" (*"l'imagination du signe"*) go?[12] Does not Moles anticipate a "permutational art" in which poetry, discarding the chaste mystery of inspiration, will openly reveal the portion of manipulation it has always contained, and will finally address itself to computers? The "poet" would program the machine, giving it a certain number of elements and setting limitations; the machine would then explore all the possible combinations, and the author would, at the end of the process, make his selection.[13]

A utopia? Or prophecy? Moles does not say it will come tomorrow, and there is no reason why one cannot extrapolate from the premises of today. Prophecies are rarely fulfilled in their predicted forms, but they are nevertheless indicative. This essay springs from the conviction that the "montage or bust" approach is not a fruitful path for film (nor, for that matter, poetry). But it should be seen that that orientation is entirely consistent with a certain spirit of modernism, which, when called cybernetics or structural science, yields results that are much less questionable.

Thus, up to a certain point, "montage or bust" partakes of a state of mind peculiar to "structural man."[14] But no sooner is it established than this similarity must be qualified by two reservations, which might actually be only one. First is the point that the height of montage came well before the flood tide of the syntagmatic mind. The latter began really only after World War II, just at the time when "montage or bust" (1925–30) was being more and more criticized and rejected by film-makers and theoreticians.[15] Second, is it not paradoxical that the cinema should have been one of the areas in which the spirit of manipulation began its career? Is not the notion of a reconstructed reality, which seeks no literal resemblance, contrary to film's essential vocation? And is not the camera's role to restore to the viewer the object in its perceptual quasi-literalness, even if what it is made to film is only a preselected fragment of a total situation? Is not the close-up itself—the absolute weapon of the theoreticians of montage in their war against visual naturalism—on a smaller scale, as respectful of the object's aspect as is the establishing shot?* Is not film the triumph of the *"pseudo-physis"* that the spirit of manipulation precisely rejects? Is it not entirely based on that famous "impression of reality," which no one challenges, which many have studied, and to which it owes its more "realistic" moments as well as its ability to realize the fantastic?[16]

In fact these two reservations are merely one: In the period when

* In fact, though, not entirely; isolated and magnified, the fragment is occasionally unrecognizable. This has been pointed out already, with reason. But this nuance, which will have to be studied separately, may be temporarily neglected in a global study.

a certain form of intellect agent becomes more aware and sure of it-self, it is natural that it should tend to abandon areas, such as the cinema, that restricted it, and should gather its forces elsewhere. Conversely, in order for it to exert a strong influence on the cinema, this mentality had to be as yet in its beginnings and not yet estab-lished.*

From "Ciné-Langue" to Cinema Language

The preceding, somewhat cavalier** view was not meant to explain everything. It was put forward as a hypothesis. The observation con-cluding it is negative and doubly so: Film did not lend itself well to manipulation, and the spirit of manipulation itself was not under-stood well. There remains a positive fact to account for: The cinema —which is not the only field in which manipulation may be, how-ever imperfectly, conceived—the cinema, in preference to other fields, was chosen (and with what fanaticism!) by certain theoreticians of manipulation.

During the same period, to be sure, montage was being affirmed elsewhere than on the screen: in mechanical arts, in engineering tech-niques, and in the constructivist theater. Eisenstein was educated at the School for Public Works of St. Petersburg before 1917. He him-self declared that his theory of the "montage of attractions" had been suggested to him by the assembling of tubular parts in engineering, as well as by the techniques of juxtaposition used in circuses and music halls.[17] He was actively engaged in the constructivist move-ment of the young Soviet theater. He was an admirer of the Kabuki

* It goes without saying that I am speaking here about cinematographic *creation*. For the author of this book is obviously in no position to maintain that syntagmatic methods are not suited to the *analysis* of film. This is some-what like the problem of the "creator" and the "theoretician"—despite their closeness in the modern period, which, though it has often been pointed out, is still insufficient—who *necessarily* approach the same object by means that are so different that they are not always able to resist the pessimistic and over-simplifying illusion that it is not the same object.
** And which strikes me as being even more cavalier today than when this article was written.

theater, which he considered to be a pure product of montage. He wrote for *Lef*, Mayakovsky's review, staged Tretyakov, worked for the Prolecult (popular theater), for the Free Experimental Theater, for Meyerhold's theater, etc. But none of these influences and contagions[18] can exempt a truly cinematographic study from examining the factors that, in the nature of film itself, could produce—even if by some quasi-misunderstanding—the specifically filmic designs of the manipulative mind.

For the error was tempting: Seen from a certain angle, the cinema has all the appearances of what it is not.* It is apparently a *kind of language* (*une sorte de langage*), but it was seen as something less, a specific *language system* (*une langue*).** It allows, it even necessitates, a certain amount of cutting and montage; its organization, which is so manifestly syntagmatic, could only be derived, one believed, from some embedded paradigmatic category, even if this paradigmatic category was hardly known. Film is too obviously a message for one not to assume that it is coded.

For that matter, any message, provided it is repeated often enough and with a sufficient number of variations—as is the case with film —becomes in time like a great river whose channels are forever shift-

---

* Despite the clumsy formulations of a man who was partly self-taught, which are scattered throughout his books (though not in his films), Eisenstein remains, to my mind, one of the greatest film theoreticians. His writings are crammed full of ideas. His thoughts on language systems (in spite of an exuberant and somewhat unfocused vocabulary), however, will have to be restated in terms of language.

** A language system (*langue*) is a highly organized code. Language itself covers a much broader area: de Saussure said that language is the sum of *langue* plus speech (*parole*). The concept of a "fact of language" (*fait de langage*) in Charles Bally or Émile Benveniste points in the same direction. If we were to define things and not words, we might say that language, in its broadest reality, is manifest every time something is said with the intention of saying it (see Charles Bally, "Qu'est-ce-qu'un signe?" in *Journal de psychologie normale et pathologique*, Paris, vol. 36, 1939, nos. 3 and 4, pp. 161–74, and especially p. 165). Of course, the distinction between verbal language (language proper) and other "sign systems" (semes) (sometimes called "languages in the figurative sense") comes to mind, but it must not confuse the issue. It is natural that semiotics be concerned with all "languages," without pre-establishing the extent and the limits of the semic domain. Semiotics can and must depend heavily on linguistics, but it must not be confused with linguistics.

ing, depositing here and there along its course a string of islands: the disjointed elements of at least a partial code. Perhaps these islands, barely distinguishable from the surrounding flood, are too fragile and scattered to resist the sweep of the current that gave them birth and to which they will always be vulnerable. Nevertheless there are certain "syntactical procedures" that, after frequent use as *speech,* come to appear in later films as a language system: They have become conventional to a degree. Many people, misled by a kind of reverse anticipation, have antedated the language system; they believed they could understand the film because of its syntax, whereas one understands the syntax because one has understood, and only because one has understood, the film. The inherent intelligibility of a dissolve or a double exposure cannot clarify the plot of a film unless the spectator has already seen other films in which dissolves and double exposures were used intelligibly. On the other hand, the narrative force of a plot, which will always be understood only too well—since it communicates with us in images of the world and of ourselves—will automatically lead us to understand the double exposure and the dissolve, if not in the first film we see them, at least by the third or fourth. As Gilbert Cohen-Séat has said, the language of film will always have the advantage of being "already entirely written out in actions and in passions important to us."[19] All experiments on filmic intellection tend to prove this. The works of B. and R. Zazzo, Ombredane, Maddison, Van Bever, Mialaret, Méliès, Lajeunesse and Rossi, Rébeillard, etc. all share the idea that it is only those syntactical procedures that have become too conventionalized that cause difficulties of understanding among children or primitive subjects, unless the film's plot and its world of diegesis, which remain understandable in the absence of such procedures, are able to make the procedures themselves understandable.

After these digressions let us now return to Rossellini's interview. "Things are," he had said. "Why manipulate them?" Obviously he was not referring to the techniques of organization in their broadest sense, but only and explicitly to the actual cinematographic theory of "montage or bust." Thus he was echoing (to the utmost joy of

Cahiers du Cinéma, which was not interviewing him innocently) a whole tendency that the *Cahiers* had incubated and of which it was practically the incarnation. While the Italian director spoke, one thought of the French film-makers and writers. Was it not in connection with Rossellini's films* that André Bazin had developed his famous theories on the sequence shot, depth of field, and continuity shooting?[20] As for all those comrades and friends, were they not all working toward the same goal, the death of a certain concept of the cinema: the erector-set film? If the cinema wants to be a true language, they thought, it must cease to be a caricature. Film has to say something? Well then, let it say it! But let it say it without feeling obliged to manipulate images "like words," arranging them according to the rules of a pseudo-syntax whose necessity seemed less and less evident to the mature minds of what is called—beyond the narrow sense of the "new wave"—the "modern" cinema? The days of Dziga Vertov's *"ciné phrase"* ("film sentence") and *"ciné langue"* ("film language-system") were gone![21]

Thus André Bazin was not alone. There was Roger Leenhardt,[22] there was Jean Renoir with his many statements in favor of the sequence shot,[23] there was—to limit ourselves to film-makers who were also theoreticians—Alexandre Astruc whose famous *"camera stylo"*[24] was, despite appearances, the exact opposite of the old notion of *ciné langue.* A pen (*stylo*) only writes what it is made to write. What Astruc wanted was a cinema as free, personal, and sharp as some novels are, but he was careful to explain[25] that his "vocabulary" would be made up of the very aspect of things, "the impasto of the world." The "montage or bust" approach, on the contrary, consisted in dismantling the immanent perception of things in order to reel it off in slices, which would become simple signs to be used wherever one pleased. Around the same time, in a work whose title itself made cinema a language,[26] Marcel Martin observed in passing[27] that the reader would not find a strict system of signs. Then, following Mer-

---

* And also in relation to Italian neorealism in general, and to certain aspects of Orson Welles, William Wyler, Jean Renoir, Erich von Stroheim, Friederich Murnau, etc.

leau-Ponty's lecture on "Le Cinéma et la nouvelle psychologie,"[28] film began to be defined here and there, or at least approached, from what one called the "phenomenological" angle: A sequence of film, like a spectacle from life, carries its meaning within itself. The signifier is not easily distinguished from the significate. "It is the felicity of art to show how a thing begins to signify, not by reference to ideas that are already formed or acquired, but by the temporal and spatial arrangement of elements."[29] This is an entirely new concept of ordering. The cinema is the "phenomenological" art *par excellence,* the signifier is coextensive with the whole of the significate, the spectacle its own signification, thus short-circuiting the sign itself: This is what was said, in substance, by Souriau, Soriano, Blanchard, Marcel, Cohen-Séat, Bazin, Martin, Ayfre, Astre, Cauliez, Dort, Vailland, Marion, Robbe-Grillet, B. and R. Zazzo, and many others in the course of one article or another. It is possible, even probable, that they went too far in this direction: For the cinema is after all not life; it is a created spectacle.* But let us put these reservations aside for the moment, and simply record what was in fact a convergence in the historical evolution of ideas about film.

Rossellini's remarks, though they may not be very philosophical, nevertheless point in the same direction. Let us listen to him some more: The cinema, he says, is a language, if one means by that a

---

* In *Esthetique et psychologie du cinéma* (Paris: Éditions Universitaries, vol. 1, 1963), Jean Mitry states matters more vigorously: After having been everything, montage now tends to be nothing, at least in some theories. But the cinema is inconceivable without a minimum of montage, which is itself contained within a larger field of language phenomena (pp. 10–11). The analogy and the quasi-fusion of the signifier and the significate do not define all of film, but only one of its constituents—the photographic material—which is no more than a point of departure. A film is made up of many images, which derive their meaning in relation to each other in a whole interplay of reciprocal implications, symbols, ellipses, etc. Thus the signifier and the significate are given a greater distance, and so there is indeed a "cinematographic language" (see especially pp. 119–23). I mention this in order to insist on the difference between such a "language" and a "film language-system." The partisans of what is called "non-montage" (the Bazin tendency), even if they have occasionally made statements on the aesthetics of film that are too exclusive, at least can be credited—on the level of a sort of intuitive and spontaneous semiotics—with rejecting any concept of the cinema as *langue* and affirming the existence of a cinematographic *language.*

"poetic language." But the theoreticians of silent film saw in it a real, specific *vehicle* (Rossellini's word) about which we are much more skeptical today. For the creator of *Open City,* who is not normally concerned with semiotics, this was a kind of conclusion. It was uttered somewhat haphazardly (in his choice of terms at any rate), spontaneously, but in fact with great felicity: It is unusual for a man of the profession, other than in his films, to suggest so many things in so few words.

A Non-System Language:
Film Narrativity

When approaching the cinema from the linguistic point of view, it is difficult to avoid shuttling back and forth between two positions: the cinema as a language; the cinema as infinitely different from verbal language. Perhaps it is impossible to extricate oneself from this dilemma with impunity.

After analyzing the "logomorphic" nature[30] of film, Gilbert Cohen-Séat came to the provisional conclusion that one must at least overcome the temptation to consider the cinema as a language.[31] Film tells us continuous stories; it "says" things that could be conveyed also in the language of words; yet it says them differently: There is a reason for the possibility as well as for the necessity of adaptations.

To be sure, it has often been justly remarked[32] that, since film has taken the narrative road—or, what F. Ricci calls the "novel's way" (*voie romanesque*)[33]—since the feature-length fiction film, which was only one of many conceivable genres, has taken over the greater part of total cinematic production, it could only be the result of a positive development in the history of film, and particularly in the evolution from Lumière to Méliès, from "cinematography" to cinema.[34] There was nothing unavoidable, or particularly natural, in this. Yet even those who emphasize the historical aspect of this growth never conclude that it was meaningless or haphazard. It had to happen, but it had to happen for a reason; it had to be that the very nature of the cinema rendered such an evolution if not certain at least probable.

There was the *demand,* what the spectator wanted. This is the main idea in Edgar Morin's analyses (which it would be superfluous to repeat with less talent). Although the spectatorial demand cannot mould the particular content of each film, Morin recently explained, it is perfectly capable of determining what one might call the spectacle's formula.[35] The ninety-minute show with its digressions (documentary, etc.) of lesser narrativity is one formula. It will perhaps not endure, but for the moment it is sufficiently pleasing; it is accepted. There have been other formulas, for example two "great movies" in a single showing. But these are all variations. The basic formula, which has never changed, is the one that consists in making a large continuous unit that tells a story and calling it a "movie." "Going to the movies" is going to see this type of story.

Indeed the cinema is eminently apt to assume this role; even the greatest demand could not have diverted it in any lasting way along a path that its inner semiological mechanism would have made improbable. Things could never have occurred so fast nor remained in the state we still find them, had the film not been a supreme story-teller and had its narrativity not been endowed with the nine lives of a cat. The total invasion of the cinema by novelesque fiction is a peculiar, striking phenomenon, when one thinks that film could have found so many other possible uses which have hardly been explored by a society that is nevertheless forever in pursuit of technographic novelty.

The rule of the "story" is so powerful that the image, which is said to be the major constituent of film, vanishes behind the plot it has woven—if we are to believe some analyses[36]—so that the cinema is only in theory the art of images. Film, which by nature one would think adapted to a transversal reading, through the leisurely investigation of the visual content of each shot, becomes almost immediately the subject of a longitudinal reading, which is precipitous, "anxious," and concerned only with "what's next." The sequence does not string the individual shots; it suppresses them. Experiments on the memory retention of film—whether by Bruce, Fraisse and de Monmollin, Rébeillard, or Romano and Botson—all come to the same conclusion, though by different means: All one retains of a film is its plot and a *few images*. Daily experience confirms this, except of course for those who, seeing very few films, retain them entirely (the child's first movie; the farmer's one film of the year; and even then). On an entirely different level, Dreyfus[37] observes that the attempts to create a certain "language" in a type of modern film (Antonioni, Godard, etc.) occasionally produce a disturbing, however talented, overabundance, since the film track itself is already and always saying something.

Narrativity and logomorphism. It is as if a kind of induction current[38] were linking images among themselves, *whatever one did,* as if the human mind (the spectator's as well as the film-maker's) were incapable of not making a connection between two successive images.

Still photography—a close relative to film, or else some very old and very distant second cousin—was never intended to tell stories. Whenever it does, it is imitating the cinema, by spatially deploying the successivity that film unfolds in time. The eye proceeds down the page of the "picture romance" magazine in the prescribed order of the photographs—which is the order they would have unreeled in on the screen. "Picture romances" are frequently used to retell the story of an existing film. This is the consequence of a deep similarity, which is in turn the result of a fundamental dissimilarity: Photography is so ill-suited to story-telling that when it wants to do so it becomes cinema. "Picture romances" are derived not from photography but from film. An isolated photograph can of course tell nothing! Yet why must it be that, by some strange correlation, two juxtaposed photographs must tell something? Going from one image to two images, is to go from image to language.

Kuleshov's experiments, as I said earlier, were considered for many years the "scientific" basis for the supremacy of montage. No one, however, has paid sufficient attention to the fact that, in the midst of the age of "montage or bust," there existed another interpretation of those famous experiments. An interpretation that seemed to provide yet more ammunition for the partisans of manipulation, but in fact implied a covertly discordant position (more modestly than it should have), which only the future was to bring to light. It was contained in Béla Balázs's book *Der Geist des Films* (1930).[39] With a kind of shrewdness peculiar to him, the Hungarian theoretician remarked that, if montage was indeed sovereign, it was so by necessity, for, when two images were juxtaposed purely by chance, the viewer would discover a "connection." That, and nothing else, is what Kuleshov's experiments demonstrated. Film-makers obviously understood this and decided that this "connection" would be their tool, to manipulate according to their will. Yet right from the beginning their hand was forced by the viewer, or rather, by a certain structure of the human mind, that obdurate diachronist. Listen to Balázs: "One presupposes an intention. . . . The viewer understands what he thinks montage wants him to understand. Images . . . are . . . linked together . . . internally through the inevitable induction of a current of signification. . . . The power [of montage] exists and is exerted, whether one wants it or not. It must be conscientiously used." In his *Esthétique et psychologie du cinéma* Jean Mitry elaborates in much greater detail an interpretation of the "Kuleshov effect" (pp. 283–85). He concludes that the famous experiments in no way authorize the theory of "montage or bust" (according to which the diegesis is marginal to the development of montage effects, which tend to produce an abstract logic, or piece of eloquence, independent of the film itself). They simply demonstrate the existence of a "logic of implication," thanks to which the image becomes language, and which is inseparable from the film's narrativity.

Thus, film montage—whether its role is the triumphant one of yesterday or the more modest one of today—and film narrativity—as triumphant now as it was in the past—are only the consequences of that current of induction that refuses not to flow whenever two poles are brought sufficiently close together, and occasionally even when they are quite far apart. The cinema is language, *above and beyond any particular effect of montage*. It is not because the cinema is language that it can tell such fine stories, but rather it has become language because it has told such fine stories.

Among the theoreticians and film-makers who have moved the

cinema away from the spectacle to bring it closer to a novelistic "writing" capable of expressing everything—its author as well as the world—of repeating and sometimes replacing the novel in the multiple task it had assumed since the nineteenth century,[40] we find precisely, and by no accident, many of those who are the least concerned with "cinematographic syntax" and who have said so, not without talent at times, in their articles (Bazin, Leenhardt, Astruc, Truffaut) or have shown so in their films (Antonioni, Visconti, Godard, Truffaut). There are individual cases, of course: With Alain Resnais, with Jean-Luc Godard, there is a body of montage which reappears, but with a new meaning; the genius Orson Welles makes films beyond any restriction—a master of visual surprise, he can use, when necessary, continuous camera shots as involved and involving as a sentence of Marcel Proust's. But, whereas individual style is one thing, the evolution of cinematographic language is another, differing from it, not in substance (for it is the film-makers who make up the cinema), but in scale and in one's approach to it. One would need forty chapters to do justice to the first, whereas, for the latter, two suffice, at least for the present: *ciné langue* (cinema language system) and cinema language. I have mentioned Antonioni, Visconti, Godard, and Truffaut because, of the directors having a style, they seem to me to belong among those, furthermore, in whom one can most clearly see the change from the will to system to the desire for language.* They frequently use the sequence shot where the partisans of montage would have cut and reassembled; they fall back on what is called, for better or worse, the "tracking shot" (and which implies nothing other than a noncodified mobility of the camera, a movement that is truly *free*)** where traditional film syntaxes distinguish between rear and forward "dolly," "pan" and "tilt," etc.[41]

Thus language is enriched by whatever is lost to system. The two phenomena are one. It is as if the code's signifying abundance were linked to that of the message in the cinema—or rather separated from

---

* This text was written in the beginning of 1964; today there would be many names to add to it.

** A very successful example: the sequence of the travel agency in *Breathless* by Jean-Luc Godard.

it—by an obscurely rigorous relationship of inverse proportions: Code, when it is present, is crude—the great film-makers who believed in it were great despite it; the message, as it becomes refined, circumvents the code. At any given moment, the code could change or disappear entirely, whereas the message will simply find the means to express itself differently.*

"Ciné Langue" and Verbal Languages:
The Paradox of the Talking Movies

In the period when the cinema considered itself a veritable language system, its attitude toward verbal languages was one of utmost disdain. It feared their competition, which had come about only by its intrusion into their midst. One might think that before 1930 the very silence of film would have given it automatic protection against the detested verbal element. Like the deaf who sleep peacefully undisturbed by any noise, the silent cinema, deriving strength from its weakness, would lead, one might think, a still and tranquil life. But not at all! No period was ever more noisy than that of the silent movies. Manifestoes, vociferations, invectives, proclamations, and vaticinations succeeded each other in denouncing always the same, ghostlike enemy: speech—speech, which was radically absent—necessarily so—from film itself and which existed finally (as victim and executioner) only in the speeches delivered against it. The young Jean Epstein; the young René Clair; Louis Delluc (who died young); the cohorts of the "pure cinema" with their impetuous Egeria, Germaine Dulac; Béla Balázs; Charlie Chaplin; and naturally the legion in close formation of Soviet pioneers: They were all full of contempt for the word. And I have mentioned only the loudest.

* Today I would no longer state the relationship between the code and the message in such strictly antagonistic terms. It now appears to me that the realities codes possess are more complex, more various, subtler—and therefore more compatible, so to speak, with the richness of messages. On these points, see the whole of Chapter 5, "Problems of Denotation in the Fiction Film," as well as passages from "The Modern Cinema and Narrativity." See also *"Problèmes actuels de théorie du cinéma,"* (not reprinted here), *Revue d'esthétique* (special issue: "Le cinéma") vol. xx, no. 2-3 (especially p. 221).

Of course it is easy to smile at them. Yet there was more truth in their paradoxical anathemas than at first appears. The old verbal structures, although officially absent from film, were nevertheless a haunting presence. The attack was not without an object: Obviously there were the explanatory titles; above all there was the gesticulation in acting, whose true reason for being—we will have to return to this —was not, as has been wrongly said, in the infirmity of the silent image, or in acting habits mechanically inherited from the theater (how to explain that in some silent pictures there is no gesticulation?), but in a subconscious attempt to speak without words, and to say without verbal language not only what one would have said with it (which is never entirely impossible), but in *the same way* it would have been said. Thus there came into being a kind of silent gibberish, simultaneously overexcited and petrified, an exuberant gabbling whose every gesture, every bit of mimicry, stood with scrupulous and clumsy literalness for a linguistic unit, almost always a sentence whose absence, which would not otherwise have been catastrophic, became abundantly obvious when the gesticulated imitation so clearly emphasized it. Yet it was sufficient for a Stroheim*—reduced like his peers to silent pictures, and as anxious as they to express a great deal despite this limitation—to circumvent speech (instead of attacking it head on, while at the same time shamefully copying it) for film to be enriched and to become quieter, for the previously clumsily localized significations to become more continuous and to reveal a full, complex meaning.

Those for whom the silent film still spoke too much were thus not entirely wrong. They anticipated many truths; however, it was in the steps of a much broader development of thought—and one that was more obscure, and more deeply motivated. They were almost *afraid* of verbal language, for even as they were defining the cinema as a nonverbal language, they were still obscurely thinking of some pseudo-verbal system within their films. Obscurely, yet clearly

* Think of the magnificent seduction scene in *Wedding March* (1927), which was entirely constructed from the imperceptible facial play of the actor-*auteur*. Not a gesture, but what expressiveness!

enough for them to see the language of words as a powerful rival forever on the point of overstepping its bounds. An analysis of the theoretical writings of the period would easily show a surprising convergence of concepts: The image is like a word, the sequence like a sentence, for a sequence is made up of images like a sentence of words, etc. By assuming this position, the cinema, for all its proclamations of superiority, was condemning itself to perpetual inferiority. In contrast to a *refined* language (verbal language), it defined itself unwittingly as a coarser duplication. It only remained for it to sport its plebeian condition (many of Marcel L'Herbier's articles seem to have no other aim), in secret fear of a more distinguished older brother.

One can see how the paradox of the talking cinema was already rooted at the heart of the silent movies. But the greatest paradox was yet to come: The advent of the talking movies, which should have changed not only the films but the theories about them, in fact modified the latter in no way, at least during the first several years. Films talked, and yet one spoke about them as if they were silent. But there was an exception: A profoundly new tendency, unjustly scorned until Bazin began to rehabilitate it,[42] was being developed in the writings of Marcel Pagnol. This tendency came from outside the cinema, and its roots were not buried in the problems of the silent film (which is what aroused the fury of its enemies). Very significantly, it began to appear only after the arrival of the talking movies.[43] It was able to avoid what I have called the paradox of the talking cinema.

The introduction of speech into the cinema did not substantially modify the attendant theoretical positions. It is known that not a few lovers of cinematographic purity hesitated before accepting this newcomer to the filmic world. They gave their word here and there that they would not use it, or that they would use it as little as possible, and in any case never realistically; furthermore, the fashion would soon pass. There was also an attempt—both a diversion and a regression—which consisted in opposing "sound" to "talking." Noise and music were accepted but not speech, which, of all the sounds in the world, in whose midst it nevertheless exists, was kept—in theory—

under a mysterious and specific taboo. This produced the "wordless talking film, the shy film, the film garnished with the creakings of doors and the tinkling of spoons; the moaning, shouting, laughing, sighing, crying, but never the talking film," as the Provençal dramatist expressed with such verve.[44] But all this was only episodic. The great debate on the statutory admission of speech into film was largely platonic, and one was hardly aware of it other than as something that occupied a large place in the theory of film. The films themselves were already talking: They began to do so very rapidly, almost all of them did so, and continued to do so.

Not the least part of the paradox is, in fact, the ease with which speech did in fact find its way into the films of all those whose pronouncements had indissolubly linked the survival of the art of film to the permanence of its silence.[45] Accepted in practice, speech was not accepted in theory. One persisted in explaining that nothing essential had changed—hardly a reasonable position!—and that the laws of cinematographic language remained what they had been in the past. Arnoux summarizes an opinion that was very common at the time when he affirms[46] that the good talking films were good for the same reason that the good silent films were, and that the "talkie" was after all only one of many technical improvements, less important all in all than the close-up shot, which had been "invented" long before.

From our greater distance in time, we can only be amazed at this obstinate refusal to see the arrival of speech as an occurrence of capital importance—at any rate an occurrence deserving to be given its place in theory, and consequently to displace older, accepted elements from their respective positions. This is the condition for any true change, as we know—linguists have shown this to be the case in diachronics, and Proust has demonstrated it with human feelings. But speech was simply added (if even that) to the theory of cinema, as if it were in excess and there were no more room for it—and this at the very time when the silent cinema (not to mention the "sound" cinema, that voluntary invalid, that stillborn child) was entirely disappearing from the screens.

This unwillingness to see, or rather to hear, is even to be found, though in a less sterile and caricatural form, among those who had the richest and most fruitful reaction to the birth of the talking film (Pagnol excepted). In the "Manifesto for Orchestral Counterpoint,"[47] Eisenstein, Alexandrov, and Pudovkin generously welcome the sound-track, in the absence of speech itself. Their attitude is positive. For them it is a matter of giving visual counterpoint an auditory dimension, of multiplying the old cinema by the new. However—and precisely because a healthy and intelligent reaction makes us regret its omission, since it provides them with such a rich frame—one notices that nowhere do the three Soviet directors take speech into consideration. For them the sound cinema is a cinema that is squared—multiplied by itself, and only by itself. The authors of the "Manifesto" were thinking of noise and music; for them a film remained an *uttered discourse.* They would not consider, they rejected, the idea that an uttering element, speech, could be inserted into film.

We should not blame them: It was more difficult to approach these subjects in 1928 than in 1964. But we can take advantage of our greater distance to note that the appearance of speech in film inevitably brought the cinema closer to the theater—contrary to an opinion too often held, and in spite of the numerous analyses (often correct in their own terms) that since 1930 have underlined the differences between cinematographic and theatrical speech. For the most part these analyses point to the same conclusion: In their different ways they all suggest that in the theater the *word* is sovereign, a constituent of the representation, whereas, in film, *speech* is governed and constituted by the diegesis. This is an important difference one can hardly challenge. In a deeper sense, nevertheless, any utterance, whether governing or governed, by nature tells us something *first,* whereas an image, or noise or music, even when it is "telling" us a great deal, must first be *produced.*

There is no way in which the division into active and passive aspects can occur in the same way for verbal language, which has always been bound to the human agent and to determined signification, and for the nonverbal "languages" of the image, of noise or even of music, which are for their part linked to the impassivity of the world and to the malleability of things; whatever one may say about it, a film dialogue is never entirely diegetic. Even if we set aside "film commentaries" (it is enough to note their existence), which would support us too easily, we observe that the verbal element is never entirely integrated into the film. It sticks out, necessarily. Speech is always something of a spokesman. It is never altogether *in* the film, but always a little *ahead* of it. The most brilliantly emphatic musical or pictorial compositions, on the contrary, never intervene between the film and the spectator; they are experienced as an integral part of the film: However rich they may be, they remain media.

Despite all that was questionable in his ideas about filmed theater, Marcel Pagnol was undoubtedly the least mistaken person during the years from 1927 to 1933, when it was indeed difficult not to be wrong. There were those who refused to admit sound. Others accepted it grudgingly. Still others had taken to it enthusiastically. Some—like the hostess who, wanting to have a great musician to dinner, invites his chattering wife as well, in the improbable hope that her dreaded manners might not after all be so dreadful—some, in a grand gesture of courageous acceptance, even considered letting a few words be added to the background noise they so highly prized. Pagnol was almost the only one to accept the *talking* cinema—that is to say, a cinema that talked.

After these few words of history, let us now try to define formally the paradox of the talking cinema, which Pagnol alone was able to avoid. When the cinema was silent, it was accused of "talking" too much. When it began to talk, one declared that it was still essentially silent and should remain so. Is there anything surprising, then, in the affirmation that, with the advent of the "talkie," nothing had changed? *And, in fact, for a certain kind of cinema, nothing had changed.* Before 1930, films chattered silently (pseudo-verbal gesticulation). After 1930, they were loquaciously silent: A torrent of words was superimposed over a structure of images which remained faithful to its old laws. *Ciné-langue* never was, and could not become, the talking cinema. Not in 1930 did films begin talking, but in 1940, or thereabouts, when little by little they changed in order to *admit* speech, which had remained waiting at the door, so to speak.*

But, one will say, it is well known that the first talking films talked too much. Certainly. But if this is so noticeable, it is because they did not really talk. Today, on the contrary, we are not shocked by speech in a film. Perhaps it is used more sparingly? Not always. But, say it is. In any event, the crux of the matter lies elsewhere: Today films talk better, and speech no longer surprises us, at least as a general rule. Let us make it clear that, as *films,* they talk better. The *text* has not necessarily improved, but it harmonizes better with the film.

For a cinema that claimed to be language but conceived of itself as a language system (a universal and "nonconventional" one, to be sure, but a language system, nevertheless, since it wanted to create a system that was fairly strict and that logically would precede any message), the verbal languages could only offer it an unwanted increase and an unseasonable rivalry: No one could think seriously of inserting, even less of fusing, them into the texture of images—one could hardly conceive of making them agree with the images. The cinema began to speak only after it had begun to conceive of itself as a language that was flexible, never predetermined, sufficiently sure of itself to do away with a permanent, ill-tempered guard in front of its own doors, and bountiful enough to be enriched by the wealth of others. The "sequence shot" did more for talking films than the advent of the talking cinema itself. As Étienne Souriau remarks in another context,[48] a technical invention can never resolve a problem in art; it can only state it, so that it can be resolved by a second, properly aesthetic, invention. This is the well-known dialectic of long-term progress and short-term regression.

In order to get a better understanding of the talking cinema, one should study a certain type of "modern" film,[49] particularly the work of the inseparable trio, Alain Resnais, Chris Marker, and Agnes Varda. In their films, the verbal, even openly "literary," element, is

---

* Today I would qualify this statement. There were good talking films right from the beginning of the talkies; the period 1930–33 was fairly rich. A little later there were also certain American comedies. Etc. . . .

given great weight in the overall composition, which is nevertheless more authentically "filmic" than ever. In *Last Year at Marienbad,* the image and the text play a sort of game of hide-and-seek in which they give each other passing caresses. The sides are equal: Text becomes image, and image turns into text. This interplay of contexts gives the film its peculiar contexture.

One is reminded of the famous problem of "cinematographic specificity" about which André Bazin, in almost every one of his articles, makes at least one or two very enlightening statements. The overt self-affirmation of a strong personality is not always the trait of those who possess the strongest personalities: And thus it was for a certain type of cinema in the past.

A State of Mind and a Stage: Criticism of Ciné Langue

We forgive the cinema of the past for its excesses, because it has given us Eisenstein and a few others. But one always excuses genius. The concept of *ciné langue* constituted a whole theoretical corpus and must be evaluated as such. The point is important, for the perspective of the critic or the historian does not coincide here with that of the theoretician. The theory is full of splendid deadends, concepts that have not survived, but while they were alive, gave us some of the greatest masterpieces of the screen.

Moreover, although a kind of "erector-set cinema" did exist, there never was an "erector-set film." The common trend in many films of the period was enshrined mainly in writings and manifestoes. It was never entirely invested in a particular film, unless perhaps in certain avant-garde productions on the borderline between normal cinema and pure experimentation (seeing these films today one begins to feel that the others were indeed normal. Let the critic evaluate the contribution of these experimental films.)

As for the historian, he will rightly observe that only through its excesses—theoretical as well as practical—could the cinema begin to gain a consciousness of itself. The cinema as a language system is also the birth of the cinema *as an art,* some time after the entirely technical invention of the cinematograph (as André Bazin said of the avant-garde in its strict sense).[50] This can be extended to include a good part of all the cinema of that period. Let the historian study everything positive—and that is a lot—in this crisis of adolescent originality.

In the broad sense used here, the language-system cinema produced a sizable portion of the best cinema of its period; through it there occurred something that affected both art and language. This is why I have spoken only about it. But one must not lose sight of the proportions: For each film of the language-system tendency, there were, as there is always, ten undistinguished films that managed to avoid the problems of the silent cinema and the paradox of the talking cinema. Before 1930, the grade-B movie director would go out and photograph African elephants; after 1930, he would record music-hall numbers, music and words included. Neither the presence or absence of speech could cramp his style.

There was another cinema, too, which was neither the *ciné langue* nor the ordinary dud. At the height of the "montage or bust" era, Stroheim and Murnau were heralding the modern cinema. It was a matter of talent and personality, because their cinema had no theory and did not at first get a following. Ideologically, manipulation was supreme. And this is normal: Stages are made to be skipped by a talented minority.*

---

* I have said nothing about the period prior to 1920, which is nevertheless of capital importance for the genesis of cinematographic language (especially D. W. Griffith). But the problems this period poses are foreign to the intent of these pages, which do not pretend to give a historical account. It is quite apparent that a director like Feuillade, to take one example out of many, is exempt from the kind of excesses for which I am blaming the *ciné-langue attitude.* The question that interests me (language or language system?) was conceivable only after the first *theories* of film made their appearance, roughly in 1920. Before then, the cinema was too busy being created. Lumière invented the cinematograph; he did not invent "film" as we know it today (a complex narrative body of considerable magnitude). The great pioneers before 1920 invented the cinema (see Mitry, *Esthétique et psychologie du cinéma, op. cit.,* pp. 267–85 of vol. I). Before the problems of semiotics raised here could even have meaning, let alone an object, the cinema had first to exist, and it had to begin thinking of itself in terms of theory.

A Seminal Concept: Cinematographic Specificity

As Rossellini said, the cinema is a language of art rather than a specific vehicle. Born of the fusion of several pre-existing forms of expression, which retain some of their own laws (image, speech, music, and noise), the cinema was immediately obliged to *compose,* in every sense of the word. From the very beginning, threatened with extinction, it became an art. Its strength, or its weakness, is that it encompasses earlier modes of expression: Some, truly languages (the verbal element), and some, languages only in more or less figurative sense (music, images, noise).

Nevertheless, these "languages" are not all found on the same plane with respect to the cinema: Speech, noise, and music were annexed at a later time, but film was born with *image discourse.* A true definition of "cinematographic specificity" can therefore only be made on two levels: that of filmic discourse and that of image discourse.

As a totality, filmic discourse is specific through its composition. Resembling true languages as it does, film, with its superior instancy, is of necessity projected "upward" into the sphere of art—where it reverts to a specific language. The film total can only be a language if it is already an art.

But within this totality there is an even more specific core, which, contrary to the other constituent elements of the filmic universe, is not found in a separate state in other arts: It is the image discourse. The proportions in its case are reversed, because a sequence of images is a language first. Perhaps, being too far removed from the language we speak, it is only a figurative language? So be it. It is nevertheless a language, in such a way that Rossellini's characterization (which was obviously directed at film as a whole) cannot be applied to it. Image discourse *is* a specific vehicle. It did not exist before the cinema; until 1930 it alone was sufficient to define film. In technical or medical films it functions exclusively as a vehicle and is not linked to any attempt at artistic realization. On the other hand, in films of fiction the language of the image tends to become an art (within a vaster sphere of art)—just as verbal language, which has a thousand utilitarian applications, is able to become incantation, poetry, theater, or novel.

The specific nature of film is defined by the presence of a *langue* tending toward art, within an art that tends toward language.

We have two things, therefore. Not three. There is indeed language system, but neither the image discourse nor filmic discourse are language systems. Whether language or art, the image discourse is an open system, and it is not easily codified, with its nondiscrete basic units (the images), its intelligibility (which is too natural), its lack of distance between the significate and the signifier. Whether art or language, the composed film is an even more open system, with its whole sections of meaning directly conveyed to the audience.*

Film as we know it is not an unstable compound, because its elements are not incompatible. And they are not incompatible because none of them are language systems. It is hardly possible to use two language systems simultaneously: If I am spoken to in English I am not spoken to in German. Languages on the other hand, are more tolerant of superimpositions, at least within certain limits: Whoever speaks to me by means of verbal language (English or German) can at the same time make use of gestures. As for the arts, they can be superimposed within even broader limits: Witness opera, ballet, and chanted poetry. Cinema gives us the impression—occasionally erroneous, by the way—of rendering everything compatible with everything else, because its field of action lies for the most part between language and art, and not within *langue*. The cinema as we know it —it may assume other shapes, some of which are already beginning to emerge in certain Cinerama spectacles—is a "formula" with many advantages: It joins consenting arts and languages in a durable union in which their individual faculties tend to become interchangeable. It is a commonwealth, as well as a marriage of love.

* Today I would not use the words "natural" and "directly." Or at least I would use them more circumspectly. See second footnote p. 78.

Film and Linguistics

Does this mean, then, that the study of film—at a time when linguistics itself, faithful on the whole to the Saussurian teachings, is mainly concerned with language systems—cannot have a linguistic dimension?

I am persuaded on the contrary that the "filmolinguistic" venture is entirely justified, and that it must be fully "linguistic"—that is to say, solidly based on linguistics itself. But how is one to interpret this statement, since the cinema is not a language system? That is what I would now like to clarify.

The study of film is concerned with linguistics at two points, two separate moments of its procedure, and in the second, not quite with the same linguistics as in the first.

It was de Saussure, we know, who made the study of language the subject of linguistics.[51] But de Saussure also laid the foundation for a much broader science—semiotics—of which linguistics was to be only one branch, although an especially important one.[52] Conversely, there were those here and there who began to study the inner mechanism of nonverbal systems (traffic signals, cartographic conventions, numbers, the gestures of politeness), or of transverbal systems (the verbal formulas of politeness, poetry, folktales, myths), or even of certain systems bridging the verbal and the nonverbal (kinship as seen by Claude Lévi-Strauss, with its dual organization into "appellations" and "attitudes,")[53] and almost all of them were fervent readers, admirers, or direct disciples of the Swiss scholar. We will return to the point. But already we can notice a rather striking point: In theory, linguistics is only a branch of semiotics, but in fact semiotics was created from linguistics. In a way it is very normal: For the most part semiotics remains to be done, whereas linguistics is already well advanced. Nevertheless there is a slight reversal. The post-Saussurians are more Saussurian than de Saussure himself: They have taken the semiotics he foresaw and are squarely making it into a translinguistic discipline. And this is very good, for the older brother must help the younger, and not the other way around. Moreover, de Saussure himself hints at the possibility of such a cross-influence: Linguistics could be of great help to semiotics, he writes, if it became more semiological.[54]

By focusing its attention on human language, linguistics proper has been able to obtain a knowledge of its subject with an often enviable rigor. It has cast a bright light, which has (not paradoxically) illuminated neighboring topics. Thus broad aspects of the image discourse that a film weaves become comprehensible, or at least more comprehensibly, when, in a first stage, they are as entities examined distinct from *langue*. To understand what film is not is to gain time, rather than to lose it, in the attempt to grasp what film is. The latter aim defines the second stage of film study. In practice, the two stages are not separable, for one always opens onto the other. I call one of them the "first stage" because it benefits from the capital of linguistics, which encourages one to begin with it. The "second stage" is properly semiological and translinguistic; it is less able to depend on previously acquired knowledge, so that, far from being helped, it must, on the contrary, participate—if it is able to—in work that is new. Thus it is condemned to suffer the present discomfort of semiotics.

Image Discourse in Relation to Langue: The Problem of Cinematographic "Syntax"

THE SECOND ARTICULATION.[55]   There is nothing in the cinema that corresponds, even metaphorically, to the second articulation.*   This

---

* Rather than to the cinema, this affirmation should in fact be applied to "cinematographic language," i.e., to the *specific level* of codification that is constituted by the signifying organizations proper to film and common to all films. Therefore it would be more correct to say that the cinema *as such* has no second articulation (and, as we will see further, no first articulation either). But the "cinema" as a totality—the sum of all that is said in films, as well as of all the signifying organizations (perceptual, intellectual, iconological, ideological, "symbolic," etc.) that affect the understanding of a whole film—the cinema as a totality represents a much vaster phenomenon, within which cinematographic language constitutes only one among many signifying levels. To that extent, it is not impossible that certain cinematographic significations are ruled by systems that, in one way or another, contain several articulations. The concept of *cinematographic language* is a methodological abstraction: This language is never present alone in films but is always in combination with

articulation is operative on the level of the signifier, but not on that of the significate: Phonemes and *a fortiori* "features" are distinctive units without proper signification. Their existence alone implies a great *distance* between "content" and "expression." In the cinema the distance is too short. The signifier is an image, the significate is what the image represents. Furthermore, the fidelity of the photographic process, which gives the image particular verisimilitude, and

---

various other systems of signification: cultural, social, stylistic, perceptual, etc.

Secondly, it is appropriate to note that, in the linguistic sense of the term, the articulations—i.e., what is called the "double articulation"—are not the only conceivable types of articulation.

For either one of these two reasons, one must make a careful distinction between two affirmations: The first, which is advanced in this text, consists in saying that cinematographic language in itself exhibits nothing resembling the double linguistic articulation. The second, for which I assume no responsibility, would consist in saying that the cinema has no articulations.

Indeed, there would be nothing absurd in supposing—and this is only an example—that the total cinematographic message brings five main levels of codification into play, each one of which would be a kind of articulation: (1) perception itself (systems for structuring space, "figures," and "backgrounds," etc.), to the degree that it already constitutes a system of acquired intelligibility, which varies according to different "cultures"; (2) recognition and identification of visual or auditive objects appearing on the screen—that is to say, the ability (which is also culturally acquired) to manipulate correctly the denoted material of the film; (3) all the "symbolisms" and connotations of various kinds attach themselves to objects (or to relationships between objects) outside of films—that is to say, in culture; (4) all the great narrative structures (in Claude Brémond's sense) which obtain outside of films (but in them as well) within each culture; and, finally, (5) the set of properly cinematographic systems that, in a specific type of discourse, organize the diverse elements furnished to the spectator by the four preceding instances.

We know that Umberto Eco has recently formulated an interesting hypothesis according to which the cinematographic message taken as a whole would involve only three main levels of articulation (*Appunti per une semiologica delle comunicazioni visivi,* University of Florence, Bompiani, 1967, pp. 139–52). In the preface of his work, *Le cru et le cuit* (Plon, 1964, p. 31, notably; *The Raw and the Cooked* [New York: Harper & Row, 1969]), one recalls, as well, Claude Lévi-Strauss distinguished two main levels of organization in pictorial art—and it is easy to apply this to cinematographic art: On one hand the objects that are represented on the canvas, and on the other hand the properly pictorial composition into which they enter. For his part, Pier Paolo Pasolini sees two principal levels of articulation in the pictorial message, somewhat like those discerned by Lévi-Strauss (*La lingua scritta dell'azione,* paper contributed to the Second Festival of New Cinema, *Pesaro II,* Italy, June 1966, reprinted in *Nuovi Argomenti,* new series, no. 2, April–June 1966, pp. 67–103).

the psychological mechanisms of participation, which ensure the famous "impression of reality," shorten the distance even more—so that
it is impossible to break up the signifier without getting isomorphic
segments of the significate. Thus the impossibility of a second articulation: Film constitutes an entirely too "intrinsic seme," to use Eric
Buyssens's terminology. If, in an image representing three dogs, I
isolate the third dog, I am necessarily isolating both the signifying
and the signified "third dog." The English logician and linguist
Ryle makes fun of a certain naïve concept of language (which de
Saussure already condemned), which he calls ironically the "FIDO-
Fido theory": The name FIDO corresponds exactly to the dog, Fido;
words stand in direct ratio to an equal number of pre-existing things.
This point of view, very backward in linguistics, is less so in the
cinema, where there are as many "things" in the filmic image as there
were in the filmed spectacle.

The theoreticians of the silent film liked to speak of the cinema as
a kind of Esperanto. Nothing is further from the truth. Certainly
Esperanto does differ from ordinary languages, but that is because it
accomplishes to perfection what they strive for but never attain: a
system that is totally conventional, specific, and organized. Film also
differs from true languages but in the opposite way. It would be more
correct to say that the true languages are caught between two Es-

---

Without going into the details of these several analyses, I will remark simply
that, in principle, they do not contradict the ideas here expressed. For it is
obvious that the authors I have mentioned (1) bring into their account aside
from cinematographic language itself one or another system of signification
that is mainly cultural and extends beyond the cinema, although it does come
into play in the deciphering of the film as totality; (2) they have in mind
levels of articulation of which they ask only that they be authentic—and I
agree with them that they are—but of which they demand no equivalence to
linguistic articulations (whereas, I want to insist, precisely on the absence of
these equivalences, without, however, maintaining that cinema has no articulation at all).

Similarly, it can be remarked that my "large syntagmatic category of the
image-track," which will be outlined further on (Chapter 5) by its very existence constitutes a specific articulation: It resembles neither the first, nor the
second articulation of verbal language—since it does not divide the film into
units comparable to phonemes or monemes—but it undoubtedly has the effect
of *articulating* (in another way—that is to say, on the level of the discourse)
the cinematographic message.

perantos: the true Esperanto (or the ido, or novial, or whatever), which is reached through an excess of linguisticity, and the other, the cinema, which has a dearth of linguisticity.

In short, the universality of the cinema is a two-fold phenomenon. Positive aspect: The cinema is universal because visual perception varies less throughout the world than languages do. Negative aspect: The cinema is universal because it lacks the second articulation. There is a solitary relationship between the two observations that must be emphasized: A visual spectacle entails a joining of the signifier to the significates, which in turn renders impossible their disjunction at any given moment and, therefore, the existence of a second articulation.

Strictly speaking, Esperanto is manufactured; it is a product of language. For the most part "visual Esperanto" is a raw material that precedes language. In this concept of filmic Esperanto there is, all the same, some truth: It is in the second articulation that languages differ most radically, one from another, and that men fail to understand each other.[56] As Roman Jakobson observes, the sentence is always more or less translatable.[57] That is because it corresponds to a real mental impulse, and not to a code unit. The word can still yield interlinguistic equivalences, imperfect to be sure, but sufficient to make dictionaries possible. The phoneme is completely untranslatable, since it is entirely defined by its position in the phonemic grid of each language. The absence of a meaning cannot be translated. Thus we return to the idea that image discourse needs no translation, and that is because, having no second articulation, it is already translated into all languages: The height of the translatable is the universal.

André Martinet believes that, strictly speaking, one cannot talk of language, except where there is double articulation.[58] In point of fact, the cinema is not a language but a language of art. The word, language, has numerous meanings, more or less strict, and each is in its own way justified. This polysemic multiplication tends—in my judgment—to branch out in two directions: Certain systems (even the least human ones) are called "languages" if their formal structure resembles that of our spoken languages: This is the case with the language of chess (which de Saussure found so interesting) or with the binary languages of computers. At the other pole, everything that expresses man to himself (even in the least organized and least linguistic way) is felt to be a "language": the language of flowers, the language of painting, even the language of silence. The semantic field of the word, language, seems to be organized along these two axes. Now it is in "language" in its most proper meaning (human phonic language) that these two vectors of metaphorical expansion are rooted: For verbal language is used by men to communicate among themselves, and it is highly organized. The two nodes of figurative meaning are already there. Keeping these conditions of usage in mind, which does not always allow us to abide by meanings one would like to be strict about, it seems appropriate to look at the cinema as a language without a system.

FIRST ARTICULATION. The cinema has no phonemes; nor does it, whatever one may say, have words. Except on occasion, and more or less by chance, it is not subject to the first articulation. It should be shown that the almost insurmountable difficulties that film "syntaxes" launch themselves into are derived for the most part from an initial confusion: The image is defined as a word, the sequence as a sentence. The case is, however, that the image (at least in the cinema) corresponds to one or more sentences, and the sequence is a complex segment of *discourse*.

The word, sentence, of course, here and on the following pages, designates the oral and not the written sentence of grammarians (a complex statement with multiple assertions, contained between two marked punctuations). I am speaking of the linguists' sentence.* In

---

* This distinction between two kinds of sentence seems less important to me today than it did when I wrote this article. First of all, from a purely linguistic point of view, Vendrys's analysis, which I used to support my argument, is subject to a number of reservations, particularly since Noam Chomsky's work has progressively shed new light on the problem of the sentence. Secondly, from a properly cinematographic point of view, it is in any case impossible to say whether the "shot" corresponds to *one* or to several sentences: The question of knowing whether these sentences would be of the "written" or "oral" type,

his famous example, designed precisely to distinguish between the two types of sentence, Joseph Vendrys[59] maintains that there are five sentences (in the sense that interests us) in the following statement: "You see that man/ over there/ he's sitting on the sand/ well, I met him yesterday/ he was at the station." I do not want to suggest that a film sequence with the same contents would have exactly these five sentences (shots). I mean simply that the image in the cinema is a kind of "equivalent" to the spoken sentence, not to the written sentence. It is not impossible that certain shots or groups of shots might, in addition, correspond to the "written" type of sentence—but that is another problem. In many respects,[60] film recalls written expression a great deal more than spoken language. But at a certain point in the division into units, the shot, a "completed assertive statement," as Benveniste would call it,[61] is equivalent to an oral sentence.

Roman Jakobson writes[62] that Shimkin, in his work on proverbs, was brought to propose that, in the proverb, "the highest coded linguistic unit functions simultaneously with the smallest poetic unit." The image discourse of the cinema represents a nonverbal area (while the proverb is transverbal). Nevertheless the shot, a "sentence" and not a word (like the proverb), is indeed the smallest "poetic" entity.

How is one to understand this correspondence between the filmic image and the sentence? First of all, the shot, through its semantic content, through what Eric Buyssens would call its "substance"[63] is closer, all things considered, to a sentence than to a word. An image

---

"simple" or "complex," is therefore quite secondary. One can say simply that a film "shot" is very different from a word, that it always constitutes an actualized unit of discourse, and that consequently it is to be situated *on the level of the sentence*. And that is indeed the observation I made in this text; but it should have exempted me from looking for more precise equivalences between the shot and one or another type of *internal phrastic structure* observable in languages. Since the shot is *not made of words,* it can "correspond" only *externally* to the sentence, i.e., in relation to discourse (see Chapter 5, part 3). As long as one seeks internal equivalences, one will be led into an impasse: Let us indeed suppose that in certain circumstances a shot can appear to be equivalent to several sentences (a thing that will not fail to occur): How are we to know if these sentences, in a written text, have always been separate sentences or if, for example, they had at one time been different "clauses" of a single complex sentence?

shows a man walking down a street: It is equivalent to the sentence "A man is walking down the street." The equivalence is rough, to be sure, and there would be much to say about it; however the same filmic image corresponds even less to the word "man," or the word "walk," or the word "street," and less still to the article "the" or to the zero-degree morpheme of the verb "walks."

The image is "sentence" less by its quantity of meaning (a concept too difficult to handle, especially in film) than by its assertive status. The image is *always actualized*. Moreover, even the image—fairly rare, incidentally—that might, because of its content, correspond to a "word" is still a sentence: This is a particular case, and a particularly revealing one. A close-up of a revolver does not mean "revolver" (a purely virtual lexical unit), but at the very least, and without speaking of the connotations, it signifies "Here is a revolver!" It carries with it a kind of *here* (a word which André Martinet rightly considers to be a pure index of actualization.[64] Even when the shot is a "word," it remains a kind of "sentence-word," such as one finds in certain languages.

CINEMA AND SYNTAX. The image is therefore always speech, never a unit of language. It is not surprising that the authors of "cinematographic grammars" have found themselves at an impasse. They claimed to have written a syntax of film, but, in fact, with their image-word, they had been thinking of something half way between a lexicon and a morphology, something that does not exist in any language. The cinema is something else.

There is a syntax of the cinema, but it remains to be made and could be done only on a syntactical, and not a morphological, basis.[65] De Saussure observed[66] that syntax is only an aspect of the syntagmatic: A thought that should be meditated on by anyone concerned with film. The shot is the smallest unit of the filmic chain (one might perhaps call it a "taxeme," as Hjelmslev uses the term[67]); the sequence is a great syntagmatic whole. One should examine the richness, exuberance even, of the syntagmatic arrangements possible in film (which will bring one to see the problem of montage under a new light), and contrast it to the surprising poverty of the paradigmatic resources of the cinema.*

THE PARADIGMATIC CATEGORY OF FILM. In the writings of theoreticians, the word, montage, in its broad sense includes cutting, but the opposite never occurs. The moment of ordering (montage) in film is somehow more important—"linguistically" at least—than the choosing of the images (cutting), no doubt because the latter, being too open, is not a choice, but rather an act of decision, a kind of creation. That is why, on the *artistic level,* the content of each shot is of great importance (although the organization is itself an art). On the level of the visual subject, there is art, if anything. Art continues on the level of the sequence or of the composed shot, and "cinematographic language" begins. Hence the condemnation of "beautiful photography" in the cinema.

* I am no longer of the opinion, as I reread this, that the two aspects of the problem can be strictly speaking "*contrasted.*" For, as I have said—but not sufficiently clearly—in the text reprinted here, they are not situated on the same level: One can speak of "paradigmatic poverty" in relation to the *image* (see pp. 65–67) and of "syntagmatic richness" in relation to the *structuring of images* (see p. 67). At the same time, however, it should be remarked that the existence of several types of image-ordering has the effect of creating (on the level of discourse) a specific paradigmatic category, which is constituted precisely by the total system of the different syntagmas. One cannot indeed conceive of a syntagmatic category with no corresponding paradigmatic category on the *same level,* (that is, a paradigmatic category related to units of the same magnitude), nor of a paradigmatic category with no corresponding syntagmatic category on the same level: by definition the syntagmatic categories and paradigmatic categories are strict correlatives. I will return to these problems in Chapter 5.
Second observation: One must not exclude the possibility that *between the images themselves* there are different kinds of paradigmatic associations, since in all human groups one finds various cultural "symbolisms" that relate to iconography. These paradigms, however, are not peculiar to cinematographic language.
Third and final observation: One must keep in mind when distinguishing between the "image" and the "structuring of images" that the first term can designate either the shot (as opposed to the sequence) or the filmed subject (as opposed to the shot, which is already the product of an initial composing or arrangement). In either case, what we call "image" is really the *photographic fact* (or phonographic fact, if we are referring to the sound-track), and what it is contrasted to is the *filmic fact.* The latter indeed unfolds on two levels: within the shot, from "subject" to "subject"; within the sequence, from shot to shot. For more on this point, see Chapter 5, particularly part 6.

The image paradigm is fragile in film; often still-born, it is approximate, easily modified, and it can always be circumvented. Only to a slight degree does the filmic image assume meaning in relation to the other images that could have occurred at the same point along the chain. Nor can the latter be inventoried; their number is, if not limitless, at least more "open" than the "most open" linguistic inventory. There is no equivalent here to the "peribolic" unraveling whose importance in verbal language has been underlined by Guillaume.[68] Charles Bally[69] observed that certain units that are opposed to an unlimited and undefinable number of terms (dependent only on context, the speakers, and the association of ideas) are often in the long run unopposed, really, to any term: This is somewhat the case with the filmic image.

Everything is present in film: hence the obviousness of film, and hence also its opacity. The clarification of present by absent units occurs much less than in verbal language. The relationships *in præsentia* are so rich that they render the strict organization of *in-absentia* relationships superfluous and difficult. A film is difficult to explain because it is easy to understand. The image impresses itself on us, blocking everything that is not itself.

A rich message with a poor code, or a rich text with a poor system, the cinematographic image is primarily speech. It is all assertion. The word, which is the unit of language, is missing; the sentence, which is the unit of speech, is supreme. The cinema can speak only in neologisms. Every image is a *hapax.** It would be fruitless to

---

* It is becoming less and less certain, in fact—especially since one has begun to understand Chomsky's work—that the sentence is a unit of speech. In one way the sentence is even the unit of language *par excellence,* since a language is a system that allows one to make sentences.

As for the filmic image, which is only a "sentence" because of its function in discourse, and not because of its internal structure, it does indeed remain a "hapax," but it also is contained by larger units that are not hapaxes. I was therefore only partially correct in saying that the cinema can only talk by neologism. I should have said that, *in order to speak,* the cinema is able to use only neologism as its basic material, but that, *in speaking* it integrates these neologisms (without however altering them in their details) into a second order not governed by the single law of proliferation. On these problems, see Chapter 5, parts 3 and 4.

search among images for true associative series or strict semantic fields. Even the cautious, flexible structuralism of a Stephen Ullmann,[70] for example, is out of place here, for it is lexicological, and a "filmolinguistic" structuralism can only be syntactic.

There is a paradigmatic category of film. But the commutable units are large signifying units. Thus, in the scholarly work of J. L. Rieupeyrout on the history of the Western, we are told that there was a period when the "good" cowboy was indicated by his white clothes and the "bad" by his black costumes. The audience, apparently, always knew which was which. This allows us to establish a rudimentary commutation as much on the level of the signifier (white/black) as on that of the significates (good/bad). The two colors are already *predicated* (since attributed to present clothes), and so are the two qualities (since it is the cowboy in the image who is either good or bad), prior to the commutation, and this is the essential difference from a lexical and *a fortiori* phonological commutation. But that is not all: The paradigm, perhaps precisely because it is engaged too much in "speech," is unstable and fragile; the convention of the cowboy in white, or in black, did not last long. It was inevitable that one fine day a film-maker, bored with the routine, should get the idea of dressing his rider in gray, or in a white shirt and black pants, and so much for the paradigm! The poverty of the paradigm is the counterpart of a wealth distributed elsewhere: The film-maker can express himself by showing us directly the diversity of the world, and in this he differs from the reciter of tales. Thus the paradigm is very rapidly overwhelmed: This is another aspect of the kind of struggle, which occurs at certain points in the cinema, between code and message. The great directors (and is it not puerile to repeat always that the cinema is not them, for who else could it be?) have avoided the paradigm.

Or at least have avoided *certain* paradigms. For the "type" *cowboy in black/cowboy in white* defines only one kind of filmic paradigm. "Syntactic" by the syntagmatic extent of its commutable segments and by their assertive status, such an opposition, however, bears, by its contents, on affective impressions ("the cowboy is good") that retain something of a "levical" quality. Other filmic oppositions, also more or less commutable are more rooted in syntax and bear more on kinds of "morphemes."* A large number of *camera movements* (rear and forward dolly) or *techniques of punctuation* (dissolve or cut) can be considered in this light.** It is a case of one relationship opposed to another relationship. In addition to the commutable elements, there is always a kind of support[71] that is ideally invariable. Rear and forward dolly shots correspond to two intentions of a "seeing"—but that "seeing" always has an object; that which the camera moves away from or approaches. It is, therefore, to the theory of syncategorematic terms that one should look here: Just as the word "but" never expresses the idea of the adversative as such, but always an adversative relationship between two realized units, a forward dolly expresses a concentration of attention, not on itself, but always on an object.

The duality of support and relationship, in a language that permits the simultaneity of several visual perceptions, explains why such procedures have something *supersegmental* to them: The support and the relationship are often perceived at the same time. Furthermore, in the cinema the "relationship" is often one and the same as the camera's (and the spectator's) "seeing" of the support object. A forward dolly on a face is a way of seeing that face. That is why so

---

* The word is taken here in the sense in which it is opposed to the term "semanteme," or the more current "lexeme," and not in the sense: minimum unit having its own signification. It seems to me that I did not sufficiently insist, in the passage above, on the fact that paradigms of this second variety—precisely because they come closer to those of true grammar—are much less easily judged than the others in terms of "originality" or "banality" when one encounters them in films. It is these paradigms that constitute "cinematographic language" itself, whereas the systems like that of the cowboy in black or white only affect a few film subjects, and only for a restricted period. I return to this problem later, in Chapter 6 (see especially pp. 221–23, including note on 223).

** And, even more so, many *codified montage orderings* (see "Problems of Denotation in the Fiction Film," especially pp. 119–33). That is why I am indeed less skeptical today about the paradigmatic category of film than I was when I wrote this article; what I had not seen is that a major part of the paradigmatic category of film must be sought for in the syntagmatic category itself—*that is to say in the interplay between various different image orderings*. On this point see also "Problems of Denotation. . . ."

many materially unreal filmic procedures are psychologically convincing, as has been occasionally noted.[72] Consider, for example, the rapid forward dolly, which makes the object grow larger to our eyes, or oblique framing, or certain extreme close-ups—they are all instances in which the appearance of the object is hardly plausible. But the super segemental aspect of the support-relationship pair displaces filmic "plausibility" toward the level of the living, constructive dynamism of perception, and away from that of the objective circumstances of the perceived situation, for in the same segment the film contains a perceived and a perceiving instance. There are many camera movements that work by bringing an implausible object to a "seeing" that makes it plausible.

Filming Intellection[73]

A film is always more or less understandable. If by chance it is not at all understood, that is as a result of peculiar circumstances, and not of the semiological process proper to the cinema. Naturally the cryptic film, like cryptic utterance, the extraordinary film, like the extraordinary book, the film that is too rich or too new, like an explanation that is too rich or too new, can very well become unintelligible. But as "language" a film is always grasped—except by abnormal persons who would not understand any other form of discourse any better, and often not as well; except by the blind, suffering from a selective impairment blocking reception of the signifier (like the deaf with speech); except, finally, in those cases where the actual substance of the signifier is materially damaged (the old film, scratched, yellowed, and undecipherable; the speaker whose voice is so hoarse he cannot be understood).

Aside from these cases, a film is always understood, but always *more or less so,* and this "more or less" is not easily quantifiable, for there are no discernible degrees, no units of signification that can be immediately counted. With two persons speaking different languages, one should—in principle, at least—be able to enumerate the quantitative degrees of their mutual understanding: *A* knows three words of the language spoken by *B*, and *B* six words of the language spoken by *A*. Within a given sentence, it is a particular word, and not its neighbor, that has not been understood; or it can be established that one certain word, by a kind of ricochet, has rendered the whole sentence unintelligible to the hearer. A linguistic unit is either *recognized* or not by the hearer, since it already exists in the language. Marcel Cohen's suggestion (to study the degrees of understanding between languages) can be successfully undertaken, despite great difficulties. But in the cinema the units—or rather, the elements —of signification that are present together in the image are too numerous and too continuous: Even the most intelligent viewer cannot discern them all. On the other hand it is sufficient to have generally understand the main elements to grasp the approximate, overall, and yet relevant meaning of the whole: Even the dimmest spectator will have roughly understood. There have been some rather interesting experiments,[74] thanks to which one has been able to isolate the *character* of what is easy or difficult to understand in film. But it cannot be inferred from this that the *degree* of understanding of a normal commercial film can easily be established for a particular viewer or category of viewers.

One must also set aside clearly all those cases—very numerous in the cinema, as well as in verbal language, literature, and even everyday life—in which the message is unintelligible because of the very nature of what is being said, without the semiological process being affected. Many films are incomprehensible (either entirely or in part and depending on the audience) because their *diegesis* contains realities or concepts that are too subtle, too exotic, or mistakenly thought to be familiar. The fact has not been sufficiently emphasized that, in these cases, it is not the film itself, but on the contrary what the film does not make clear, that is incomprehensible. And the reason this has not been emphasized is because the current fashion is to insist that *everything* is language, to such an extent that what is *said* is overpowered and reduced to nothing by how one *says* it. This is a very common illusion. The angry lover shouts to his faithless mistress, "You don't understand me!" But she understands him only too well; the case is simply that she no longer loves him. Whether filmic or verbal, language cannot suppress reality; on the contrary, it is rooted in reality. If men do not "understand" each other, it is not only because of words, but also because of what the words contain. How many "misunderstandings" are actually the result of too great an understanding! People always see a lack of understanding where there is real disagreement. A whole army of Korzybskis and "general semanticists"(!) cannot put a stop to antagonism, stupidity, and indifference. The audience of local shopkeepers* who booed Antonioni's *L'Avventura* at the Cannes Film Festival had understood the film, but either they had not grasped, or were indifferent to, its message. Filmic intellection had nothing to do with their attitude; what bothered them was simply "life" itself. It is normal that the problems of the couple as stated by Antonioni should leave a large section of the audience indifferent, puzzled, or derisive.**

* They are given free tickets by the municipality of Cannes and constitute what one refers to as the Festival audience.

** In this passage reprinted here, the material has been considered too exclusively from the *point of view of the cinema*, and I have not paid sufficient attention to the possibilities of a general semiotics of culture. To be sure, it was not the cinematographic language in *L'Avventura* (which was utilized in a particularly clear fashion) that put off the Cannes "shopkeepers"; in this sense one can say that it was the subject of the film, and therefore "life," that had annoyed them. If all that is wanted is to show that the particular problem of filmic intellection is not relevant in such cases, the argument suffices. But if one wants to go further, one must then indeed observe that the "subject" of the film (as well as "life" itself) is, in turn, liable to be more or less understood—again depending on the audience, and on the form in which it is presented—*according to a set of cultural systems* that, though they are foreign to the cinema, nevertheless do constitute organized systems of signifiers.

In other words, the distinction referred to between what is said and how it is said should be made relative: One can identify what pertains to the "saying" and what belongs to the "said" only in relation to the instance of "saying" with which one is occupied in each particular analysis. When analyzing another set of signifiers, one might well find that what was part of the "saying" now comes under the "said." In every human phenomenon of some magnitude—the cinema included—various cultural systems intervene together and overlap in complex ways. A "content" determined by one of these systems can be annexed by another (which encloses it although it did not determine it) within the same overall "message." What we call "the cinema" is not only cinematographic language itself; it is also a thousand social and human significations that have been wrought elsewhere in culture but that occur also in films. Furthermore, the "cinema" is also each individual film as a unique composition, with signifying

Cinema and Literature:
The Problem of Filmic Expressiveness

The cinema is not a language system, because it contradicts three important characteristics of the linguistic fact: a language is a *system* of *signs* used for *intercommunication*. Three elements to the definition.[75] Now, like all the arts, and because it is itself an art, the cinema is one-way communication. As we have already seen, it is only partly a system. Finally, it uses only very few true signs. Some film images, which, through long previous use in speech, have been solidified so that they acquire stable and conventional meanings, become kinds of signs. But really vital films avoid them and are still understood. Therefore the nerve center of the semiological process lies elsewhere.

The image is first and always an image. In its perceptual literal-

and signified elements distinct from those of cinematographic language in general. In the case of *L'Avventura,* one can isolate at least three autonomous factors of signification (sets of signifiers) that are present at the level of the concrete message: (1) cinematographic language (a much larger category but one that does not exclude the film), (2) *L'Avventura* as a work of art (which, on both the levels of expression and content, *adds* to cinematographic language many particular structures that do not belong to the general "writing" of the cinema), and (3) a peculiar ideology (that of the "modern couple," of the "exhaustion of feeling," etc.) derived from a historical and sociocultural situation foreign to the cinema, but liable to be reflected in films. The insufficiently educated audience in my example did not understand the film, not because it could not grasp system 1, but surely because it was unable to decipher correctly systems 2 and 3. The cinematographic "saying" was not responsible. But nor was the "said" entirely so either—or, if it was, it was so only in relation to the previous "saying"— since it comprised on the one hand a particular "Antonionian" content and on the other a certain "socio-ideological" content. So that, in a way, it is still true that the cause lay with the "saying" and not with what was "said"; yet in another way the responsibility was in the "said" and not in the "saying." In the study of a determined signifying system many things that appear to be pure substance actually correspond to significations derived from elsewhere, where they existed as forms and not as substances. Unless one entirely abandons the endeavour to speak about Man, one cannot avoid the enclosing of meaning. The reason that the cinema as a totality gives a first impression of being a collective body lacking in any kind of strict organization is in large part becasue it is one of the locations where a very large number of signifying systems, each having its relative autonomy, come together from the four corners of culture: cinematographic language itself is only one of those systems. Whatever cinematographic language does not account for is not necessarily condemned to formlessness; simply, it has been formed elsewhere.

ness it reproduces the signified spectacle whose signifier it is; and thus it becomes what it shows, to the extent that it does not have to *signify it* (if we take the word in the sense of *signum facere,* the special making of a sign). There are many characteristics to the filmic image that distinguish it from the preferred form of signs—which is arbitrary, conventional, and codified. These are the consequences of the fact that from the very first an image is not the indication of something other than itself, but the pseudopresence of the thing it contains.

The spectacle recorded by the film-maker may be natural ("realistic" films, scenes shot in the street, *cinéma verité,* etc.) or arranged (the film-operas of Eisenstein's last period, Orson Welles's films, and, in general, the cinema of the unreal, or of the fantastic, expressionist cinema, etc.). But it is basically all one thing. The *subject* of the film is either "realistic" or not; but, whatever the case, the film itself only shows whatever it shows. So we have a film-maker, realistic or not realistic, who films something. What happens? Whether natural or arranged, the filmed spectacle already had its own expressiveness, since it was after all a piece of the world, which always has a meaning. The words a novelist uses also have pre-existing meanings, since they are segments of language, which is always significant. Music and architecture have the advantage of being able to develop *immediately* their properly aesthetic expressiveness—their style—in materials (sound or stone) that are purely impressionable and do not *designate.*[76] But literature and the cinema are by their nature condemned to connotation,[77] since denotation always precedes their artistic enterprise.*

Film, like verbal language, can be used merely as a vehicle, without any artistic intention, with designation (denotation) governing alone. Consequently, the art of the cinema, like verbal art, is, so to speak, driven one notch upward:[78] In the final analysis it is by the wealth of its connotations that Proust's great novel can be distin-

---

* "Prior" to literature, denotation is secured through *idiom.* "Prior" to the art film, it is secured: (1) through perceptual analogy, (2) through the cinema language that contains a partial denotative code (derived incidentally from the earlier search for connotations). On this point see Chapter 5, pp. 117–19.

guished—in semiological terms—from a cookbook, or a film of Visconti's from a medical documentary.

Mikel Dufrenne believes that in any work of art the *world that is represented* (denoted) never constitutes the major part of what the author has to say. It is merely a threshold. In the nonrepresentational arts it is even missing: The art of stone and the art of sound do not designate anything. When it is present its function is only to introduce the *expressed world*:[79] the artist's style, the relationship of themes and values, a recognizable "accent"—in short, the connotative universe.

In this respect, however, there is an important difference between literature and the cinema. In the cinema, aesthetic expressiveness is grafted onto natural expressiveness—that of the landscape or face the film shows us. In the verbal arts, it is grafted, not onto any genuine prior expressiveness, but onto a conventional *signification*—that of language—which is generally inexpressive. Consequently the introduction of the aesthetic dimension—expressiveness added to expressiveness—into the cinema is made with ease: An easy art, the cinema is in constant danger of falling victim to this easiness. It is so easy to create an effect when one has available the natural expression of things, of beings, of the world! Too easy. The cinema is also a difficult art: For, Sisyphus-like, it is trapped under the burden of its facility. There are very few films which do not have a little art in them; fewer still contain a great deal of art. Literature—especially poetry—is a so much more improbable art! How can that insane craft ever succeed?—To bestow an aesthetic expressiveness (that is, *in a natural way*) upon those "words of the tribe" Mallarmé railed against—where linguists agree in recognizing only a small portion of expressiveness and a very large portion of arbitrary signification, even when one considers the modifications brought to the famous theory of the "arbitrary" since de Saussure (the presence in language of partial motivation—whether phonic, morphological, or semantic—brought to light principally by Ullmann; the motivations by the signifier and other "implicit associations" analyzed by Charles Bally; and, in general, the various studies on the "motivated" areas of language). But when the

poet has succeeded in his initial alchemy and has made words expressive, the greater part of his task is done: In this respect, literature, which is a difficult art, enjoys at least that advantage. Its endeavor is so arduous that the weight it bears is hardly a danger. There
are a great number of books entirely lacking in art; there are a few
books possessing enormous art.

The concept of *expression* is used here as defined by Mikel Dufrenne. There is expression when a "meaning" is somehow immanent
to a thing, is directly released from it, and merges with its very form.*
Some of Eric Buyssens's "intrinsic semes" perhaps fall under this definition. *Signification,* on the contrary, links from the outside an iso-
lable signifier to a significate that is itself—this has been known since
de Saussure[80]—a concept and not a thing. These are the "extrinsic
semes" Buyssens writes about.[81] A concept is signified; a thing is expressed. Being extrinsic, signification can only derive from a convention; it is of necessity obligatory, since one would deprive it of its
only support—consensus—by rendering it optional. This, one recognizes, is the famous "thesis" of the Greek philosophers. There is *more
than one difference* between expression and signification: One is
natural, the other conventional; one is global and continuous, the
other divided into discrete units; one is derived from beings and
things, the other from ideas.**

* Gestalt, and not graphic contour.
** Today, I would say rather that expressiveness is a meaning established
without recourse to a *special* and explicit code. But not without recourse to vast
and complex sociocultural *organizations,* which are represented by other forms of
codification. On this point, see Chapter 5, pp. 110–14 and 140–42. In general,
if the sum of the effects of meaning we call *expressive,* or *motivated,* or *symbolic,* etc., appears to be "natural"—and is indeed so in a certain way, for example to a phenomenology or a psychology of meaning—it is mainly because the
effects are very deeply rooted in cultures, and because they are rooted at a
level that, in these cultures, lies far beyond the various explicit, specialized, and
properly informative codes. One can of course argue whether these deep significatory organizations existing at these distant levels can rightly be considered as
proper codes. But, whatever the case, they are more or less organized systems,
which can convey meaning and vary from one human group to another. If as a
general rule the system-user experiences them not as codes but as effects of
natural meaning, that is because he has sufficiently "assimilated" them to the
extent that he does not possess them *in a separate state.* Thus, as a paradoxical
consequence, the deepest cultural codifications are experienced as the most

The expressiveness of the world (of the landscape or face) and the expressiveness of art (the melancholy sound of the Wagnerian oboe) are ruled essentially by the same semiological mechanism: "Meaning" is naturally derived from the signifier as a whole, without resorting to a code. It is at the level of the signifier, and only there, that the difference occurs: In the first case the author is nature (expressiveness of the world) and in the second it is man (expressiveness of art).

That is why literature is an art of heterogeneous connotation (expressive connotation added to nonexpressive denotation), while the cinema is an art of homogeneous connotation (expressive connotation added to expressive denotation). The problem of cinematographic expressiveness should be studied from the point of view I have just outlined, for it would bring one to consider style, and therefore the author. In Eisenstein's *Que Viva Mexico,* there is a famous shot of the tortured, yet peaceful faces of three peons buried to their shoulders being trampled by the horses of their oppressors. It is a beautiful triangular composition, a well-known trademark of the great director. The denotative relationship yields a signifier (three faces) and a significate (they have suffered, they are dead). This is the "subject," the "story." There is natural expressiveness: Suffering is read on the peons' faces, death in their motionlessness. Over this is superimposed the connotative relationship, which is the beginning of art: The nobility of the landscape as it is structured by the triangle of the

---

natural. Other codifications—which are cultural too, but are more superficial or more specialized—are, on the contrary, much more easily identified by the user as conventional and separate systems.

In the text above, I gave, among other examples of *expressiveness,* what we quite rightly call "facial expression." Certainly it is not through the effect of "cinematographic language" (nor of any other explicitly informative code) that the film spectator is able to decipher the expressions he reads on the hero's face. However, it is not through the effect of nature itself either, for the expressions of the face have meanings that vary considerably from one civilization to another (think of the difficulty one experiences in trying to understand the facial expressions in a Japanese film). Nevertheless it remains true that in films of our own culture we understand them quite naturally—that is to say, through the effect of a knowledge that is very old and very deep in us, that functions by itself, and that—for us—is henceforth merged with perception itself.

faces (*form* of the image) expresses what the author, by means of his style, wanted it to "say": The greatness of the Mexican people, his certainty of their eventual victory, a kind of passion in that man from the North for all that sunny splendor. Therefore, aesthetic expressiveness. And yet still "natural": The strong and savage grandeur rises very directly out of the plastic composition that turns suffering into beauty. Nevertheless, two languages exist side by side in this image, since one can identify two signifiers: (1) three faces in a barren stretch of land; (2) the landscape given a triangular shape by the faces—and two significates—(1) suffering and death; (2) grandeur and triumph. One notices that, as usual, the connoted expression is much "vaster" than the denoted expression, and is also disconnected from it.[82] One finds the denotative material (signifier and significate) functioning as the signifier of the connotation: The solemn, sorrowful victory that the image connotes is expressed by the three faces themselves (signifiers of denotation) as well as by the martyrdom they exhibit (significate of denotation). The signifier of the aesthetic language is the sum of the signifier-significate of a prior language (the anecdote, the subject) with which it is interlocked. This is precisely Hjelmslev's definition of connotation; the linguist, we know, does not use the terms "signifier" and "significate," but *expression* and *content* ("*cénématique*" and "*plérématique*"). However, for the student of the cinema the word *expression* (as distinct from *signification*) is too useful to be given the meaning of "signifier," for the result would be a very annoying polysemic collision. From our point of view, therefore, "expression" does not designate the signifier, but rather the relationship between a signifier and a significate, when that relationship is "intrinsic."* It would even be possible, in the case of expressive semes, to use *expresser* and *expressed*, re-

* This terminological problem does not seem as serious to me today; it suffices to indicate clearly in each case what one is talking about. Moreover the relationship between expression and signification no longer seems to me to be as adversative; the distinction retains all of its value for a phenomenology of meaning, but for a semiological analysis it may be a matter of codified organizations in both cases, although each has a different character and is situated at a different level. See Chapter 5, pp. 110–14.

serving "signifier" and "significate" for nonexpressive relationships (signification proper). But one hesitates dropping such established terms, which, since de Saussure, have been linked to so many important analyses, as the words *signifier* and *significate*.

Comparisons are frequently made between the cinema and "language," where the identity of the latter is uncertain and variable. At times it is literature (the art of language), and at other times it is ordinary language that one contrasts to film. In such a muddle it is impossible to see clearly. The art of words and the art of images, as we have seen, are located along the same semiological horizon; on the connotative level they are neighbors. If the art of the cinema is compared to ordinary language, however, everything is changed; the two members are no longer on the same plane. The cinema begins where ordinary language ends: at the level of the "sentence"—the filmmaker's minimum unit and the highest properly linguistic unit of language. We then no longer have two arts; what we have is one art and one language (in this particular case, language itself). The strictly linguistic laws cease when nothing is any longer obligatory, when ordering becomes "free."* But that is the point where film begins; it is immediately and automatically situated on the plane of rhetoric and poetics.

How then is one to explain such a curious lack of symmetry, a lack that insidiously confuses scholars and renders books obscure? On the

---

* The quotation marks were placed around the word "free" to indicate that the freedom I am talking about is never total—since, in the next sentence I mention "rhetoric and poetics" (to which one might add, incidentally, the various Barthesian "writings"). In many ways "cinematographic language" is one of these "writings"—on this point, see note, Chapter 6, p. 223. Simply, it is true, as Roman Jakobson noted, that, as one considers syntagmatic units of increasing magnitude, the portion of freedom available to the speaker becomes increasingly important. In this respect, the *level of the sentence* is a kind of threshold, below which the speaker is ruled (for the most part anyway) by the law of idiom, beyond which he falls under various laws of "composition," "rhetoric," etc., which are less restrictive—or perhaps have other restrictions?—than those of idiom. One can, if not ignore them, at least circumvent them, play with them, bend them, etc. That is indeed why the most authentic creativity (or "originality") is by no means inseparable from a total *freedom:* The French classical writers of the seventeenth century understood this perfectly, and it was bourgeois romanticism that made us forget it.

verbal side two levels—verbal language and literature—are readily distinguished. On the filmic side there is only and always the "cinema." To be sure, one can make a distinction between films that are purely utilitarian (educational films, for example) and films that are artistic. Nevertheless one senses that this is not altogether satisfactory and that the distinction is not as clear cut as that between the poetic or dramatic word and a conversation in the street. There are, of course, borderline cases that obscure the division: The films of Flaherty, Murnau, or Painlevé, which are both documentaries (biological and ethnographic) and works of art. In the verbal order, however, one may find many equivalent examples. The crux of the matter must, therefore, lie elsewhere. In truth there is no totally aesthetic use of the cinema, for even the most connotative image cannot avoid being also a photographic representation. Even in the period when filmmakers like Germaine Dulac dreamed of a "pure cinema," the most nonrealistic avant-garde films, the films that were the most resolutely devoted to the exclusive concerns of rhythmic composition, still represented something—whether it was the variations of changing cloud patterns, the play of light on water, or the ballet of pistons and connecting rods. Nor is there a totally "utilitarian" cinema, for even the most denotative image has some connotations. The most literal educational documentary cannot prevent itself from framing its images and organizing their sequence with at least something like an artistic concern; when a "language" does not already exist, one must be something of an artist to speak it, however poorly. For to speak it is partly to invent it, whereas to speak the language of everyday is simply to use it.

All this is derived from the fact that in the cinema connotation is homogeneous with denotation, and like it, is expressive. One is forever shifting from art to non-art, and vice-versa. The beauty of the film is governed to some extent by the same laws as the beauty of the filmed spectacle; in some cases it is impossible to tell which of the two is beautiful and which of the two is ugly. A film by Fellini differs from an American Navy film*—made to teach the art of tying knots

---

* Let us not forget that there are thousands of films of this type.

to new recruits—through its talent and through its intention and not through its most intimate semiological workings. Purely vehicular films* are made in the same way others are, whereas a poem by Victor Hugo is not shaped in the same way as a conversation between two office workers: First of all, one is written while the other is oral; a film, however, is always filmed. But that is not the main point. It is because of its heterogeneous connotation (that is, the fact that it imparts a value to words that are in themselves nonexpressive) that the gap between the functional use of the verb and its aesthetic use came into being.**

Thus the impression of having on the one hand two realities (ordinary language and literature) and on the other only one (the "cinema").† And thus—finally—the truth of that impression. Verbal language is used at every hour, at every moment. In order to exist, literature assumes that a book must first be written by a man—a special, costly act that cannot be diluted in ordinary activity. Whether "utilitarian" or "artistic," a film is always like a book and not like a conversation. It must always be created. Like a book still, and unlike the spoken sentence, a film does not automatically entail a direct answer from an interlocutor present to give an immediate reply in the same language; and in this sense film is expression rather than signification. There is a somewhat obscure but perhaps essential solidary

* Like those of the American Navy I have just mentioned, or even like the technical films of the French Institut de Filmologie, or technological films in general. The documentaries one sees in movie theaters are something else; they are, in purpose at least, already art films.

** In fact, even in the verbal order, pure denotation is very rare. Everyday language carries strong connotations. In *Le Langage et la vie* (Geneva, 1926), Charles Bally analyzes the spontaneous expressiveness of everyday or "popular" language at length and shows that in essence it is no different from literary or poetic expressiveness. But this is another problem. The "gap" I am referring to still exists—in the verbal order, not in the cinema—between expressive connotation (whether it is "literary" or "ordinary") and pure denotation (i.e., the inexpressive code of *langue*).

† In *Esthétique et psychologie du cinéma,* vol. I, Jean Mitry notes quite rightly (p. 48) that the word "cinema" designates three different things: A means of mechanical recording, which lies this side of art (animated photography); cinematographic art, which is also language (filmic fact); and, finally, a means of broadcasting (cinematographic fact).

relationship between *communication* (bilateral relation) and "arbitrary" signification; conversely, unilateral messages often depend on (nonarbitrary) expression—a relationship that is easier to grasp. A thing or a being yields its *singularity* through expression in a message that implies no answer. Even the most harmonious love is not a dialogue so much as it is a kind of duet. Jacques tells Nicole of his love for her; Nicole tells Jacques of her love for him. They are therefore not speaking about the same thing, and one says rightly that their love is "shared" (divided). They do not answer each other—indeed how can one really answer a person expressing himself?

Shared, their love is divided into two loves, which yield two expressions. For Jacques and Nicole, expressing as they did two different sentiments, to evolve, rather than the give-and-take of a dialogue, the agreement of a true encounter tending toward a fusion that abolishes all dialogue, there had to be a kind of coincidence—hence the rareness of the occurrence—rather than that interplay of influences and after-the-fact adjustments by which a dialogue is characterized. Like Jacques (without Nicole) or like Nicole (without Jacques), films and books express themselves and are not really answered. But if, using ordinary language, I ask, "What time is it?" and someone answers, "Eight o'clock," I have not been expressing myself; I have signified, I have communicated, and I have been answered.

It is therefore true that we identify only one cinema, unlike the double term literature-language, and furthermore that that one cinema resembles literature rather than language.

Cinema and Translinguistics:
The Large Signifying Units

By initially casting light on what the cinema is not, and thanks to its analysis of language systems, linguistics—and especially that part of it which leads to translinguistics (semiotics)—gradually allows us to glimpse what the cinema is. The smallest filmic unit is the "sentence," the assertion, the actualized unit. This suggests certain comparisons.

A whole tendency of modern research, mostly in the straight line of the Saussurian enterprise, has come to be concerned precisely with the sentence. Joseph Vendryes[83] notes that a gesture of the hand is equivalent to a sentence rather than to a word. Eric Buyssens makes a similar observation[84] about traffic signs and, more generally, about all semes that cannot be broken down into signs. Claude Lévi-Strauss defines the smallest unit of the myth—the *"mythème"*—as the assigning of a predicate to a subject—that is to say, as an assertion; he even adds[85] that each *mythème* can perhaps, when it is first transcribed onto cards, be relevantly summarized by a sentence; and, at a later stage in formalization, the *"grand mythème"* is still, he says, a package of predicative relationships—in short, a set of sentences having a recurrent theme. In his study of proverbs, already mentioned, Shimkin sees the smallest poetic unit in the largest coded linguistic unit. Vladimir Propp's analysis of Russian folktales is undertaken in a similar spirit.[86] Roland Barthes has defined the modern myth as a unit of speech,[87] and has emphasized—precisely in relation to the cinema— the "large signifying units."[88] Georges Mounin[89] believes that certain "nonlinguistic systems of communication" have become so important in modern society that the time has arrived to undertake seriously the semiotic de Saussure had dreamt of (and this is what Eric Buyssens had been saying already in the very first lines of his book), instead of dispatching it in a few sentences clapped on to the end of textbooks of linguistics. Roman Jakobson believes that poetry could be studied in a more linguistic spirit, on the condition that linguistics in turn be concerned with units larger than those of the sentence.[90] These are all converging perspectives.*

* Since this article was written (February 1964) this trend has become even more pronounced. One would now have to add to the list—to mention only those contributions of a general, theoretical nature, and more especially those applicable to significatory bodies other than verbal languages—the work of Algirdas Julien Greimas and Luis J. Prieto, whose precise significance have become more clearly apparent now that each writer has outlined his thought in a coherent, over-all exposé: *Sémantique structurale* (1966) for Greimas, and *Messages et signaux* (also 1966) for Prieto. Similarly, the gathering of several of Émile Benveniste's articles into a single volume, *Problèmes de linguistique generale* (again 1966) has contributed to clarifying the notion of *discourse.* Also, since 1964 a number of semiological investigations have been undertaken, which, on questions such as narration and discourse, partly overlap on the

The "nonlinguistic systems" Georges Mounin refers to[91] are those of numbers (telephone, social security, etc.), traffic signals, cartography, the symbology of tourist guidebooks, and advertising images. He does not speak of the cinema. Nevertheless he does observe that, in the modern world, the image tends gradually to lose its original decorative role and to acquire an informative function. Above all he underscores the fact that many of these nonlinguistic systems are ruled by a single articulation. "Semanteme by semanteme," he says,[92] "never phoneme by phoneme." However it seems that many nonlinguistic systems are broken down into "sentences," rather than into semantemes. Many, but not all. Those Mounin mentions, which can be analyzed into words (like the symbols of international tourism signifying "restaurant," "hotel," or "garage"), do indeed exhibit a single articulation. It is these systems, as the author says, that justify André Martinet's question: Can a perfect "ideographic system" exist, "a language that would no longer be spoken but that one would continue to write," a "system in which the units of content would merge with those of expression"—whereas the second articulation divides discourse into expressive units without corresponding content? In the cinema, as in other nonlinguistic systems, the units of content are also "merged" with those of expression, but in a different sense—on the level of the "sentence."* Any traffic sign is a sentence in the impera-

---

semiotics of film: literary studies, mythological studies, studies of narrativity, etc., in France (see, for example, *Communications,* no. 8, special issue on the structural analysis of the narrative, 1966), as well as elsewhere (Italy, the United States, Poland, the Soviet Union, Czechoslovakia, etc. . . . with various resulting conferences). As for the cinema itself, the successive roundtable discussions (1965, 1966, 1967) conducted within the framework of the *New Cinmea Festival* (Pesaro, Italy) have allowed various contributions to come to light, like those of Pier Paolo Pasolini or of Umberto Eco, which are mentioned elsewhere in this book. There was also the second volume of Jean Mitry's *Esthétique et psychologie du cinema* (1965). Etc.

* I am not suggesting that each *shot* equals a *single* sentence. That is why I have placed the word *sentence* between quotation marks throughout this passage. The "correspondence" between shot and sentence is on a global scale and is derived from the fact that a shot is an actualized unit, a unit of discourse, and is inherently dissimilar to the word. The filmic shot is of the *magnitude of the sentence,* so to speak.

This is not the case—it is a notable difference within a deeper resemblance

tive mode, rather than a semanteme. The jussive may actualize as clearly as the indicative. "Do Not Pass!" Two elements are identified: the lexeme (concept of "passing") and the imperative morpheme, which simultaneously actualizes and constitutes the sentence. This double function of "verbs" and more generally of predicates (which provide a lexemic content, and also constitute the statement as such) has been studied by linguists like Jean Fourquet, Louis Hjelmslev, Émile Benveniste, and André Martinet,[93] especially in relation to the

---

—with traffic signs, which are discussed a little further on in the text: They are also of the magnitude of the sentence, but, in addition, it is possible to find more precise equivalences between a highway sign and a sentence (like my example, "Do not Pass"). Among other things, this obviously derives from the fact that a traffic sign constitutes a signifying unit that is poorer and easier to analyze than cinematographic language. That is why I hesitate to use the word *seme* in connection with the cinema (and particularly with the shot). This term—in one of its acceptations at least, for authors like Bernard Pottier and Greimas use it differently—is the one that Eric Buyssens and Luis Prieto use to designate precisely the *units of signification of the magnitude of the statement,* such as one finds in various signifying systems; the statement proper thus becomes the specifically linguistic form of the seme. (On this problem, see my article "Sème" in *Supplément scientifique à la Grande Encyclopédie Larousse,* 1968, and "Remarque sur le mot et le chiffre. À Propos des conceptions de Luis J. Prieto," in *La Linguistique,* 1967, vol. 2—texts that are not reprinted in this book.) In many nonlinguistic signifying bodies one finds units clearly different from the "word," and clearly on the magnitude of the sentence—up to this point, exactly as in the cinema—but which are, moreover, finite in number, relatively easy to enumerate, and each one of which is equivalent, through its semantic substance, to a sentence that can be more or less reconstructed (as is the case with sign boards). The concept of the "seme," particularly since it has been remarkably developed by Luis Prieto, seems to me to be henceforth "ready" for the analyses of all instances of this kind (and there are many). On the other hand the concept of the seme in its present form could not be applied to signifying bodies like cinematographic language where one encounters units which, although they are of the magnitude of the statement, are infinite in number, impossible to enumerate, and none of which permits an exact equivalence with *a* sentence, but only very vague "equivalences" with a large segment of linguistic discourse comprising an indeterminate number of successive sentences. I have, incidentally, nothing better to suggest for "replacing" the concept of the seme in such cases; one can only note that the general history of semiotics has nothing to offer on this point so far (at least to my knowledge); that is why I use paraphrases like "units of the magnitude of the sentence, but which . . . etc." For that matter it may be that this lacuna is permanent (that it is not really a lacuna), and that the difficulty derives simply from the fact that "cinematographic language" has no specific units *on the level of the image,* but only on the level of the ordering of images.

famous problem of nominal sentences, which can be compared to the problem of close-ups in the cinema, or to the problem of sign boards and signals: A telephone sign does not just mean "telephone" (a purely lexical unit), but "telephone HERE." It is a self-sufficient statement, which implies the existence of something in reality; it is therefore not a word.

One can be misled, however, by the fact that in systems that are by nature *poor,* the breakdown of the "sememe" into sentences (and consequently the absence, really, of the first articulation itself) is not necessarily accompanied by a numerical multiplication of the units, which remain small in number and more or less stable. This makes it appear that there is an articulation—and in a certain sense there is one indeed, since it is true that the units are fairly stable and they can be at least approximately enumerated. But the discretion of discrete units does not prevent them from being "sentences." It is the natural poverty of the things signified that, in this case, guarantees a kind of automatic economy rendering the first articulation superfluous, and performing the same function as the articulation, yields the impression that the poverty has been derived from the articulation—for one lends only to the rich; furthermore, as André Martinet insists, the first articulation provides verbal language with a function of economy.[94] As for the sememes of sign boards, they benefit from a prior retrenchment, since the number of institutions designated is restricted: In this case it is the small number of the referents that functions as the first articulation. Since verbal language is a sememe containing many more "things that have to be said," it therefore requires the first articulation in order to reduce the infinite multiplication of sentences to the controlled amplitude of a lexicon. The cinema, like language, has much to say, but, like sign boards, it actually escapes the first articulation. It proceeds by "sentence," like sign boards, but, like verbal language, its sentences are unlimited in number. The difference is that the sentences of verbal language eventually break down into words, whereas, in the cinema, they do not: A film may be segmented into large units ("shots"), but these shots are not *reducible* (in Jakobson's sense) into small, basic, and specific units.

One can of course conclude that the cinema is not a language, or that it is so only in a sense that is altogether too figurative, and, consequently, it should not be dealt with through semiotics. But this is a very negative point of view, particularly in the case of a social fact as important as the cinema. The result of this attitude would be that one would study traffic signals because they have a very obvious paradigmatic structure, while paying no attention to a means of expression that after all carries a little more human weight than roadside signs! The alternative approach is to look at the semiological endeavor as open research, permitting the study of new forms; "language" (in the broad sense) is no simple thing—whole flexible systems may be studied as flexible systems, and with the appropriate methods.

Under these circumstances—and despite the fact that the names mentioned on these pages indicate a strong Saussurian legacy—problems of strict compliance can of course arise. But it suffices to point them out. Naturally, anything that even approximately resembles a *linguistics of speech* is a departure, it would seem, from the thought of the Genevan scholar. The objection had to be pointed out. It is, however, not insurmountable,* and it would be to respect the great linguist very narrowly indeed if one were to block all innovative research under the pretext that one could not risk even grazing a study of speech. And I say: *grazing.* For it often happens in the study of nonverbal means of communication that the actual nature of the material under consideration causes one to resort to a "linguistics" that is neither that of language nor that of speech, but rather is one of *discourse* in Émile Benveniste's sense[95] (or even in the way Eric Buyssens used the word in a text in which he was attempting precisely

---

* In the present state of research in linguistics and semiotics, it is becoming less and less insurmountable. The fact that Chomsky's work—and among other contributions, his reformulation of the "language system/speech" duality in terms of "competence/performance" with all that this implies—is now better known in France is only one of the reasons. There is also the concept of *discourse* (neither pure language system nor pure speech) in Émile Benveniste; Zellig Harris's *discourse analysis;* Greimas's *transphrastic* analysis; Luis Prieto's concept of the seme (extralinguistic unit of the same order as the statement), etc. A certain, too brutal, or too literally Saussurian, concept of the "language system/speech" dichotomy is becoming less and less tenable.

to broaden the famous Saussurian bipartition in order to be able to analyze more diverse "language systems"). Between words—pure "sign events" as they are called in American semiotics, events that never occur twice and cannot give rise to a scientific study—and language (human language, or the more systematic and formalized language of machines), which is an organized, coherent instance, there is room for the study of "sign designs," sentence patterns,[96] transphrastic organizations, "writings" in the Barthesian sense, etc.—in short, *types of speech.*

Conclusion

There have been, up to now, four ways of approaching the cinema. I will leave aside the first two (film criticism and the history of the cinema), which are foreign to my purpose even if some of their basic notions, which fall under the category of "general cinematographic culture," are clearly indispensable to anyone who wants to speak about the cinema. One must go and see films, and one must of course have at least an approximate idea of their dates. The third approach is what has been called the "theory of cinema." Eisenstein, Béla Balázs, and André Bazin are its great names. The "theoreticians" were either film-makers, enthusiastic amateurs, or critics (and it has often been pointed out that criticism itself is a part of the cinematographic institution[97]): This is a fundamental point (about the cinema, or about film, according to the case), whose originality, whose interest, whose range, and whose very definition are after all derived from the fact that the theory was made within the cinematographic universe. The fourth approach is that of filmology—of the scientific study conducted from outside by psychologists, psychiatrists, aestheticians, sociologists, educators, and biologists. Their status, and their procedures, place them outside the institution: It is the cinematographic fact rather than the cinema, the filmic fact[98] rather than the film, which they consider. Theirs is a fruitful point of view. Filmology and the theory of film complement each other. There are even some border-line cases between the two, some of which are quite important: Who is to say whether Rudolf Arnheim, Jean Epstein, or Albert Laf-

fay were "filmologists" or "theoreticians?" Filmology proper also has
its great names: Gilbert Cohen-Séat and Edgar Morin. Both filmology and the theory of the cinema are indispensable to the approach I
am proposing. Their division is justifiable only when it allows for a
reciprocity of perspectives. If it becomes a true separation, if it is
made into an antagonism, it can only be damaging. The major book
Jean Mitry has just published, *Esthétique et psychologie du cinéma*,
a true sum of all the thought that the cinema has provoked up to
present, is an example of the deep reconciliation of these two complementary approaches, which one can only applaud.

Very much to one side of both filmology and the theory of the cinema—unfortunately—is linguistics* and its semiological extensions.
The discipline is an old one—it was known by Bopp and Rask—
and old age seems to suit it, since it is very much alive and well. It is
sure of itself—therefore it inspires confidence. That is why one has
sought its aid unhesitatingly—it can hardly be overburdened by a few
extra demands placed on it, and in any case, the study of the cinema
is far from being its only concern. It is a well-known fact that the
busiest people are always those who find the time to concern themselves with others—as Proust remarked about Monsieur de Norpois.

These few pages were written in the belief that the time has come
to start making certain conjunctions. An approach that would be derived as much from the writings of the great theoreticians of the cinema as from the studies of filmology and the methods of linguistics
might, gradually—it will take a long time—begin to accomplish, in the
domain of the cinema, and especially on the level of the large signifying units, the great Saussurian dream of studying the mechanisms by
which human significations are transmitted in human society.

De Saussure did not live long enough to remark on the importance
the cinema has assumed in our world. No one disputes this importance. The time has come for a semiotics of the cinema.

---

* In his *Essais sur les principes* . . . (*op. cit.*), G. Cohen-Séat had very
clearly indicated what importance the linguistic approach would have for the
filmic fact. But there has been no development since then. One still speaks innocently about "language" in the cinema as if no one had ever studied language. Was Meillet then a service-station attendant, and Trubetskoy a butcher?

4 Some Points in
the Semiotics of the Cinema

The purpose of this text is to examine some of the problems and difficulties confronting the person who wants to begin undertaking, in the field of "cinematographic language," de Saussure's project of a general semiotics:[1] to study the orderings and functionings of the main signifying units used in the filmic message. Semiotics, as de Saussure conceived it, is still in its childhood,[2] but any work bearing on one of the nonverbal "languages," provided that it assumes a resolutely semiological relevance and does not remain satisfied with vague considerations of "substance," brings its contribution, whether modest or important, to that great enterprise, the general study of significations.

The very term "cinematographic *language*" already poses the whole problem of the semiotics of film. It would require a long justification, and strictly speaking it should be used only after the in-depth study of the semiological mechanisms at work in the filmic message had been fairly well advanced. Convenience, however, makes us retain, right from the start, that frozen syntagma—"language"—which has gradually assumed a place in the special vocabulary of film theoreticians and aestheticians. Even from a strictly semiological point of view, one can perhaps at this time give a preliminary justification for the expression "cinematographic language" (not to be confused with "cinematographic *langue*" (language system), which does not seem to me acceptable)—a justification that, in the present state of semiological investigations, can only be very general. I hope to outline it in this essay and especially on the next-to-the-last page.

Cinema and Narrativity

A first choice confronts the "film semiologist": Is the corpus to be made up of feature films (*narrative films*) or, on the contrary, of short films, documentaries, technological, pedagogical, or advertising films, etc.? It could be answered that it depends simply on what one wants to study—that the cinema possesses various "dialects," and that each one of these "dialects" can become the subject of a specific analysis. This is undoubtedly true. Nevertheless, there is a hierarchy of concerns (or, better yet, a methodological urgency) that favors—in the beginning at least—the study of the narrative film. We know that, in the few years immediately before and after the Lumière brothers' invention in 1895, critics, journalists, and the pioneer cinematographers disagreed considerably among themselves as to the *social function* that they attributed to, or predicted for, the new machine: whether it was a means of preservation or of making archives, whether it was an auxiliary technography for research and teaching in sciences like botany or surgery, whether it was a new form of journalism, or an instrument of sentimental devotion, either private or public, which could perpetuate the living image of the dear departed one, and so on. That, over all these possibilities, the cinema could evolve into a machine for telling stories had never been really considered. From the very beginnings of the cinematograph there were various indications and statements that suggested such an evolution, but they had no common measure with the magnitude that the narrative phenomenon was to assume. The merging of the cinema and of narrativity was a great fact, which was by no means predestined—nor was it strictly fortuitous. It was a historical and social fact, a fact of civilization (to use a formula dear to the sociologist Marcel Mauss), a fact that in turn conditioned the later evolution of the film as a semiological reality, somewhat in the same way—indirect and general,* though effective—that "external" linguistic events (conquests, colonizations, transformations of language) influence the "internal" functioning of idioms. In the realm of the cinema, all nonnarrative genres—the documentary, the technical film, etc.—have become marginal provinces, border regions so to speak, while the *feature-length film of novelistic fiction,* which is simply called a "film,"—the usage is significant**—has traced more and more clearly the king's highway of filmic expression.

This purely numerical and social superiority is not the only fact concerned. Added to it is a more "internal" consideration: Nonnarrative films for the most part are distinguished from "real" films by their social purpose and by their content much more than by their "language processes." The basic figures of the semiotics of the cinema —montage, camera movements, scale of the shots, relationships between the image and speech, sequences, and other large syntagmatic units—are on the whole the same in "small" films and in "big" films. It is by no means certain that an independent semiotics of the various nonnarrative genres is possible other than in the form of a series of discontinuous remarks on the points of difference between these films and "ordinary" films. To examine fiction films is to proceed more directly and more rapidly to the heart of the problem.

There is, moreover, an encouraging diachronic consideration. We know, since the observations of Béla Balázs,[3] André Malraux,[4] Edgar Morin,[5] Jean Mitry,[6] and many others, that the cinema was not a specific "language" from its inception. Before becoming the means of expression familiar to us, it was a simple means of mechanical recording, preserving, and reproducing moving visual spectacles—whether of life, of the theater, or even of small *mises-en-scène,* which were specially prepared and which, in the final analysis, remained theatrical—in short, a "means of reproduction," to use André Malraux's

---

* Except, of course, for specific lexical facts.

** As in statements like "The short was terrible, but the film was great" or "What are they showing tonight, a series of shorts or a film?" etc.

term.[7] Now, *it was precisely to the extent that the cinema confronted the problems of narration* that, in the course of successive gropings, it came to produce a body of specific signifying procedures. Historians of the cinema generally agree in dating the beginning of the "cinema" as we know it in the period 1910–15. Films like *Enoch Arden*,[8] *Life for the Czar*,[9] *Quo Vadis?*,[10] *Fantomas*,[11] *Cabiria*,[12] *The Golem*,[13] *The Battle of Gettysburg*,[14] and above all *Birth of a Nation*[15] were among the first films, in the acceptation we now give this word when we use it without a determinant: Narration of a certain magnitude based on procedures that are supposed to be specifically cinematographic. It so happens that these procedures were perfected in the wake of the narrative endeavor. The pioneers of "cinematographic language"—Méliès, Porter, Griffith—couldn't have cared less about "formal" research conducted for its own sake; what is more (except for occasional naïve and confused attempts), they cared little about the symbolic, philosophical or human "message" of their films. Men of denotation rather than of connotation, they wanted above all to tell a story; they were not content unless they could subject the continuous, analogical material of photographic duplication to the *articulations*— however rudimentary—of a narrative discourse. Georges Sadoul[16] has indeed shown how Méliès, in his story-teller's naïveté, was led to invent double exposure,[17] the device of multiple exposures with a mask and a dark backdrop,[18] the dissolve and the fade-in,[19] and the pan shot.[20] Jean Mitry, who has written a very precise synthesis of these problems,[21] examines the first occurrences of a certain number of procedures of filmic language—the close-up, the pan shot, the tracking shot, parallel montage, and interlaced, or alternate, montage—among the film primitives. I will summarize the conclusions he reaches: The principal "inventions" are credited to the Frenchmen Méliès and Promio, to the Englishmen A. G. Smith and F. Williamson, and to the American E. S. Porter; it was Griffith's role to define and to stabilize— we would say, to codify—the *function* of these different procedures in relation to the filmic *narrative,* and thereby unify them up to a certain point in a coherent "syntax" (note that it would be better to use the term *syntagmatic category;* Jean Mitry himself avoids the word syntax[22]). Between 1911 and 1915, Griffith made a whole series of films having, more or less consciously, the value of experimental probings, and *Birth of a Nation*, released in 1915, appears as the crowning work, the sum and the public demonstration of investigations that, however naïve they may have been, were nonetheless systematic and fundamental. Thus, it was in a single motion that the cinema became narrative and took over some of the attributes of a language.

Today still, the so-called filmic procedures are in fact filmic-narrative. This, to my mind, justifies the priority of the narrative film in the filmosemiological enterprise—a priority that must not of course become an exclusivity.

Studies of Denotation and Studies of Connotation in the Semiotics of the Cinema

The facts I have just reviewed lead to another consequence. The semiotics of the cinema can be conceived of either as a semiotics of connotation or as a semiotics of denotation.[23] Both directions are interesting, and it is obvious that on the day when the semiological study of film makes some progress and begins to form a body of knowledge, it will have considered connotative and denotative significations together. The study of connotation brings us closer to the notion of the cinema as an art (the "seventh art"). As I have indicated elsewhere in more detail,[24] the art of film is located on the same semiological "plane" as literary art: The properly aesthetic orderings and constraints—versification, composition, and tropes in the first case; framing, camera movements, and light "effects" in the second —serve as the connoted instance, which is superimposed over the denoted meaning. In literature, the latter appears as the purely linguistic signification, which is linked, in the employed idiom, to the units used by the author. In the cinema, it is represented by the literal (that is, perceptual) meaning of the spectacle reproduced in the image, or of the sounds duplicated by the sound-track. As for connotation, which plays a major role in all aesthetic languages,* its significate is the literary or cinematographic "style," "genre" (the epic, the western, etc.), "symbol" (philosophical, humanitarian, ideological, and so on), or "poetic atmosphere"—and its signifier is the whole denotated semiological material, whether signified or signifying. In American gangster movies, where, for example, the slick pavement of the waterfront distills an impression of anxiety and hardness (significate of the connotation), the scene represented (dimly lit, deserted wharves, with stacks of crates and overhead cranes, the significate of denotation), and the technique of the shooting, which is dependent on the effects of lighting in order to produce a certain *picture* of the docks (signifier of denotation), converge to form the signifier of connotation. The same scene filmed in a different light would produce a different impression; and so would the same technique used on a different subject (for example, a child's smiling face). Film aestheticians have often remarked that filmic effects must not be "gratuitous," but must remain "subordinate to the plot."[25] This is another way of saying that the significate of connotation can establish itself only when the corresponding signifier brings into play *both* the signifier and the significate of denotation.

The study of the cinema as an art—the study of cinematographic expressiveness—can therefore be conducted according to methods derived from linguistics. For instance, there is no doubt that films are amenable to analyses comparable (*mutatis mutandis*) to those Thomas A. Sebeok has applied to Cheremis songs,[26] or to those Samuel R. Levin has proposed.[27] But there is another task that requires the careful attention of the film semiologist. For also, and even first of all, through its procedures of *denotation*, the cinema is a specific language. The concept of *diegesis* is as important for the film semiologist as the idea of art. The word is derived from the Greek διήγησις, "nar-

---

* Aesthetic language practices a kind of promotion of connotation, but connotation occurs as well in various phenomena of expressiveness proper to ordinary language, like those studied by Charles Bally (*Le Langage et la vie,* Geneva, Payot, 1926).

ration" and was used particularly to designate one of the obligatory parts of judiciary discourse, the recital of facts. The term was introduced into the framework of the cinema by Étienne Souriau.[28] It designates the film's *represented* instance (which Mikel Dufrenne contrasts to the expressed, properly aesthetic, instance[29])—that is to say, the sum of a film's denotation: the narration itself, but also the fictional space and time dimensions implied in and by the narrative, and consequently the characters, the landscapes, the events, and other narrative elements, in so far as they are considered in their denoted aspect. How does the cinema indicate successivity, precession, temporal breaks, causality, adversative relationships, consequence, spatial proximity, or distance, etc.? These are central questions to the semiotics of the cinema.

One must not indeed forget that, from the semiological point of view, the cinema is very different from still photography whence its technique is derived. In photography, as Roland Barthes has clearly shown,[30] the denoted meaning is secured entirely through the automatic process of photochemical reproduction; denotation is a visual transfer,* which is not codified and has no inherent organization. Human intervention, which carries some elements of a proper semiotics, affects only the level of connotation (lighting, camera angle, "photographic effects," and so on). And, in point of fact, there is no specifically photographic procedure for designating the significate "house" in its denoted aspect, unless it is by showing a house. In the cinema, on the other hand, a whole semiotics of denotation is possible and necessary, for a film is composed of *many* photographs (the concept of montage, with its myriad consequences)—photographs that give us mostly only partial views of the diegetic referent. In film a "house" would be a shot of a staircase, a shot of one of the walls taken from the outside, a close-up of a window, a brief establishing shot of

* I am speaking here as a semiologist and not as a psychologist. Comparative studies of visual perception, both in "real" and in filmic conditions, have indeed isolated all the optical distortions that differentiate between the photograph and the object. But these transformations, which obey the laws of optical physics, of the chemistry of emulsions and of retinal physiology, do not constitute a signifying system.

the building,* etc. Thus a kind of filmic *articulation* appears, which has no equivalent in photography: It is the denotation itself that is being constructed, organized, and to a certain extent codified (*codified*, not necessarily *encoded*). Lacking absolute laws, filmic intelligibility nevertheless depends on a certain number of dominant habits: A film put together haphazardly would not be understood.

I return to my initial observations: "Cinematographic language" is first of all the literalness of a plot. Artistic effects, even when they are substantially inseparable from the semic act by which the film tells us its story, nevertheless constitute another level of signification, which from the methodological point of view must come "later."

Paradigmatic and Syntagmatic Categories

There is a danger that the semiotics of the cinema will tend to develop along the syntagmatic rather than along the paradigmatic axis. It is not that there is no filmic paradigm: At specific points along the chain of images the number of units liable to occur is limited, so that, in these circumstances, the unit that does appear derives its meaning in relation to the other members of the paradigm. This is the case with the "fade-dissolve" duality within the framework of the "conjunction of two sequences":** a simple commutation, which the users —that is to say, the spectators—perform spontaneously, makes it possible to isolate the corresponding significates: a spatiotemporal break with the establishing of an underlying transitive link (dissolve), and a straightforward spatiotemporal break (fade). But in most of the *po-*

* Even if this over-all view is the only one shown us in the film, it is still the result of a choice. We know that the modern cinema has partially abandoned the practices of visual fragmentation and excessive montage in favor of the continuous shot (cf. the famous "shot-sequence" controversy). This condition *modifies* to the same extent the semiotics of filmic denotation, but it in no way dismisses it. Simply, cinematographic language, like other languages, has a diachronic side. A single "shot" itself contains several elements (example: switching from one view to another through a camera movement, and without montage).

** Fades, or dissolves, can also occur in other settings, especially at the center of sequences. In such cases, their value is different.

sitions of the filmic chain, the number of units liable to appear is very much open (though not infinite). Much more open, in any case, than the series of lexemes that, by their nonfinite nature, are nonetheless opposed to the series of grammatical monemes in linguistics.[31] For, despite the difficulty, already emphasized by Joseph Vendryes in *Le Langage*, of accurately enumerating the words of an idiom, it is at least possible to indicate the maximum and minimum limits, thus arriving at the approximate order of magnitude (for example, in French the lexeme *"lav-"* exists, but the lexeme *"patouf"* does not*). The case is different in the cinema, where the number of images is indefinite. Several times indefinite, one should say. For the "profilmic" spectacles** are themselves unlimited in number; the exact nature of lighting can be varied infinitely and by quantities that are nondiscrete; the same applies to the axial distance between the subject and the camera (in variations which are said to be scalar—that is, scale of the shot),† to the camera angle, to the properties of the film and the focal length of the lens, and to the exact trajectory of the camera movements (including the stationary shot, which represents zero degree in this case). It suffices to vary one of these elements by a perceptible quantity to obtain *another* image. The shot is therefore not comparable to the word in a lexicon; rather it resembles a complete statement (of one or more sentences), in that it is already the result of an essentially free combination, a "speech" arrangement. On the other hand the word is a syntagma that is precast by code—a "vertical" syntagma, as R. F. Mikus would say.[32] Let us note in this connection that there is another similarity between the image and the

---

* The lexemic unit *"lav-"* corresponds to *"wash-"* in English; *"patouf"* is no more of a lexeme in English than it is in French.—TRANSLATOR.

** As defined by Étienne Souriau (see reference 28). The "profilmic" spectacle is whatever is placed in front of the camera, or whatever one places the camera in front of, in order to "shoot" it.

† In *Le Langage cinématographique* (Paris, 1962), François Chevassu maintains (p. 14) that the "scale of shots" is coded. I would say instead that it is the technical terminology ("close-up," "thirty-degree angle shot," "medium shot," etc.) that is coded. The actual scale of the shots constitutes a continuous gradation, from the closest to the furthest shot. Codification intervenes at the metalinguistic level (studio jargon) in this case, and not on that of the language object (that is, cinematographic language).

statement: Both are actualized units, whereas the word in itself is a purely potential unit of code. The image is almost always assertive—and assertion is one of the great "modalities" of actualization, of the semic act.[33] It appears therefore that the paradigmatic category in film is condemned to remain partial and fragmentary, at least as long as one tries to isolate it on the level of the *image*. This is naturally derived from the fact that *creation* plays a larger role in cinematographic language than it does in the handling of idioms: To "speak" a language is to use it, but to "speak" cinematographic language is to a certain extent to invent it. The speakers of ordinary language constitute a group of users; film-makers are a group of creators. On the other hand, movie *spectators* in turn constitute a group of users. That is why the semiotics of the cinema must frequently consider things from the point of view of the spectator rather than of the film-maker. Étienne Souriau's distinction between the filmic point of view and the *"cinéastique,"* or film-making, point of view[34] is a very useful concept; film semiotics is mainly a *filmic* study. The situation has a rough equivalent in linguistics: Some linguists connect the speaker with the message, while the listener in some way "represents" the code,[35] since he requires it to understand what is being said to him, while the speaker is presumed to know beforehand what he wants to say.

But, more than paradigmatic studies, it is the syntagmatic considerations that are at the center of the problems of filmic denotation.[36] Although each image is a free creation, the arrangement of these images into an intelligible sequence—cutting and montage—brings us to the heart of the semiological dimension of film. It is a rather paradoxical situation: Those proliferating (and not very discrete!) units—the *images*—when it is a matter of composing a film, suddenly accept with reasonably good grace the constraint of a few large syntagmatic structures. While no image ever entirely resembles another image, the great majority of narrative films resemble each other in their principal syntagmatic figures. *Filmic narrativity*—since it has again crossed our path—by becoming stable through convention and repetition over innumerable films, has gradually shaped itself into forms that are more or less fixed, but certainly not immutable. These forms represent a synchronic "state" (that of the present cinema), but if they were to change, it could only be through a complete positive evolution, liable to be challenged—like those that, in spoken languages, produce diachronic transformations in the distribution of aspects and tenses. Applying de Saussure's thought[37] to the cinema, one could say that the large syntagmatic category of the narrative film *can change*, but that no single person can make it change over night.* A failure of intellection among the viewers would be the automatic sanctioning of a purely individual innovation, which the system would refuse to confirm. The originality of creative artists consists, here as elsewhere, in tricking the code, or at least in *using* it ingeniously, rather than in attacking it directly or in violating it—and still less in ignoring it.

An Example: The Alternating Syntagm

It is not within the scope of this paper to analyze the principal types of *large* filmic *syntagma*. Instead, as an example, I will simply indicate some of the characteristics of one type, the *alternating syntagma* (for example, image of a mother-image of her daughter-image of the mother, etc.). The alternating syntagma rests on the principle of alternating distribution of two or more diegetic elements. The images thus fall into two or more *series*, each one of which, if shown continuously, would constitute a normal sequence. The alternating syntagma is, precisely, a rejection of the grouping by continuous series (which remains potential), for reasons of connotation—the search for a certain "construction" or a certain "effect." This type of syntagma apparently made its first appearance in 1901 in England, in a film by Williamson, *Attack on a Mission in China*, one of those "re-enacted news reels" that were popular at the time. In it, one saw images of a mission surrounded by Boxers (during the rebellion of that name)

---

* But then, I should have added, by the same token, that this syntagmatic category contains a paradigmatic category, and consequently I should have shown less skepticism as to the possibilities of a paradigmatic category in the cinema. On this point, cf. above, note, pp. 68–69. Also Chapter 5, part 9.

alternating with shots of marines coming to the rescue.* Subsequently the procedure becomes more or less usual.

The alternation defines the form of the signifier, but not necessarily, as we shall see, that of the significate—which amounts to saying that the relationship between the signifier and the significate is not always analogous in the alternating syntagma. If one takes the nature of the *significate of temporal denotation* as a relevant basis, one can distinguish three cases of alternating syntagma. In the first case (which might be called the *alternator*), the alternation of the signifiers refers to a parallel alternation of the significates (analogous relationship). Example: two tennis players framed alternately, at the moment each one is returning the ball. In the second case (which would be the *alternate syntagma*), the alternating of the signifiers corresponds to a simultaneity of the significates. Example: the pursuers and the pursued. Every spectator understands that he is seeing two chronological series which are contemporaneous at each instant, and that, while he is seeing the pursued galloping away (locus of the signifier, on the screen), the pursuers are nonetheless continuing the chase (locus of the signifier, in the diegesis). Thus the semiotic *nexus* —alternating simultaneity—is no longer analogous. But it does not become "arbitrary" because of that: It remains motivated (remember that analogy is one of the forms of motivation), and the understanding of this kind of syntagma by the viewer is relatively "natural." The motivation must be explained by the spontaneous psychological mechanisms of filmic perception. Anne Souriau[38] has shown that sequences of the "pursued-pursuing" variety are readily understood, with little previous exposure, by the spectator (on the condition, only, that the rhythm of the alternation not be too slow), for he "interpolates spontaneously" the visual material that the film presents. He guesses that series 1 continues to unfold in the plot while he is seeing series 2 in the image. The third case could be called *parallel syntagma:* Two series of events are mixed together through montage without having any relevant temporal relationships on the level of

* "Alternation" means simultaneity here. It pertains therefore to the alternate *syntagma,* as I am about to define that term.

the significate (diegesis), at least with respect to denotation. It is this variety of syntagma that film theoreticians sometimes refer to with expressions like "neutral temporal relationships."[39] Example: a sinister urban landscape at night, alternating with a sunny pastoral view. There is nothing to indicate whether the two scenes are simultaneous or not (and if not, which precedes and which follows). It is simply a matter of two motifs brought together for "symbolic" reasons by montage (the rich and the poor, life and death, reaction and revolution, etc.) and without their literal location in time as a pertinent factor. It is as if the denoted temporal relationship had yielded to the rich, multiple values of connotation, which depend on the context as well as on the substance of the significate.

The three varieties of alternating syntagma constitute a small system whose internal configuration recalls somewhat the structure of verbal grammatical persons as conceived by Émile Benveniste.[40] A first correlation (presence or absence of relevant temporal denotation) allows us to distribute parallel montage to one side (absence), and alternate and alternator montage to the other (presence). Within the second term, another correlation (nature of the significate of temporal denotation) distinguishes between the alternate (significate equals simultaneity) and the alternator (significate equals alternation).*

---

* I have retained this passage because it gives a simple example of what commutation can be in the filmic corpus, but the factual conclusions presented here no longer correspond to the current state of my investigations of the considered point. First of all, the study of various passages of films has made it appear that the "alternator" cannot always be distinguished from the "alternate" syntagma (or, in rarer cases, from the parallel syntagma) by any really probing difference: In the example of the tennis players, it can also be considered that the two partners are both supposed to be engaged in action continuously and simultaneously (i.e., alternate syntagma). Thus—and although certain cases seem to subsist where the alternate syntagma appears, more clearly than in other cases, as a *variant* similar to what I have called here the "alternator"—I have not retained the alternator as a separate type or subtype. Then, there are cases where the alternating of images on the screen corresponds to temporal relationships not mentioned in this article: For example, one finds "alternating syntagmas" that interweave a "present" series with a "past" series (a kind of alternating flashback), and in which consequently the relationship of the two series can be defined neither by simultaneity nor by the term "neutral temporal relationship." One will note also that the concept of "alternating syntagma" has a certain obscure correspondence to that of the "frequentative syntagma" (see

Other Problems

These very brief remarks provided an example of what the syntagmatic study of filmic denotation could be. There are important differences between the semiotics of the cinema and linguistics itself. Without repeating those mentioned elsewhere,[41] let me recall some of the main points: Film contains nothing corresponding to the purely distinctive units of the second articulation; all of its units—even the simplest, like the dissolve and the wipe—are directly significant (and moreover, as I have already pointed out, they only occur in the actualized state). The commutations and other manipuations by which the semiotics of the cinema proceeds therefore affect the large significatory units. The "laws" of cinematographic language call for *statements* within a narrative, and not monemes within a statement, or still less phonemes within a moneme.

Contrary to what many of the theoreticians of the silent film declared or suggested ("*Ciné langue,*" "visual Esperanto," etc.), the cinema is certainly not a language system (*langue*). It can, however, be considered as a *language,* to the extent that it orders signifying elements within ordered arrangements different from those of spoken idioms—and to the extent that these elements are not traced on the perceptual configurations of reality itself (which does not tell stories).[42] Filmic manipulation transforms what might have been a mere visual transfer of reality into discourse. Derived from a kind of signification that is purely analogous and continuous—animated photography, cinematography—the cinema gradually shaped, in the course of its diachronic maturation, some elements of a proper semiotics, which remain scattered and fragmentary within the open field of simple visual duplication.*

---

notes pp. 122, 123). In the final analysis, however, the reason I have dropped the "alternator" *as a general category of classification* is less because of the drawbacks I have just pointed out (and which various adjustments could suppress) than because of an over-all *reformulation* of the table of the main types of filmic arrangement, as presented in Chapter 5 of this work (pp. 119–34). Taken separately, the analysis developed above remains partially valid.

* But I should have added here that the significations that analogy and mechanical duplication yield—although they do not pertain to *cinematographic*

The "shot"—an already complex unit, which must be studied—remains an indispensable reference for the time being, in somewhat the same way that the "word" was during a period of linguistic research. It might be somewhat adventurous to compare the shot to the *taxeme*, in Louis Hjelmslev's sense,[43] but one can consider that it constitutes the largest *minimum segment* (the expression is borrowed from André Martinet[44]), since at least one shot is required to make a film, or part of a film—in the same way, a linguistic statement must be made up of at least one phoneme. To isolate several shots from a sequence is still, perhaps, to analyze the sequence; to remove several frames from a shot is to destroy the shot. If the shot is not the smallest unit of filmic *signification* (for a single shot may convey several informational elements), it is at least the smallest unit of the filmic chain.*

One cannot conclude, however, that every minimum filmic segment is a shot. Besides shots, there are other minimum segments, *optical devices*—various dissolves, wipes, and so on—that can be defined as visual but not photographic elements. Whereas images have the objects of reality as referents, optical procedures, which do not represent anything, have images as referents (those contiguous in the syntagma). The relationship of these procedures to the actual shooting of the film is somewhat like that of morphemes to lexemes; depending on the context, they have two main functions: as "trick" devices (in this instance, they are sorts of semiological exponents influencing contiguous images), or as "punctuation." The expression "filmic punctuation," which use has ratified, must not make us forget that optical procedures separate large, complex statements and thus correspond to the articulations of the literary narrative (with its pages

---

language as a specific system—nevertheless do have the effect of bringing structures and elements that belong to *other* systems which are also cultural, which also carry meaning and which are also more or less organized, into the cinema (as a whole). On this point, see pp. 110–14; note, p. 61; note, p. 214.

* Similarly, the phoneme is not the minimum distinctive unit, since the latter is the "feature," but it is the minimum element of the spoken *sequence*, the threshold below which an order of consecutiveness yields to an order of simultaneity.

and paragraphs, for example), whereas actual punctuation—that is to say, typographical punctuation—separates sentences (period, exclamation mark, question mark, semicolon), and clauses (comma, semicolon, dash), possibly even "verbal bases," with or without characteristics (apostrophe, or dash, between two "words," and so on).

In Conclusion

The concepts of linguistics can be applied to the semiotics of the cinema only with the greatest caution. On the other hand, the methods of linguistics—commutation, analytical breakdown, strict distinction between the significate and the signifier, between substance and form, between the relevant and the irrelevant, etc.—provide the semiotics of the cinema with a constant and precious aid in establishing units that, though they are still very approximate, are liable over time (and, one hopes, through the work of many scholars) to become progressively refined.

5 Problems of Denotation in the Fiction Film

The film semiologist tends, naturally, to approach his subject with methods derived from linguistics. Consequently wherever the language of cinematography differs from language itself, film semiology encounters its greatest obstacles. Let us begin immediately with the points of *maximum difference*. There are two of them: There is the problem of the *motivation* of signs (see Part 1) and that of the *continuity* of meanings (see Part 3). Or, if one prefers, the question of the arbitrariness of signs (in the Saussurian sense) and the question of discrete units.

1. Cinematographic Signification Is Always More or Less Motivated, Never Arbitrary

Motivation occurs on two levels: on that of the relationship between the denotative signifiers and significates, and that of the relations between the connotative signifiers and significates.

Denotation: The motivation is furnished by analogy—that is to say, by the perceptual similarity between the signifier and of the significate. This is equally true for the sound-track (the sound of a cannon on film resembles a real cannon sound) as for the image track (the image of a dog is like the dog).

We therefore have visual analogy and auditory analogy; for the cinema is derived from photography and from the phonograph, which are both modern technologies of *mechanical duplication*. Of course the duplication is never perfect; between the object and its image there are many perceptible differences, which film psychologists have studied. But, from the point of view of semiotics, it is not necessary that the signifier and the significate be *identical*. Simple analogy provides sufficient motivation.

For, even when it partially distorts its model, mechanical duplication does not *analyze* into specific units. There is no actual transformation of the object, but a simple partial *distortion,* which is purely perceptual.

Connotation: Connotative meanings are motivated, too, in the cinema. But in this case the motivation is not necessarily based on a relationship of perceptual analogy. We should remember that, in his distinction between intrinsic and extrinsic semes, Eric Buyssens had already observed that analogy is only one of the forms of motivation.

We will not insist upon the problems of cinematographic connotation here, for this is a study of denotation. Suffice it to say that cinematographic connotation is always symbolic in nature: The significate motivates the signifier but goes beyond it. The notion of *motivated overtaking (depassement motivé)* may be used to define almost all filmic connotations. Similarly, one says that the cross is the symbol of Christianity because, although Christ died on a cross (the motivation), there are many more things in Christianity than there are in a cross (the "overtaking").

The *partial motivation* of filmic connotations does not prevent them from giving rise quite often to codifications or to conventions, which are more or less extended according to the case. Here is a simple example: In a talking film in which the hero has, among other diegetic peculiarities, the habit of whistling the first bars of a certain tune—and provided that this fact has been clearly impressed upon the spectator from the beginning of the film—the mere appearance of the tune on the sound-track (in the visual absence of the hero himself) will be sufficient to suggest the totality of the character later in the film after the hero has gone on a long journey or even vanished. It is not without powerful connotations that the character may have been thus designated. In this simplified example we see that the hero has not been "symbolized" by some arbitrary characteristic, but by a feature entirely his own (thus, lack of *total* arbitrariness). Yet in the whole character there was more than just the familiar tune; other features, which belong to him also, could have been chosen to "symbolize" him (and would have involved other connotations). There is, then, some arbitrariness in the relationship between the connotative signifier (the melody) and the connotative significate (the character).*

Even the subtlest and most ingenious cinematographic connotations are based then on this simple principle, which we might state as follows: A visual or an auditory theme—or an arrangement of visual and auditory themes—once it has been placed in its correct syntagmatic position within the discourse that constitutes the whole film, takes on a value greater than its own and is increased by the additional meaning it receives. But this addition itself is never entirely "arbitrary," for what the theme symbolizes in this manner is an integral situation or whole process, *a part of which in fact it is,* within the story told by the film (or which the spectator knows to be an actual part of life). In short, the connotative meaning *extends over* the denotative meaning, but without *contradicting* or *ignoring* it. Thus the partial arbitrariness; thus the absence of total arbitrariness.

2. Range and Limits of the Concept of Analogy

The concept of analogy must nevertheless be handled with caution. It is true that, for an actual semiotics of the cinema, analogy serves as

---

* This amounts to saying that *ellipsis* and *symbol,* regarded in their deepest principle, are no longer two different things in the cinema. Rather they constitute the present face (symbol) and the absent face (ellipsis) of a single representation, through which the film, *by the mere fact that it must always select what it shows and what it does not show,* transforms the world into articulated discourse.

a kind of stopping block: Wherever analogy takes over filmic signification (that is, notably the meaning of each visual element taken
separately), there is a lack of specifically cinematographic codification. That is why I believe filmic codes must be sought on other
levels: the codes peculiar to connotation (including partially "motivated" codes, for the pure "arbitrary" does not exhaust the codifiable
field) or the codes of denotation-connotation related to the discursive
organization of image groups (see also, for example, the "large syntagmatic category in the image track," pages 119–34). But, for a
general semiotics, the analogous portions of filmic signification would
not constitute a point of stopping off; for many things that are assumed to be "acquired" by the film analyst and therefore are a kind
of absolute beginning *after which* the cinematographic experience
unfolds, are in turn the complex, terminal products of *other* cultural
experiences and various organizations whose field of action, being
more general, includes a great deal more than the cinema alone.
Among the codes that are extracinematographic by nature, but that
nevertheless intervene on the screen under cover of analogy, one
must point out as a minimum—without prejudice to more complex
and sensitive enumerations—the *iconology* specific to each sociocultural group producing or viewing the films (the more or less institutionalized modalities of object representation, the processes of recognition and *identification* of objects in their visual or auditive
"reproduction," and, more generally, the collective notions of what an
image is), and, on the other hand, up to a certain point, *perception*
itself (visual habits of identification and construction of forms and
figures, the spatial representations peculiar to each culture, various
auditory structures, and so on). Characteristically, codes of this type
function, so to speak, at the heart of analogy and are experienced by
the viewers as a part of the most ordinary and natural visual or auditory decipherment.

Contrary to what I believed four years ago (notably in "The
Cinema: Language or Language System?"[1]), it does not seem at all
impossible to me, today, to assume that *analogy is itself coded without, however, ceasing to function authentically as analogy in relation*

to the codes of the superior level—which are brought into play only on the basis of this first assumption. Many of the misunderstandings and arguments about these subjects derive from the fact that no one has yet attempted to draw up a half-way complete list of the different heterogeneous and superimposed codes copresent in any cultural activity of some importance, and no one has yet tried to clarify the precise organization of their interactions.*

In any event, it seems to me that one can distinguish at least two main types of signifying organization: *cultural* codes and *specialized* codes. The first define the culture of each social group; they are so ubiquitous and well "assimilated" that the viewers generally consider them to be "natural"—basic constituents of mankind itself (although they are clearly *products,* since they vary in space and time). The handling of these codes requires no *special* training—that is to say, no training other than that of living, and having been raised, in a society. On the other hand the codes I have called "specialized" concern more specific and restricted social activities. They appear more explicitly as codes, and they require a special training—to a large or small extent depending on the case (relatively "small" in the cinema)—that is to say, a training even the "native" person, possessing the culture of his group, cannot dispense with.

This bipartition is fairly useful in the study of gesticulatory codes, which I take here simply as examples. The so-called expressive, affective, spontaneous, natural, or speech-accompanying gestures *already* constitute a first level of codification, since it is known that the same gesture has different meanings from culture to culture, while the same meaning is expressed by different gestures. Gestures like those that make up the "sign language" of the deaf and dumb (and in general all gestures said to be "artificial," "conventional," "codi-

---

* The discussions that have taken place in recent years about the semiotics of the cinema have made it appear more and more clearly that *the cinema as a whole* is a locus where many signifying systems are superimposed and interwoven—and that *cinematographic language* is only one of these systems. As for me, I would willingly classify the totality of the "codes" that intervene in the total cinematographic message into five main levels of organization that would be superimposed in a hierarchy (see Chapter 3, pp. 61–63, note p. 61). But this is only a hypothesis.

fied," or "ruled," and so on) represent *another* level of codification, which is used in particular social situations and the training for which constitutes a separate activity. A Frenchman, born and raised in France, does not need to be specially taught the gestures expressing anger, refusal, resigned acceptance, or the gesture that stands for "Come here!"—but, though he is French, he will need to be specially taught the sign language of the deaf and dumb (in his own language), otherwise he will never know it.

The purely cinematographic signifying figures studied here (montage, camera movements, optical effects, "rhetoric of the screen," interaction of visual and auditory elements, and so on) constitute specialized codes—although relatively "easy" ones, as we will see later—that function above and beyond photographic and phonographic analogy. The iconological, perceptual, and other codes are cultural codes, and they function in good part *within* photographic and phonographic analogy, as Umberto Eco,[2] to whom the hypothesis advanced in these pages owes much, has rightly pointed out.

———————

So far, I have been speaking about denotation (the literal sense of the film). But, among the large body of connoted significations in the cinema (the "symbolic sense" of all varieties), there are a certain number that, outside of the specifically cinematographic codifications, intrude into the film by means of perceptual analogy each time an object or an ordering of objects (visual or auditory) "symbolizes" within the film what it would have symbolized outside of the film— that is to say, within culture (with the chance that it will carry *in addition,* and only in the film, symbolic significations that will then derive from its location within the cinematographic discourse proper). "Objects" (and characters must also be included)—that is to say, the different basic elements of filmic discourse—do not enter the film in a virgin state; they carry with them, before even "cinematographic language" can intervene, a great deal more than their simple literal identity—which does not prevent the spectator belonging to a given culture from deciphering this "increment" at the same time that he identifies the object. This is the concept of the *"im-segno"* as formulated by Pier Paolo Pasolini, who does not, however, sufficiently insist on the fact that the *"im-segno,"* in the cinema, is located at the very center of the perceptual analogy between the object and its image.[3]

This new specific level of organization, which is constituted by the cultural connotations peculiar to objects, has an extremely complex relationship to *iconology* (about which I spoke a little earlier); complex in itself, even more complex when it occurs in the framework of a film. Between these two levels of intelligibility there is all the difference that separates denotation from connotation—but also the similarity implied by their common root in the actual perception of the spectators. This is why, provisionally, I use the term *iconography* to designate the prefilmic connotations of objects, in order to distinguish them from—and at the same time draw them closer to—the *iconology* (likewise prefilmic) that organizes the denotation of those same objects.

3. *The Cinema as Such Has Nothing Corresponding to the Double Articulation of Verbal Languages*

Let us note first that the cinema has no *distinctive* units (I mean distinctive units of its own).* It does not have anything corresponding to the phoneme or to the relevant phonic feature on the level of expression, nor, on the level of content, does it have anything equivalent to the seme in Algirdas Julien Greimas's sense,[4] or in Bernard Pottier's sense.[5]

---

* I mean to say that cinematographic language as such lacks distinctive units. For, as a totality, the cinema contains various other signifying systems, each one of which behaves differently in relation to the problem of articulations. On this point, see above, Chapter 3, footnote, pp. 61–63.

The most obvious example—there are others less apparent—of the superposition of codes within the total cinematographic institution (superpositions that complicate the problem of the articulations in the cinema) is provided by the occurrence of the *verbal element* in talking films: The effect of its intervention is to integrate the doubly articulated significations into the global message of the film, but not into the specific language of the "cinema."

Even with respect to the signifying units, the cinema is initially deprived of discrete elements. It proceeds by whole "blocks of reality," which are actualized with their total meaning in the discourse. These blocks are the "shots." The discrete units identifiable in the filmic discourse on another level—for, as we shall see, there is another level—are not equivalent to the first articulation of spoken languages.

Certainly, it is true that montage is in a sense an analysis, a sort of articulation of the reality shown on the screen. Instead of showing us an entire landscape, a film-maker will show us successively a number of partial views, which are broken down and ordered according to a very precise intention. It is well known that the nature of the cinema is to transform the world into discourse.

But this kind of articulation[6] is not a true articulation in the linguistic sense. Even the most partial and fragmentary "shot" (what film people call the close-up) still presents a complete segment of reality. The close-up is only a shot taken closer than other shots.

It is true that the film *sequence* is a real unit—that is to say, a sort of coherent *syntagma* within which the "shots" react (semantically) to each other. This phenomenon recalls up to a certain point the manner in which words react to each other within a sentence, and that is why the first theoreticians of the cinema often spoke of the shot as a word, and the sequence as a sentence. But these were highly erroneous identifications, and one can easily list five radical differences between the filmic "shot" and the linguistic word:[7]

(1) Shots are infinite in number, contrary to words, but like statements, which can be formulated in a verbal language.

(2) Shots are the creations of the film-maker, unlike words (which pre-exist in lexicons), but similar to statements (which are in principal the invention of the speaker).

(3) The shot presents the receiver with a quantity of undefined information, contrary to the word. From this point of view, the shot is not even equivalent to the sentence. Rather, it is like the complex statement of undefined length (how is one to describe a film shot completely by means of natural language?).

(4) The shot is an actualized unit, a unit of discourse, an assertion, unlike the word (which is a purely virtual lexical unit), but like the statement, which always refers to reality or a reality (even when it is interrogative or jussive). The image of a house does not signify "house," but "Here is a house"; the image contains a sort of index of actualization,[8] by the mere fact that it occurs in a film.

(5) Only to a small extent does a shot assume its meaning in paradigmatic contrast to the other shots that might have occurred at the same point along the filmic chain (since the other possible shots are infinite in number), whereas a word is always a part of at least one more or less organized semantic field. The important linguistic phenomenon of the clarification of present units by absent units hardly comes into play in the cinema. Semiologically, this confirms what the aestheticians of the cinema have frequently observed: namely, that the cinema is an "art of presence" (the dominance of the image, which "shuts out" everything external to itself).

The filmic "shot" therefore resembles the statement rather than the word. Nevertheless, it would be wrong to say that it is equivalent to the statement. For there are still great differences between the shot and the linguistic statement. Even the most complex statement is reducible, in the final analysis, to discrete elements (words, morphemes, phonemes, relevant features), which are fixed in number and in nature.

To be sure, the filmic shot is also the result of an ordering of several elements (for example, the different visual elements in the image—what is sometimes called the *interior montage*), but these elements are indefinite in number and undefined in nature, like the shot itself. The analysis of a shot consists in progressing from a nondiscrete whole to smaller nondiscrete wholes: One can decompose a shot, but one cannot reduce it.

All that can be affirmed, therefore, is that a shot is less unlike a statement than a word, but it does not necessarily resemble a statement.

4. The "Grammar" of Cinema:
A Rhetoric or a Grammar?

After the preceding paragraphs one might suppose that the "grammar" of cinema is a rhetoric rather than a true grammar, since the *minimum unit* (the shot) is not determined, and consequently codification can affect only the *large units*.

Thus, the *dispositio* (or large syntagmatic category), which is one of the principal parts of classical rhetorics, consists in prescribing determined orderings of undetermined elements: Judiciary discourse, for example, must contain five parts (*exordium,* recital of facts, and so on), but each one of these parts remains free in length and internal composition. Practically all the figures of "cinematographic grammar"—that is to say, the corpus of units that (1) signify (as opposed to being "distinctive"), (2) are discrete, (3) are of large magnitude, and (4) are proper to the cinema and common to all films—obey this same principle. Thus "alternate montage" (alternating images equals simultaneity of the referents) is an ordering that is both *codified* (i.e., the fact of alternating itself) and *significant* (since the alternating signifies simultaneity). But the length and the internal composition of the ordered elements (i.e., the alternating images) remain entirely free.

Nevertheless, it is at this point that one of the main difficulties in the semiotics of the cinema arises. *For this rhetoric I have just mentioned is also, in other aspects, a grammar*—and, as Pier Paolo Pasolini rightly points out,[9] the nature of the semiotics of film is that grammar and rhetoric are not separate in it.

Why do filmic orderings that are codified and significant constitute a grammar? Because they organize not only filmic connotation, but also, and *primarily,* denotation. The specific significate of alternate montage involves, as we have seen, the literal temporality of the plot—the first message of the film—even if the alternating order automatically entails various denotations.

It is impossible to maintain that the "grammar" of film concerns primarily denotation, unless one immediately defines what is meant by *primarily*. It is, so to speak, a synchronic *primarily:* The thing that characterizes the *functioning* of filmic orderings is that it is primarily thanks to them that the spectator understands the literal sense of the film. From the *diachronic* perspective, on the contrary, filmic orderings are codified primarily for purposes of connotation, rather than denotation. One can always "tell a story" merely by means of iconic analogy, and indeed that is what the earliest film-makers did (when, for example, they photographed a music-hall sketch) in the period when a specific cinematographic language did not yet exist (1895–1900 and even, in part, the period of 1900–15). The principal figures of cinematographic language were originally elaborated with the aim of making the story more "alive" or more "moving,"—that is to say, for connotative purposes. The empirical history of the cinema leaves us in no doubt on this matter. Nevertheless there immediately occurred a kind of vast semiological cross-fertilization: The concern with connotation resulted in increasing, organizing, and codifying denotation, thus putting an end to the *exclusive* rule of iconic analogy as a means of denotation. Here again is the example of alternate montage: It was invented in order to permit certain "effects of style" and composition, but it became a pattern of denotative intelligibility, since movie spectators henceforth knew that the alternating of images on the screen was always liable to signify that, in the most literal temporality of the fiction, the events presented were simultaneous.

It is therefore quite true, as the film aesthetician Jean Mitry[10] has remarked, that, in the cinema, even more than elsewhere, connotation is nothing other than a form of denotation. Consider our example again: a film-maker wants to show two events that are simultaneous in the fiction (significate of denotation equals, among other things, simultaneity). He has the choice, for a corresponding denotative signifier, between alternate montage and a more ordinary form of montage in which the two events are presented one after the other without alternating (the second event being then antedated by some device, such as a title saying "Meanwhile," or some indication in the dialogue, or in some detail of the image, etc.). The impression that the spectator will finally derive (i.e., significate of connotation) will not at all be the same in the two instances, and the concrete feeling of a close simultaneity between the two facts will be stronger with the use of alternate montage. Yet the significate of denotation (i.e., approximate simultaneity) will have been correctly understood in both cases, while the form of denotation will not have been the same in the two instances, and consequently the connotation will have been modified.

In short, films are able to connote without generally requiring *special* (i.e., separate) connotors because they have the most essential signifiers of connotation at their permanent disposal: the choice between several ways of structuring denotation. On the other hand, it is because *denotation itself is structured*,[11] because today it is no longer the mere automatic functioning of iconic analogy, and because the cinema is a great deal more than just photography, that films can connote without the permanent assistance of discontinuous connotors. Thus, by way of semiotics, we arrive at an observation that film aestheticians frequently make: Namely, that *pre-existing* symbols (whether social, psychoanalytic, etc.) that are artificially "tacked on" to filmic continuity represent a poor and simplistic approach, and that the essential part of cinematographic symbolism lies elsewhere (the symbol must be "born out of the film").

5. The Large Syntagmatic Category of the Image Track

So far, I have examined only the status of "cinematographic grammar," and I have said nothing about its *content*. I have not given the table of the codified orderings of various kinds used in film.

It is not possible here to give this table in its complete form, with all the explanations required by each one of the indicated orderings, and with the *principles of commutation* between them (and consequently to enumerate them).[12]

Let us content ourselves, then, with the almost unpolished "result," —the table itself in a summarized form—and only that part of it that outlines the large syntagmatic category of the image track (i.e., the codified and signifying orderings on the level of the *large** units of the film, and ignoring the elements of sound and speech). Naturally this problem constitutes only one of the chapters of "cinematographic syntax."

In order to determine the number and the nature of the main syntagmatic *types*** used in current films, one must start from common observation (existence of the "scene," the "sequence," "alternate montage," etc.) as well as on certain "presemiotic" analyses by critics, historians, and theoreticians of the cinema ("tables of montage," various classifications, etc.).† This preliminary work must account for

---

* That is to say, on a level roughly corresponding to that of the "sequence" in the usual sense of that word. The term "large syntagmatic category" is therefore meant to indicate the difference between this approach and, for example, a shot-by-shot analysis, or an analysis within the shot itself. But one must not forget that an even broader syntagmatic level also exists: groups of sequences, "main parts" of the film, return or repetition of extended motifs, etc.

In fact, as we will see further on (Part 10 of this chapter) it may well be that all the units making up cinematographic language are "large." But they are more or less so, since they do not belong all to the same type.

My "large syntagmatic category" consists in breaking the film down into segments of a certain magnitude. But this is not the only magnitude possible. For example one must point out that, in the Italian review *Cinema e film* (no. 2, Spring 1967, pp. 198–207, "Premesse sintagmatiche ad un' analisi di 'Viaggio in Italia' "), Adriano Apra and Luigi Martelli analyzed a passage from Rossellini's *Viaggio in Italia* on several simultaneous levels: They isolated "autonomous segments," using my chart, but they also identified (and rightly so) units that were larger and smaller than my "autonomous segments." Similarly, when a linguist refers to a given verbal statement, he may give a complete account of it—*represent* it integrally, as Noam Chomsky would say—in terms of phonemes *or* in terms of morphemes.

What we call a film is a set of sequences; it is also a series of shots, and a succession of "episodes" as well, etc. Each of these levels alone may account for the total material of the film; but, in order to know the film's total structure, one must, at least theoretically, have analyzed the film successively on all its levels.

** The word "type" is used here in the sense that one speaks, for example, of the ablative absolute as a type peculiar to Latin. A type in grammar is a productive analogical matrix.

† Among the authors who have devised tables of montage, or classifications of various kinds—or who have studied separately a specific type of montage—I am indebted notably to Eisenstein, Pudovkin, Kuleshov, Timochenko, Béla Balázs, Rudolf Arnheim, André Bazin, Edgar Morin, Gilbert Cohen-Séat, Jean Mitry, Marcel Martin, Henri Agel, Francois Chevassu, Anne Souriau . . . and one or two others perhaps whom I have unintentionally overlooked. (*Continued*)

several points of importance—that is why it in no way precludes the viewing of numerous films—and it must then be organized into a co-herent body—that is to say, into a list of all the main types of image-orderings occurring in films under the various headings into which they are naturally classified.

One thus arrives at a first "tabulation" of the syntagmatic compo-nents of films—a chart remaining fairly close to the concrete filmic material, but which, from the point of view of semiological theory, is as yet insufficiently developed. I will not trace here this first stage, which is indispensable but which one must go beyond, for it has al-ready been outlined in *Communications* (no. 8, 1966),[13] and orally, at the Second Film Festival of Pesaro (Italy, May 1966).[14] I will re-mind the reader simply that I had distinguished six main types: the autonomous shot, the scene, the sequence, the descriptive syntagma, the alternating syntagma (including three subcategories: alternate, alternating, and parallel), and the frequentative syntagma (also with three subtypes: full frequentative, "bracket" frequentative, and semi-frequentative).

Since then, I have sought to establish a second general table of syntagmatic categories in film. This was described in the review *Image et son* (no. 201, 1967);[15] it was also presented at the Confer-ence of Semiotics at Kazimierz, Poland, in September 1966;[16] it is the table found at the end of this chapter.[17]

This second table differs from the first on two specific points and on a question of general method. The specific points: First, it ap-peared that the "frequentative"—which is by the way relatively rare—is not a type of image-ordering to be placed on the same level as the

---

Because there is not enough room here. I will not (at least in this text) in-dicate how the various classifications of these authors are distributed in relation to each specific point of my chart. But it must not be forgotten that, among the various "image constructions" identifiable in films, some were defined and ana-lyzed (very ingeniously at times) before the appearance of an actual semio-logical method. There were also larger attempts at classification, which are ex-tremely instructive even in their failings. Semiotics as we now understand it must always rest on a double support: On the one hand, upon linguistics, and, on the other hand, upon the theory peculiar to the field under consideration.

others; rather it is a specific modality liable to affect in certain precise cases some of the remaining types.* Second, the unitary status I had given to the "alternating syntagma" (which included, notably, the alternate and parallel syntagmas, relegating them to the position of subtypes) strikes me as being a little artificial today, for the appearance on the screen of images alternating in series is a fairly common phenomenon, and can give rise to very different significa-

---

* What I used to call the "full frequentative" ("*fréquentatif plein*"—see *Communications*, no. 8, p. 122) is in fact, with its images alternating in series, simply a frequentative variant of the parallel syntagma or the alternate syntagma, depending on the case. Indeed it became apparent that the "close succession of repetitive images" (*ibid.*, p. 121) could not be distinguished from the alternating of images in series (which characterizes parallel and alternate syntagmas) by any strict initial commutation—that is to say, by a commutation made before the analyst is supposed to have isolated the *significate* of the alternating. It is precisely the fact that the viewer who is well acquainted with the cinema always (and already) knows the significates which had led me to believe mistakenly that, on a purely formal level (i.e., the distributional level), an alternating/ABAB . . . / is always an alternating/A-B-A-B . . ./, so that the relevant difference between "ordinary" alternating (parallel or alternate syntagmas) and "frequentative" alternatings (i.e., frequentative variations of the same syntagmas) must be sought on another level—and this brings us to the level of subtypes. (It is known well enough to what degree, in linguistics, too great a familiarity with the significate cuts off, or distorts, one or another characteristic of the signifier, which is theoretically very apparent; thus, when one analyzes a foreign language subconsciously using the grammatical categories of one's own language).

What I used to call the "semifrequentative" (*Communications* no. 8, p. 122) is also a frequentative variant—but of the episodic sequence in this instance. On this point, see further, pp. 130–32. Similarly, and for the same reasons, what I used to call the bracket frequentative is simply a frequentative variant of the bracket syntagma. See further, pp. 125–27.

The unitary classification into a large syntagmatic type on the same level as other syntagmatic types of several frequentative variants affecting different image structures in different ways presented an additional drawback, because it resulted in artificial unifications that partially distorted the reality of the facts of filmic ordering. Test analyses directed at passages of various films have shown specifically that, although the frequentative modality was accompanied by an alternating of images in series, in the instance of my earlier "full frequentative," the same modality of the *significate* was able to establish itself perfectly well without any alternating effect, in the instances of my earlier "bracket frequentative" or "semifrequentative" categories. Consequently, the relative unity, which will doubtless have to be retained for the totality of the frequentative variants of different segments, will probably have to be sought elsewhere than in the mere fact of alternation.

tions.* The alternating syntagma and the frequentative syntagma therefore are no longer indicated as such in the new chart.

As for the difference of method: It appears that the different types and subtypes that composed the first table, where they were presented in the purely enumerative form of a list, can be redistributed into a system of successive dichotomies, according to a procedure commonly used in linguistics. This scheme gives us a better outline of the *deep structure* of the choices that confront the film-maker for each one of the "sequences" of his film. In this way, an empirical and purely inductive classification was later able to be converted into a deductive system; in other words, a factual situation, initially ascertained and clarified, later showed itself to be more logical than one might have predicted (see table).

At present, then, I distinguish eight main types of autonomous segments, that is, "sequences" (but henceforth I will reserve the term sequence for only two of these eight types, numbers 7 and 8).

The autonomous segment is a subdivision of the first order in film; it is therefore a part of a film, and not a part of a part of a film. (If an autonomous section is composed of five successive shots, each one of these shots is a part of a part of the whole film—that is to say, a nonautonomous segment). It is clear nevertheless that the "autonomy" of the autonomous segments themselves is not an *independence,* since each autonomous segment derives its final meaning in relation to the film as a whole, the latter being the *maximum syntagma* of the cinema.

In distinguishing between the "shot" and the "sequence," everyday language clearly indicates that there are two things in the cinema

---

* On this question, see note, p. 103. The fact that, in my new table, there is no longer a *single* large syntagmatic type that is defined *only* by the fact of alternating does not imply that the *criterion of alternating* has no reality (the problem is to determine on what level it occurs); for it is quite evident that there are passages in films where images alternate in series, and others where they do not. But it has not appeared productive to state this relevance *right from the beginning* of the classification, for other criteria, in the same place, allow us to establish general conclusions more rapidly (see the problems of "convenience" and "simplicity" in linguistic formalization).

(without prejudice to eventual intermediate levels): On the one hand there is the minimum segment, which is the shot (see above, pages 106-7), and on the other hand the autonomous segment. This, as we will see shortly, does not prevent a minimum segment from being occasionally autonomous.

Let us now examine our eight syntagmatic types.

(1) A first relevance allows us to distinguish autonomous segments constituted by a single shot—that is to say, *autonomous shots*—from the seven other varieties of autonomous segment, which all contain several shots. The latter are therefore all *syntagmas* (autonomous segments having more than one minimum segment). In the case of the autonomous shot, on the contrary, a single shot presents an "episode" of the plot. The autonomous shot is therefore the only instance where a single shot constitutes a primary, and not a secondary, subdivision of the film. Similarly, in literature the sentence is a unit smaller than the paragraph, but some paragraphs contain only one sentence (in linguistics the same could be said of the relation between the phoneme and the moneme, or between the moneme and the statement; in other words, we are dealing with a phenomenon that is common in semiotics). In short, some of the autonomous segments of a film are syntagmas,* and others are not; conversely, some of the shots in a film are autonomous and others are not.

The autonomous shot includes several subtypes: There is, on the one hand, the famous "sequence shot" of the modern cinema (an entire scene treated in a single shot; the shot derives its autonomy

---

* My table therefore contains eight syntagmatic types, but only seven syntagmas. The autonomous shot is by definition not a syntagma; it is nevertheless a syntagmatic type, since it is one of the types that occur in the global syntagmatic structure of the film. More generally speaking, syntagmatic analysis is a part of semiotics in which one is *initially* confronted with "discourses" that are always syntagmas of different magnitudes, but in which the units one *isolates as one proceeds* are not necessarily all syntagmas—for some of them may not be divisible in every case.

It was the existence of autonomous shots that led me to use the term "autonomous segments" (rather than "autonomous syntagmas") for the different syntagmatic types, in order to have a term corresponding to all of the types ("autonomous segment" had the further advantage of being contrasted to "minimum segment").

from the unity of "action"); on the other hand, there are the various kinds of shot that owe their autonomy to their status as syntagmatic *interpolations* and could be collectively termed *inserts*. If one selects the *cause* of their interpolative nature as a principle of classification, one will notice that up to now there have been only four types of insert in the cinema: the *nondiegetic* insert (i.e., image having a purely comparative function; showing an object which is external to the action of the film); the *subjective* insert (i.e., image conveying not the present instance, but an absent moment experienced by the hero of the film.[18] Examples: images of memory, dream, fear, premonition, etc.); the *displaced diegetic* insert (an image that, while remaining entirely "real," is displaced from its normal filmic position and is purposely intruded into a foreign syntagma. Example: Within a sequence showing the pursuers, a single shot of the pursued is inserted); and, finally, the *explanatory* insert (the enlarged detail, in a magnifying-glass effect. The detail is removed from its empirical space and is presented in the abstract space of a mental operation. Example: close-up of a visiting card or letter).

(2 and 3) Among the syntagmas (autonomous segments composed of several shots), a second criterion allows us to distinguish between *nonchronological* and chronological syntagmas. In the first variety, the temporal relationship between the facts presented in the different images is not defined by the film (i.e., temporary withdrawal of the significate of temporal denotation); in the second kind it is.

I have so far identified two main types of nonchronological syntagma. One of them is well known by film aestheticians and is called "parallel montage sequence" (I prefer to say *parallel syntagma*, to save the word "sequence" for other uses). Definition: montage brings together and interweaves two or more alternating "motifs," but no precise relationship (whether temporal or spatial) is assigned to them—at least on the level of denotation. This kind of montage has a direct symbolic value (scenes of the life of the rich interwoven with scenes of the life of the poor, images of tranquillity alternating with images of disturbance, shots of the city and of the country, of the sea and of wheat fields, and so on).

The second type of nonchronological syntagma has not (to my knowledge) been identified before, but it is easily isolated in films. Definition: a series of very brief scenes representing occurrences that the film gives as typical samples of a same order of reality, without in any way chronologically locating them in relation to each other* in order to emphasize their presumed kinship within a category of facts that the film-maker wants to describe in visual terms. None of these little scenes is treated with the full syntagmatic breadth it might have commanded; it is taken as an element in a system of allusions, and therefore it is the series, rather than the individual, that the film takes into account. Thus the series is equivalent to a more ordinary sequence, and so it constitutes an autonomous segment (this is a kind of filmic equivalent to conceptualization). Example: the first erotic images of *Une Femme mariée* (Jean-Luc Godard, 1964) sketch a global picture of "modern love" through variations and partial repetitions; or again, the succeeding shots of destruction, bombings, and grief at the beginning of *Quelque part en Europe* (Geza Radvanyi, 1947) are an exemplary illustration of the idea of the "Disasters of War."

Let us call this construction of images the *bracket syntagma*, since it suggests that, among the occurrences that it groups together, there is the same kind of relationship as that between the words in a typographical bracket. In the bracket syntagma it is frequently the case that different successive evocations are strung together through optical effects (dissolves, wipes, pan shots, and, less commonly, fades).

* It was this circumstance (brief interruption of the vectoral temporality that constitutes the usual order of films) that, in my first version of the table of the large syntagmatic categories (see *Communication*, no. 8, p. 122), lead me to subsume this type of montage under the "frequentative" category. But in fact it appears more and more clearly that, in the cinema, the order of temporal consecutiveness may be interrupted more than one way (see, for example, the parallel syntagma, or the descriptive syntagma), and that the bracket construction per se is not necessarily iterative (it links together several facts of the same order, but without especially suggesting that each one of these facts occurred several times; similarly, although "thematic repetitions" are not excluded from this construction, they are not the rule, either). The fact remains that the bracket syntagma, by its very nature, may often appear with a frequentative modality as well (whence my initial error).

This use, which has a redundant function, provides the sequence with a common thread and confirms the viewer's impression that the sequence must be taken as a whole, and that he must not attempt to link the short partial scenes directly to the rest of the narrative. Example: in *The Scarlet Empress* (Joseph von Sternberg, 1935), the sequence that constructs the terrifying yet fascinating image of Tzarist Russia that the future empress imagines as a little girl (prisoners tied to giant bell clappers, the executioner with his axe, and so on).*

Thus, among the nonchronological syntagmas, it is the presence or absence of a systematic alternating of images in interwoven series that allows us to distinguish between the parallel syntagma and the bracket syntagma (presence equals parallel syntagma; absence equals bracket syntagma). The bracket syntagma directly groups all the images together; the parallel syntagma contains two or more series, each one having several images, and these series alternate on the screen (A B A/B, etc.).

(4) In the *chronological* syntagmas, the temporal relationships between the facts that successive images show us are defined on the level of denotation (i.e., literal temporality of the plot, and not just some symbolic, "profound" time). But these precise relationships are not necessarily those of consecutiveness; they may also be relations of simultaneity.

There is one syntagmatic type in which the relationship between *all* the motifs successively presented on the screen is one of simultaneity: the descriptive syntagma (i.e., various filmic descriptions).[19] It is the only case of consecutiveness on the screen that does not correspond to any diegetic consecutiveness. (Remember that the screen is the location of the signifier, and the diegesis is the location of the significate). Example: the description of a landscape (a tree, followed by a shot of a stream running next the tree, followed by a view of a hill in the distance, etc.). In the descriptive syntagma, the only in-

---

* In this example the optical device employed was the dissolve. Moreover the same sequence is also a good example of the bracket syntagma with a frequentative modality.

telligible relation of coexistence between the objects successively shown by the images is a relation of *spatial* coexistence.

This in no way implies that the descriptive syntagma can only be applied to *motionless* objects or persons. A descriptive syntagma may very well cover an action, provided that it is an action whose only intelligible internal relationship is one of spatial parallelism at any given moment in time—that is to say, an action the viewer cannot mentally string together in time. Example: a flock of sheep being herded (views of the sheep, the shepherd, the sheepdog, etc.). In the cinema as elsewhere, description is a modality of discourse, and not a substantial characteristic of the object of discourse; the same object can either be *described* or *told,* depending on the logic of what is said about it.

(5) All chronological syntagmas other than the descriptive syntagma are *narrative syntagmas*—that is to say, syntagmas in which the temporal relationship between the objects seen in the images contains elements of consecutiveness and not only of simultaneity.* But within the narrative syntagmas there are two divisions: The syntagma may interweave several distinct temporal progressions, or, on the contrary, it may consist of a single succession encompassing all of the images. Thus, the alternate narrative syntagma (or *alternate syntagma*) is distinguished from the various sorts of linear narrative syntagma.

The alternate syntagma is well known by theoreticians of the cinema under the names "alternate montage," "parallel montage," "synchronism," etc., depending on the case. Typical example: shot of the pursuers, followed by a shot of the pursued, and back to a shot of the pursuers. Definition: The montage presents alternately two or more series of events in such a way that within each series the temporal relationships are consecutive, but that, between the series taken

* For one will *also* find simultaneities in filmic narratives: Even when the film narrates, it does so with the image, and it is the nature of the latter frequently to show several things at the same time. It is therefore not the *presence of simultaneity,* but the *absence of consecutiveness,* that allows us to distinguish between "description" and "narration" in the cinema.

as wholes, the temporal relationship is one of simultaneity (which can be expressed by the formula "Alternating of images equals simultaneity of occurrences").*

(6) Within the *linear narrative syntagmas* (i.e., a single succession linking together all the acts seen in the images), a new criterion lets us make yet another distinction: Succession may be *continuous* (without break or ellipsis) or discontinuous (jumps). Naturally one must not count as true ellipses—that is to say, as *diegetic breaks*— what might be called simple camera breaks (i.e., temporal continuity is interrupted by a displacing of the camera, or by a cutaway, and is then taken up again at the exact chronological point it had meanwhile reached).

When succession is continuous (i.e., with no diegetic breaks), we have the only kind of syntagma in the cinema that resembles a "scene" in the theater—or a scene in everyday life—that is to say, it represents a spatio-temporal integrality experienced as being without "flaws" (by "flaw" I mean those brusque effects of appearance or disappearance that are the frequent corollaries of the very multiplicity of shots, which film psychologists[20] have studied and which constitute one of the major differences between filmic perception and real perception). This is the *scene properly speaking* (or simply scene). It was the only construction known to the early film-makers; it still exists today, but merely as one type among other types (it is therefore commutable). Example: conversation scenes (the presence on the sound-track of a coherent succession of linguistic statements has the effect of rendering a unitary, "flawless" visual construction more probable—though not obligatory).

Thus, through means that are *already* filmic (separate shots that are later combined), the scene reconstructs a unit *still* experienced as being "concrete": a place, a moment in time, an action, compact and

---

* Next to the alternating syntagma, there is one (and perhaps several) specific ordering(s) of images whose precise place in the "film's logic" is not yet clear to me. I have temporarily placed this type, with a question mark, under the alternating syntagma, from which it is less removed than from any other type of syntagma.

specific. The signifier is fragmentary in the scene—a number of shots, all of them only partial "profiles" (*Abschattungen*)—but the signifi- cates is unified and continuous. The profiles are interpreted as being taken from a common mass—for what one calls "viewing a film" is in fact a very complex phenomenon, constantly involving three distinct activities (perception, restructuring of the visual field, and immediate memory), which propel each other on, and, as fast as it comes in, never cease working on the information they furnish to themselves.

(7 and 8) Distinct from, and opposed to, the scene are the various kinds of linear narrative syntagma in which the temporal order of the facts presented is *discontinuous*. They are the *sequences proper*. (In cinematographic circles, the term "sequence" used to indicate a purely filmic construction—in contrast to "scene" in the theater—but, in time, the word has come to designate any sequence of shots having a unity—that is to say, any autonomous segment except the autono- mous shot. Therefore, in current usage, "sequence" is equivalent to what I would call the *autonomous syntagma*, of which my table lists seven varieties. That is why I specify "sequences proper" for the two kinds of sequence I will now define.)

Within the sequence proper (i.e., single, discontinuous temporal order), one finds two species. The temporal discontinuity may be unorganized and, so to speak, scattered—and the viewer skips the moments that have, to his mind, no direct bearing on the plot: This is the *ordinary sequence,* a syntagmatic type very common in the cinema. On the other hand, the discontinuity may be *organized* and may therefore be the principle of structure and intelligibility in the sequence, in which case we have what I would call the *episodic se- quence*. Definition: The sequence strings together a number of very brief scenes, which are usually separated from each other by optical devices (dissolves, etc.) and which succeed each other in chronologi- cal order.* None of these allusive little scenes is treated with the syntagmatic thoroughness it might have commanded, for the scenes

* That is the major difference between the episodic sequence and the bracket syntagma. Otherwise, as one can readily see, the two types have many character- istics in common.

are taken not as separate instances but only in their totality, which has the status of an ordinary sequence and which therefore consti- tutes an autonomous segment. In its extreme form (that is, when the successive episodes are separated by a long diegetic duration), this construction is used to condense gradual progressions. In Orson Welles's *Citizen Kane* (1941), the sequence portraying the gradual deterioration of the relationship between the hero and his first wife shows a chronological series of quick allusions to dinners shared by the couple in an atmosphere that is decreasingly affectionate; the scenes, treated in a succession of pan shots, are connected over inter- vening periods of months. In a less spectacular but structurally iden- tical form, the episodic sequence is used to represent, through a series of regularly distributed (and less "striking") abridgements, various kinds of minor diegetic progression of less extended total duration by systematically isolating some of their succeeding "moments."

The ordinary sequence and the episodic sequence are both se- quences in the proper—including the extracinematographic—sense of the word: the concept of a single concatenation plus the concept of discontinuity. However, in the episodic sequence, each one of the images constituting the series appears distinctly as the symbolic sum- mary of one stage in the fairly long evolution condensed by the total sequence. In the ordinary sequence, each one of the units in the nar- rative simply presents one of the unskipped moments of the action. Consequently, in the first case each image stands for more than it- self* and is perceived as being taken from a group of other possible images representing a single phase of a progression** (which, in re-

---

* This is true even on the denotative level (literal meaning of the film). It is, so to speak, the basic rule for this type of syntagma. The fact that on the conno- tative level (affective repercussions, symbolic extensions, etc.) every image in- dicates more than it shows is another problem and is not germane to this analysis.

** This circumstance explains why, in the first version of my syntagmatic table (see *Communications*, no. 8, p. 122), I had associated this variety of mon- tage with the "frequentative" category (though with the reservation implied in calling it "semifrequentative"). In fact, however, since this structure somehow consists in delegating an image to exemplify a virtual body of other images, it is based on a technique of *condensation* more than on a form of *iteration* (and there is no iteration either on the level of the syntagma taken as a whole, since the images, like the corresponding phases of the evolution the film condenses,

lation to the integrality of the syntagma, does not prevent each of the allusions from having its own location along the axis of time). But in the ordinary sequence each image represents only what it shows.

For all that, the ordinary sequence itself already constitutes a more specifically filmic narrative unit, and one that is more removed from the conditions of real perception, than the film scene (and *a fortiori* the theater scene); unlike the scene, the sequence is not the locus of the coincidence—even in principle—of screen time and diegetic time (time of the signifier and time of the significate). The sequence is based on the unity of a more complex action (although it is still single, contrary to what occurs, for example, in the parallel syntagma or in the bracket syntagma), an action that "skips" those portions of itself it intends to leave out and that is therefore apt to unfold in several different locations (unlike the scene). A typical example is the sequence of escape (in which there is an approximate unity of place, but one that is essential rather than literal: that is, the "escape-location," that paradoxical unit, the mobile locus). Thus, one encounters diegetic breaks within the sequence (and not just camera interruptions, as in the scene), but these hiatuses are considered insignificant—at least on the level of denotation*—and are to be distinguished from those indicated by the fades or by any other optical device between two autonomous segments.** Indeed, the latter are reputed to be over-significant, even in denotation: We are told nothing, yet we are informed that a great deal could be told us (the fade is a segment that shows nothing but is very visible), and the "skipped moments" emphasized in this way are presumed to have influenced the events narrated by the film (unlike diegetic breaks within the se-

---

succeed each other in chronological order). Therefore the syntagmatic type considered here has nothing *inherently* frequentative about it. It nonetheless is liable—as are certain other of the eight main types of montage (cf. note p. 192 ff)—to appear at times under a variant form with the addition of a frequentative modality—whence my initial error.

* Since, for the understanding of the connotative significates (and notably the style of the different films and film-makers), the number and the nature of these interruptions are obviously of great importance.

** This, of course, does not imply that optical effects always occur between two contiguous autonomous segments.

quence) and to be therefore necessary in some way, despite their absence, to the literal intellection of whatever follows.

———————————

This second version of my table of the large syntagmatic category is not necessarily the last one,* for it is the nature of intellectual investigation to be progressive and, of semiotics, to be a work of patience. Furthermore, the requirements known in linguistics under the name *formalization* usually lead one to proceed in gradual stages, particularly in an area that is, semiologically, still unexplored. After all, the more important point is perhaps not that a certain structure of images, subsumed here under a single type, may one day be more exactly analyzed (whether by me or by someone else) as corresponding, according to the specific case, to two different types—or other adjustments of this variety. The semiotics of the cinema is still taking its first steps. But it is precisely for that reason that my intention in this essay was to give the reader an idea of the problems confronting the student of film when he begins to use methods derived from linguistics and applies them in ways that are altogether new.

* It is possible, in particular, that the autonomous shot (Type 1 of my table) is a class rather than a single, terminal type, for it includes fairly numerous and varied image structures; it is the only one of my types having so many subtypes— and this sort of "bulge" may indicate insufficient formalization of the corresponding point. Also, as we shall see in Part 6 below, the autonomous shot is somehow apt to "contain" all the other varieties of shot. Finally, it can be said that the first dichotomy—which separates the autonomous shot from the seven other types, i.e., from all the syntagmas—is based on a characteristic of the *signifier* (i.e., "a single shot, or several shots?"), whereas the distinctions between the syntagmas are derived from the *significate* (despite various identifiable traits in the corresponding signifiers). These three reasons might eventually compel us to revise the status of the autonomous shot which would entail bringing some changes to the general disposition of the chart. Perhaps there are even *two* tables of the syntagmatic category in the image track (ultimately very similar to each other, or at least *homologous* on many points); a table of the syntagmas and one of the combinations internal to the autonomous shot ("free" and "determined" syntagmatic categories, as with morphemes in American linguistics)? The situation would then resemble—in methodology if not in substance—that of many languages, whose phonological systems are more easily understood if one conceives of them as comprising two subsystems, one of "vowels" and one of "consonants." I remind the reader also that the problems raised by the category of "alternating syntagmas" (see above, pp. 105–7, and note, p. 122) have not been entirely resolved.

6. Relations Between the Large Syntagmatic Category and the Concept of Cinematographic "Montage"

Each of the eight main syntagmatic types—with the exception of the autonomous shot, where the problem does not occur—may be effected in one of two ways: either by recourse to *montage proper* (as was usually the case in the cinema of the past) or by means of *subtler forms of syntagmatic ordering* (as is often the case in the modern cinema). Combinations that avoid *collage*-juxtaposition (i.e., continuity shooting, long shots, sequence shots, use of the "wide" screen, and so on) are nonetheless *syntagmatic* constructions, examples of montage in the broad sense, as Jean Mitry has clearly shown.[21] It is true that the concept of montage as irresponsible, magical, and all-powerful manipulation has become obsolete. However, montage as the *structuring of intelligible coherence by means of various "conjunctures"* is by no means "outmoded," since film is always *discourse,* and therefore the locus of many different actualized elements.[22]

Example: A filmic description can be made in a single "shot," apart from any kind of montage, simply through camera movements: The intelligible structure ordering the different visual elements is the same as that linking the different *shots* within a classical descriptive syntagma. Montage proper is an *elementary* form of the large syntagmatic category of film, for each "shot" theoretically isolates a single visual element. Thus the *relation between visual elements* coincides with the relation between shots, rendering analysis easier than in the complex (and culturally "modern") forms of the cinematographic syntagmatic category.

Consequence: A deeper analysis of the syntagmatic category in modern films would require revising the status of the autonomous shot—at the very least in its form of "sequence shot"—because, up to a certain point, it may contain image structures that, in the seven other syntagmatic types, continue to exist in a free "undetermined" state. (This is the phenomenon expressed very approximately, in a simple juxtaposition of words, by the term "sequence shot.")

7. Remark on the Diachronic Evolution of Cinematographic Codes

The large syntagmatic category of the cinema is not immutable; it has a diachronic aspect. It evolves distinctly *faster* than languages do, a circumstance derived from the fact that art and language are more closely interrelated in film than in the verbal field. The creative film-maker exerts more influence on the diachronic evolution of cinematographic language than the imaginative writer on the evolution of his idiom, for idiom may exist in the absence of art, whereas the cinema must be an art to become a language[23] with a partial denotative code. Remember, also, that film-makers constitute a limited social group (creative group), whereas the users of language are coextensive as a group with society itself (user group).[24]

Nevertheless the large syntagmatic category of the cinema ensures a codification that is coherent for every diachronic "state." Too great a deviation from this codification at any given moment results in the nonintelligence—for the mass of the spectators—of the film's literal meaning (example: certain "avant-garde" films).

8. "Natural Logic" and Conventional Codification in Filmic Ordering

Cinematographic "grammar" is codified, but it is not arbitrary. The distinction between the arbitrary and the motivated does not at all coincide, in this case, with that between the "free" and the codified.

The syntagmatic types in which denotation is not *analogous* retain a certain amount of *naturalness*[25] in their relationship of the significate to the signifier. Thus, in the alternate syntagma, denotation is not analogous—since the images alternate while the facts are presumably simultaneous and not alternating—yet, it has been shown[26] that the intelligibility of this kind of montage is based on a spontaneous form of interpolation that the spectator practices quite naturally (i.e., as soon as the rhythm of the alternating becomes sufficiently rapid, the spectator is able to guess that a series of events, A, is continuing to unfold in the diegesis, while only a fragment of the series of events, B, is being shown on the screen).

But this "natural" characteristic is not total, and therefore we can speak only of partial codification. Among the possible image structures (a fairly large number of which should exist), only a few are conventionalized; among the more or less natural (or *logical*) patterns of intelligibility on which the cinema *could* build its syntagmatic orderings, only a very few are retained—and they become *effective* patterns of intellection and are almost always grasped by the normal, adult spectator belonging to a society acquainted with the cinema. It is striking that, compared to all the conceivable image orderings, only a very small number is actually used. Just as in semantics there is the arbitrariness of lexicalization, in the cinema one has the arbitrariness of grammaticalization.

This alliance between natural logic and conventional codification has a consequence that has been singled out, with varying degrees of clarity, by psychosociologists, educators, filmologists, and the specialists of "popular animation": The practice of the cinema, both in its creating and in its viewing, requires a certain *apprenticeship,* but this apprenticeship is very *slight* compared to the one language demands. On the phylogenetic level, the evolution of cinematographic language took approximately twenty years (from 1895 to 1915 roughly: from Lumière to Griffith)—this is both a long time and a very short time. On the ontogenetic level, it is known that, before approximately the age of twelve years, a child is not able to grasp the literal meaning of an ordinary modern feature film in its whole continuity, but after that age he is gradually able to do so without having to undergo massive schooling such as the learning of a foreign language (or even a thorough knowledge of the mother tongue) requires. This is also true of adults in societies without cinema (black Africa, etc.): At first contact, they do not immediately understand the complex films of our societies, but later they are able to grasp them quite rapidly. All investigations agree on these points.[27]

9. Syntagmatic and Paradigmatic Categories in the "Grammar of Film"

The large syntagmatic category outlined above also constitutes a *paradigmatic category*—since, at any given moment in the making of his film, the film-maker must choose from a limited series of types of syntagmatic ordering. Thus we have *paradigms* of *syntagmas,* and, to a certain extent, this situation resembles that which exists in the syntaxes of many languages (example: the choice among several types of clause: final clause, consecutive clause, and so on).

"Paradigmatic" and "syntagmatic" must not, as Louis Hjelmslev pointed out,[28] be assimilated, respectively, to "smallest units" and "largest units." The distinction between *ordering* and *choice* is one thing; the distinction between *large segments* and *small segments* is something else. There are syntagmatic phenomena on the level of the small segments (i.e., the syllable in verbal languages), and, conversely, paradigmatic phenomena on the level of the large segments (such as, precisely, the aspects mentioned here of the grammar of the cinema).*

10. The Respective Positions of the "Large" and the "Small" Elements In Relation to the Definition of a Properly Cinematographic Signifying System

It is even possible—although it is still too early to affirm this positively —that the *paradigmatic category of the large units* constitutes by itself—in a certain way that will be explained—the major part of the total paradigmatic category of "cinematographic language." In this respect there are already four remarks that can be made.

(1) Various filmic paradigms, which remain to be studied and have not been examined here (camera movements, internal structures of

---

* This distinction between two distinctions is fairly simple in principle. But it is much less simple to discern clearly its application in a new and concrete area: This is, indeed, where I failed in earlier investigations. On this point, see Chapter 3, second footnote, p. 74.

the "shot," "dissolves" and other optical devices, main types of relationship between sound and sight, etc.), share with the paradigms
I have just analyzed the common characteristic of being concerned
with syntagmatic elements that are already quite "large": This is true
of entire *shot sequences,* of the entire *shot* itself, of the *relationship*
of visual elements (that is, the relationship between two or more
visual or sound elements that are isolated from the totality of the
shot but that are themselves taken as totalities with their various per-
ceptive aspects), and of the *relationship between the aspects* of the
visual elements (each one of these "aspects," even when isolated from
the other aspects of the same object, still possesses a complex and
global quality). In linguistic terms, one might say that the *frame of
reference*—or the *domain,* as Zellig Harris uses the word—of the different properly cinematographic figures remains remarkably "large,"
even when it is at its "smallest."

(2) Although, since the advent of the talking movie, *speech* has
become an important element in films (occasionally the most important) and although its very presence introduces units that are really
small—since they are the units of language—into the total cinematographic message, only a portion of the study of this verbal element—
precisely a portion that considers large segments—pertains to a specifically filmic semiotics: that is, the analysis of the principal types
of relationship between speech and image, or between speech and
the rest of the sound-track (music, "real noises," etc.). For the investigation of the filmic aspects of speech must not make us forget that
the reason speech has become so important in the cinema is because,
precisely, it is speech—that is to say, because it enriches film with the
faculties of language; to this extent, its study (and therefore, of
course, the study of the smallest units) falls largely outside of the
theory of the cinema itself.

(3) Among the other *facts* of the paradigmatic category of films
that should be studied, the greater number pertain to *differential
analyses*—that is, analyses that, taking the "filmic fact"[29] as more or
less acquired, direct their attention to its specific manifestations,
whether they are films as unique "works," the different parts of films

as unique parts, or even the different kinds of film groups (always unique) corresponding, depending on the case, to the total *"œuvre"* of a film-maker, the cinematographic "genre" (western, etc.), the "style" of a "period," of a country, of a "school," etc. (See, for example, the concept of "film stylistics" that Raymond Bellour outlines in great detail.*) These are all investigations quite separate from the study of actual cinematographic language—for the latter is an independent signifying system, and each film (or part of a film or group of films) is in turn another independent signifying system. Moreover—and although these differential analyses may, as a whole, ultimately consider elements that are smaller than those examined in the study of cinematographic language—these smaller elements risk remaining fairly "large," at least in the sense outlined in paragraph 1.

(4) Finally, if one day (whether through the study of films in general or through the study of a particular film) elements are isolated that, in comparing their syntagmatic magnitude to the total "scope" of the film-track, deserve, in one way or another, to be qualified as "small," one may well discover that they have no discrete units (and consequently no paradigms) other than those that might be derived from a general semantics, or a semiotics of cultures or objects, etc. That is to say, one would find no discrete units specific to cinematographic language; for what defines the latter, indeed, is a certain mode of reproducing and ordering "fragments of reality" that are not specifically filmic in themselves (this is what is called "making a film"). The mechanical character of the basic filmic operation (pho-

* "Pour une stylistique du film," *Révue d'esthétique,* vol. XIX, no. 2, April-June 1966, pp. 161–78. To exclude from the field of the "semiotics of the cinema" studies like Bellour's, when they are rigorously conducted, would only result in a quibbling over terms and definitions, which, in the present state of cinematographic studies, would be altogether useless and unresolvable. It is nevertheless true that, relative to the body of work remaining to be done, such studies can only be a *phase,* or an immediate *task* distinct from the study of cinematographic language in general. It is therefore important whether one considers the stylistics of film as a part of film semiotics or as a separate area of investigation. Even in the verbal domain the relationship between stylistics and pure linguistics is far from being clear. One way or another, the term "stylistics" seems to me well suited to the kind of investigation described by Raymond Bellour.

tographic and phonographic duplication) has the consequence of integrating into the final product chunks of signification whose internal structure remains afilmic, and which are governed mainly by cultural paradigms. When some of these "fragments of reality" have been specially produced for the film (i.e., *mise en scène*), this production itself—other than the fact that it is never a radical reconstruction, for objects cannot be made over (or only in language can they be recast) —is never entirely obedient to systems that are unique to the art of film, but rather in large part to those same cultural significations that intrude into the filming of an object or of a more or less pre-existing occurrence.

———————

What I am saying is this: In the current state of the semiotics of film (and of the general theory of semiotics, for that matter), it is impossible to locate precisely the threshold separating elements we call "large" from those we term "small." Is its place in the *filmed object*— that is to say, in the visual or sound element (i.e., "automobile" in a certain image, the "train sound" accompaying another image)? If this is the case, how is one to *break down* and *categorize* such "objects"? Does the threshold extend to the *aspect* of the filmed object (the "color" and "size" of the automobile; the "violent roar" of the train sound)? And if this is the case, how, again, is one to isolate these aspects? Perhaps, even, it is located in the *parts* of the filmed object (the "hood" of the car, the "beginning" of the train sound)? How are these parts to be handled?

For the time being, these problems all seem insoluble. *Languages* indeed break down into precise units the same experiences that the cinema presents in another way; and that is why one considers as acquired to the cinema units that in fact derive directly from the maternal language of the film-analyst. That, however, is also why filmic analysis requires a metalanguage that, although it is better suited to the realities of the film thanks to its significates, is nevertheless obliged to borrow those significates from one or another natural language. Simply, this metalanguage is at present still at the stage of stammering.

And yet, however uncertain its location, the existence of the threshold between the small and the large elements is beyond doubt. There are two reasons for this—and perhaps they are really one and the same reason.

(1) Even in the cases where the filming manipulates the filmed object to a maximum—whether it is by previous *mise en scène,* in the actual *shooting* (angle and axial distance, choice of film, choice of lens, etc.), or by *break down* of the shots and *montage* (i.e., discursive ordering of the various shots)—it is unable, *beyond a certain degree,* to analyze and to reconstruct the very thing it is manipulating: This derives from that incoercible minimum, photographic fidelity—that is to say (despite everything else), from the mechanical nature of the basic filmic operation. Even in trick or stunt sequences, the constituent fragments themselves are not "faked" except for those trick sequences based, not on decomposition, but on a total alteration (accelerated sequence)—even then, however, certain aspects cannot be faked (the form and the direction of motion are retained in the accelerated sequence). Consequently, no matter how far one displaces the threshold between the "large" and the "small" toward the "small," one will always encounter elements beyond that threshold that should, with precision, be termed "small," if one agrees to designate thus the level of magnitude below which and beyond which the filmic vehicle as such is no longer able to effect commutations among the elements it integrates and can then only reproduce them—and, by the same token, it is no longer able to reproduce, by means of the elements themselves, all the significations (whether literal or variously symbolic, entirely or only partially systematized) that cluster around them, *beyond the film*—that is to say, in culture.

(2) *From the semantic point of view,* these elements, however "small" they may be, are always larger than the smallest units of verbal language (Greimas's semes, for example) and even some linguistic units that are already quite large (the word). In the case of the visual elements or aspects of visual elements I have just discussed, the smallest of the filmic elements still contained a *quantity of information* that could not be conveyed by anything less than a sen-

tence in language. As a result, we may state that, *for a semantic body of the same magnitude,* languages *already* provide a highly complex analysis (for the sentence comprises several monemes, a syntax, etc., and, in fact, carries the integrality of idiom)—whereas cinematographic language has not *even begun* to speak. In this same respect it is also a very refined language: It allows others to speak before intervening, and when it does intervene, its discourse is enriched by all that it previously refrained from delivering.

Thus, when it reaches the level of the "small" elements, the semiotics of the cinema encounters its limits, and its competence is no longer certain. Whether one has desired it or not, one suddenly finds oneself referred to the myriad winds of culture, the confused murmurings of a thousand other utterances: the symbolism of the human body, the language of objects, the system of colors (for color films) or the voices of chiaroscuro (for black and white films), the sense of clothing and dress, the eloquence of landscape. In each of these cases—and in each of the cases not mentioned here—the study (indispensable, by the way) of the properly filmic creations of the appropriate significations will provide us with no essential paradigm: for those great creative tropes of meaning and of humanity will remain imbedded in culture where only a very general semantics can illuminate them—even if their deep scattered appearance in films contributes, in return, to their partial reformulation.*

Verbal language can display specific units already on the level of its smallest elements (relevant phonic and semantic features, phonemes, monemes, etc.) because it analyzes and reconstructs human experience *from end to end,* providing the different aspects of this experience with phonic substitutes that, in themselves, have nothing in common with what they are meant to indicate. Conversely, "cinematographic language" can begin displaying specific units only after

---

* Further on in this book, I will return to this problem in a somewhat different perspective, in the context of an analysis of Pasolini's theory of the "im-segno." Cf. Chapter 8, "Modern Cinema and Narrativity," pp. 211–16 . See also my analysis of *L'Avventura,* Chapter 3, footnote, p. 74.

it has reached the level of fairly large elements, because its analysis and reconstruction of human experience are only *partial*. In a way peculiar to it, it orders and states the different aspects of this experience, which it begins by taking in the form of "blocks" that are largely pre-existent to its enterprise. Thus we are brought around to some of the favorite observations—though formulated differently—of film aestheticians: That the cinema is a language of reality—and that its specific nature is to transform the world into discourse, but so that its "worldness" is retained. Note, also, that it is to a great extent thanks to this characteristic of total reconstruction that verbal language is, in fact, language proper, human language *par excellence*— and that the absence of a similar virtue contributes greatly to the fact that cinematographic language (resembling in this respect many other systems of signification) cannot presume to have an anthropological importance as central, permanent, ancient, and universal as language itself, even in recent industrial societies where "audiovisual" semiotics plays a capital role.

11. *Film and Diegesis: The Semiotics of the Cinema and the Semiotics of the Narrative*

The reader will perhaps have observed in the course of this article (and especially in the definition of the different types of autonomous segment) that it is no easy matter to decide whether the large syntagmatic category in film involves the *cinema* or the cinematographic *narrative*. For all the units I have isolated are located *in* the film but in *relation* to the plot. This perpetual see-saw between the screen instance (which signifies) and the diegetic instance (which is signified) must be accepted and even erected into a methodological principle, for it, and only it, renders commutation possible, and thus identification of the units (in this case, the autonomous segments).

One will never be able to analyze film by speaking *directly* about the diegesis (as in some of the film societies, *ciné clubs,* in France and elsewhere, where the discussion is centered around the plot and the human problems it implies), because that is equivalent to examining the significates without taking the signifiers into consideration.

On the other hand, isolating the units without considering the diegesis *as a whole* (as in the "montage tables" of some of the theoreticians of the silent cinema) is to study the signifiers without the significates—since the nature of narrative film is to narrate.

The autonomous segments of film correspond to as many diegetic *elements,* but not to the "diegesis" itself. The latter is the *distant significate* of the film taken as a whole: Thus a certain film will be described as "the story of an unhappy love affair set against the background of provincial bourgeois French society toward the end of the nineteenth century," etc. The partial elements of the diegesis constitute, on the contrary, the *immediate significates* of each filmic segment. The immediate significate is linked to the segment itself by insoluble ties of semiological reciprocity, which form the basis of the principle of commutation.

The necessity of this see-sawing I have just described is nothing other than the consequence of an underlying cultural and social fact: The cinema, which could have served a variety of uses, in fact is most often used to *tell stories*—to the extent that even supposedly nonnarrative films (short documentary films, educational films, etc.) are governed essentially by the same semiological mechanisms that govern the "feature films."[30]

Had the cinema not become thoroughly narrative, its grammar would undoubtedly be entirely different (and would perhaps not even exist). The reverse of this coin, however, is that a given narrative receives a very different semiological treatment in the cinema than it would in a novel, in classical ballet, in a cartoon, and so on.

There are therefore two distinct enterprises, neither of which can replace the other: On the one hand, there is the semiotics of the narrative film, such as the one I am attempting to develop; on the other hand, there is the structural analysis of actual narrativity—that is to say, of the narrative taken *independently from the vehicles carrying it* (the film, the book, etc.).[31] The study of the narrative, we know, is currently enjoying a great deal of interest. A scholar like Claude Brémond, for example, is directing his investigations toward that very precise "layer of signification" (*couche signifiante*) that a narrative constitutes before the intervention of the narrative "props." I agree entirely with this author as to the autonomy of the narrative layer itself:[32] The *narrated event,* which is a significate in the semiotics of narrative vehicles (and notably of the cinema), becomes a signifier in the semiotics of narrativity.

Conclusion

The concept of a "cinematographic grammar" is very much out of favor today; one has the impression, indeed, that such a thing cannot exist. But that is only because it has not been looked for in the right place. Students have always implicitly referred themselves to the *normative grammar of particular languages* (namely, their maternal languages), but the linguistic and grammatical phenomenon is much vaster than any single language and is concerned with the *great and fundamental figures of the transmission of all information.* Only a general linguistics and a general semiotics (both nonnormative and simply analytical disciplines) can provide the study of cinematographic language with the appropriate methodological "models." It does not suffice merely to observe that there is nothing in the cinema corresponding to the consecutive clause in French, or to the Latin adverb, which are extremely particular linguistic phenomena, are not necessary, and are not universal. The dialogue between the film theoretician and the semiologist can commence only beyond the level of such idiomatic specifications or such restrictive prescriptions. *The fact that must be understood is that films are understood.* Iconic analogy alone cannot account for the intelligibility of the co-occurrences in filmic discourse. That is the function of the large syntagmatic category.

GENERAL TABLE OF THE LARGE
SYNTAGMATIC CATEGORY OF THE IMAGE-TRACK

In italics: the syntagmatic types that are initially identifiable in films (inductive method), but which are arrived at last in the system (deductive method)—that is to say, the eight main syntagmatic types.

Each of these types is given the number it had in the text.

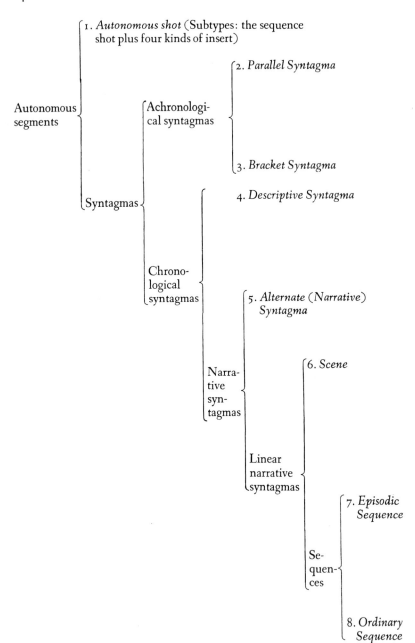

III SYNTAGMATIC ANALYSIS OF THE IMAGE TRACK*

* The following analysis was conducted with the assistance of Michèle Lacoste.

6 Outline of the Autonomous Segments in Jacques Rozier's film *Adieu Philippine*

In the following outline, the autonomous segments are listed in the order of their appearance in the film. They have been identified with reference to the criteria outlined in Chapter 5, of this book (pp. 119–33). These criteria allow one to define the different types of segments by means of successive dichotomies.

The analysis is only summarized here and is given in detail only for the first few sequences and in a few instances where the determination was difficult or doubtful.

Filmic punctuation has also been noted. Three different cases appear:

1. Two segments are joined by ordinary montage (for example, the first two syntagmas: 1–2 = ○).

2. An optical device separates the two segments: a fade, a dissolve, or a wipe, etc. (in which case it is clearly indicated in the outline).

3. There is a surprising, deliberate absence of any punctuational signifier at a point along the filmic chain where one can expect to find one (for example, between two segments very different from each other in subject or in tone)—the consequence of which is to release a very marked punctuational significate (emphasis by zero sign). One might call this type of montage, in contrast to ordinary

montage, montage with effect. It is the filmic equivalent of the asyndeton. (This type is also clearly indicated in the analysis.)

I. BRACKET SYNTAGMA

The film begins with a rapid succession of contrasting shots representing partial views of a television studio set on which we see musicians, cameramen, and technicians moving around. The ordinary sequence is, in this case, the only type of sequence that might be confused with the bracket syntagma. But the actors, who are, purposely, barely characterized, are picked up and abandoned by the camera in such a way that their activity is never organized into a true consecutiveness. Their actions are not followed in their vectoral unfolding, but are merely chosen as representative of a certain reality: work in a television studio. The peculiar world of television, or, more generally, the world of filmic creation, constitutes an underlying theme of *Adieu Philippine*. Here, Jacques Rozier has chosen to signify this world by means of a specifically cinematographic device: drawing together into a rhythmical entity a number of discontinuous images whose common denominator is simply their ability to suggest a particular atmosphere. The function of the first syntagma is, therefore, to place the film under the general heading "theme of cinema-television" upon which the plot impinges.

A difficulty arises when we try to *limit* this syntagmatic unit, because shot number 8 fits in with the preceding shots although it is also an integral part of the following sequence. During this rather long shot, the image still shows us the set in the television studio, but then it focuses on a cameraman next to whom we see Michel, the hero of the film. We are made to understand that a part of the camera is missing and that the cameraman is instructing Michel to fetch it. At this point, the real action of the film begins—individualized characters pursuing a definite goal—and, at the same time, the dialogue begins, redundantly indicating the change of filmic unit. Thus, we are dealing with a phenomenon of overlapping that is already well known in semiotics and is quite common in the cinema: The final segment of one large unit is also the first segment of the following unit.*

2. SEQUENCE

1–2 = o.

Because of this overlapping, there is no punctuation between the first two syntagmas. The new unit that appears corresponds to the definition of the sequence: A single action presented in its chronological order though certain moments of it are skipped. We see Michel leaving the studio to fetch an earphone. He encounters two young girls in the entrance hall, climbs into the television mobile unit where the director is working, returns, and, on his way back, talks to the girls, whom he then brings into the studio. After the broadcasting of the show is over, he goes up to them and makes a date to meet them in a café.

It will perhaps be felt that this summary of the action indicates an alternation of work scenes with scenes of conversation with the two girls. But this alternation, which is barely suggested, appears as the diegetic succession of the hero's actions and has no independent semiological status,** and, therefore, one cannot call it an alternate syntagma.

3. SCENE

2–3 = *montage with effect.*

The scene begins with the sudden close-up of a juke-box in a café (montage with a clear punctuational effect). Michel and the two girls, Juliette and Liliane, are seated. During the dialogue with the waiter while they are ordering, and then during the conversation between the three friends, a series of shot–reverse shots shows us alternately each of the speakers as he or she is speaking. The alternation of shots among the waiter, Michel, and the two girls does not impede the action of the scene, which is a conversation in a café. This fragmentary nature of the signifier is a peculiarity of film scenes. The

* Compare with certain musical constructions.
** On this point, see p. 164, footnote.

impression of continuity does not derive from the constant simultaneous presence of all the diegetic components but from the juxtaposition of partial views that, when combined, suggest another sort
of continuity. To check that in this case we are dealing with a scene
and not with an alternate syntagma, one can try to commute the
scene in one's mind with an autonomous shot. The communication
is perfectly possible: A single shot would have allowed one to treat
the same subject with no difference other than that of connotation.
The alternation, a simple switching back and forth of the camera,
has no *distinctive* function in this instance.

The filmic signifier in this syntagma is also discontinuous, but in
another sense, because an insert is introduced into the middle of the
scene, dividing it into two segments. On either side of this insert
shot, the two parts connect with no discontinuity; after the interruption, the characters and the dialogue are picked up again at the exact
moment in which they had been dropped. Moreover, the insert introduces no new information liable to modify the rest of the syntagma:
It serves merely to illustrate Michel's amusing boastfulness, which is
also expressed by many other signs throughout the scene.

As concerns the discrimination, at times very subtle, between the
scene and the sequence, I remind the reader of the distinction suggested earlier (p. 129) between camera breaks, which are very frequent in this scene, and diegetic breaks, of which there are none.

4. AUTONOMOUS SHOT

3–4 = 0.

A quick image, inserted without punctuation into the preceding syntagma, shows Michel in the studio. He has just been boasting about
his absolutely vital position in the television studio ("When I make
a mistake the whole show stops"), but now the flash shot puts him
in his true place: While qualified technicians are busy in front of us,
we see Michel sitting alone in the background with nothing to do.
This shot, which constitutes an enclave in the scene described above,
is foreign to the immediate context of the film—the café—but not to
the diegesis. (Despite the fact that no chronological specification is

given us: It doesn't matter at what moment the episode actually occurred; all that counts is its contrastive value to the syntagma in which it is placed.) The humor derives from the allusion, in the midst of the café conversation, to Michel's position in another life situation, already indicated at the very beginning of the film. This interpolative status, which is "real" however and not "subjective," defines the displaced diegetic insert.

5. EPISODIC SEQUENCE
   3–5 = *dissolve.*

The sequence as a whole shows us Michel going out to the country with the two girls. The narrative is organized into three quite distinct short scenes, selected from the number of similar episodes that might have characterized that Sunday outing. The time of the sequence is highly condensed relative to the time of the diegesis, which covers several hours. Such ellipsis is characteristic of the episodic sequence.

The three brief episodes have meaning only as they are taken together, for alone they are treated too allusively for them to acquire any autonomy:

1. Paris railroad station. Michel meets Liliane and Juliette as prearranged.
2. In the country. The three are walking through a field, joking.
3. Airfield. They are talking and watching the planes.

The summary effect is emphasized by the internal punctuation of the syntagma: montage of episodes removed from each other in space and in time. Furthermore, the continuity of the dialogue during the entire sequence, and through the different locations, secures two complementary functions: By challenging the viewer's common sense, it actually emphasizes the separation of the episodes by antithesis, while at the same time its very presence gives us a concrete illustration of the unity of the sequence.

6. SCENE
   5–6 = *dissolve.*

This scene takes place, on another Sunday, in front of a café where

Michel meets several friends. Their conversation is about a car they want to buy together. As in every scene, the filmic time (duration of the shots constituting the segment) coincides with the diegetic time: The meeting of the friends really lasts only a few moments.

If we are to consider the *large parts* of the film, we must connect this scene to a greater entity that would also include the following sequence, as well as scene 8, integrating them into a broad narrative unit. But, on the level of the autonomous segments, the *contrastive* features* are the important ones: We now move from a *scene* of conversation to a *sequence* built around an action.

7. EPISODIC SEQUENCE
  6–7 = *dissolve.*

It is indeed an action—test-driving the car—that establishes the unity of this sequence, fragmented as it is into several episodes. There is a distinct condensing of the diegetic time: What has taken place over several hours is related to us in a matter of minutes. This condensing is systematic, for the selected episodes are clearly separate, though successive. (In an ordinary sequence, the breaks tend to be insignificant, on the contrary, and to cancel each other out in the viewer's perception of them.)

The narrative is divided into five episodes:

  1. Garage. Michel and his friends are examining the car.
  2. Shots of the car going forward and then in reverse.
  3. Car stopped by a breakdown.
  4. Car moving again. Inside, Michel and his friends are singing. They are following some girls.
  5. Inside the car. The girls have climbed in and are participating in the conversation.

The impact of the images is increased by the use of montage with effect *between the episodes:* Thus, by simple juxtaposition, we proceed from a shot of the car going at full speed to one of the car stopped by the side of the road.

---

* In the sense used by André Martinet, in *Éléments de linquistique générale* (A. Colin, 3rd, ed., 1963), p. 52.

8. SCENE

7–8 = o.

In the beginning of the scene, we see the car pulling up in front of the Café des Sports, already familiar to the viewer. Michel emerges, goes to greet a friend, Dédé, then returns to his friends to speak about buying the car.

It seems to me that this unit should not be considered a part of the preceding sequence; rather, it constitutes an autonomous segment. My reason for believing this is the introduction of a new element into the theme of the car (Dédé); Michel's meeting with Dédé cannot be separated from what comes immediately after this scene. Let us note also that there is an effect of symmetry in relation to scene 6, of which this scene constitutes, at least on the formal level, a sort of repetitive variant: After an excursion through a succession of undifferentiated locations, we are returned to the same, familiar spot, where a similar conversation had taken place earlier. A closing scene, beyond the central sequence, echoes the opening scene of the narrative series constituted by segments 6, 7, and 8.

9. SCENE

8–9 = o.

Noon of the same Sunday. Michel's parents are dining with friends. Michel and Dédé, arriving late, join them, and a lively conversation ensues between the two generations. Very simply constructed, this scene presents no difficulties of notation.

10. SCENE

9–10 = *dissolve*.

Same place, same characters, several moments later. A simple reading of the image allows us to identify the passage as a new unit: The meal, just begun at the end of the preceding scene, has now ended, and we see coffee cups on the table. Despite this diegetic reference and despite changes in the development of the conversation, the filmmaker has thought it necessary to use punctuation to emphasize the break between the two moments of the meal. The punctuational

effect of the dissolve corresponds to his intention of treating this episode as two distinct syntagmas.

11. SCENE
$10-11 = fade.$
A brief scene during which we see the two girls, Juliette and Liliane,
waiting in the hall of a projection studio. We are made to understand
that they have shot an advertising film for a producer, Pachala, who
is supposed to come with a client to view the rushes. Unity of location, coincidence between the filmic time and the diegetic time: This
is, therefore, a scene.

12. ALTERNATE SYNTAGMA
$11-12 = 0.$
Inside the screening room. We see alternately the room itself (with
the two girls, Pachala, and the client) and the screen on which the
rushes of an unsuccessful commercial are flickering by. Between these
rushes, increasingly funny, are interspersed shots of the spectators.
The two series are not equally developed: The originality of this passage rests entirely on the use of the rushes, but the shots of the spectators are not fragmentary enough and are repeated too purposefully to
be considered simple inserts.* Furthermore, at least one of the images
of the spectators (in all other respects similar to the others) comprises
two consecutive shots.

  If we were to consider this autonomous segment as a scene interrupted by presumably "contemporaneous" discontinuous diegetic inserts, we would be able to give just as exact an account of the literalness of the narrated events, but we would not be able to account for
the construction that organizes their narration; the alternating effect
is clearly deliberate and systematic.

  The difference in the diegetic status between the two interlaced
series (typical procedure of the "film within a film") characterizes
this variety of alternate syntagma in which one of the narrative
threads reflects on the other with no possible reciprocity: The commer-

* On these problems, see p. 164, footnote.

cial provokes the client's irritation, the girls' laughter, and Pachala's resignation but is in no way modified by these reactions.

Note also that the regular alternation between the screen and the room corresponds to a total relationship of simultaneity between the two series: As we are seeing the faces of the spectators, we never doubt that the rushes are still being projected on the screen.

13. SCENE
$12-13 = 0.$
A small room next to the screening room. The client leaves, extremely dissatisfied. Pachala attempts to restrain him.

14. AUTONOMOUS SHOT
$13-14 = fade.$
Pachala enters the elevator with Juliette and Liliane; autonomous shot commutable with a scene (sequence shot).

15. SEQUENCE
$14-15 = dissolve.$
In the street, Liliane leaving with Pachala. They climb into a car, which, soon after, breaks down. This short sequence is an example of a doubtful case: It is fairly close to the scene, for the temporal discontinuity is hardly felt, is not even certain. The rest of the film does not make it clear whether a moment has been skipped between the entrance into the car and the breakdown. It seems to me, however, that the coherence of the narrative and of our perception of it presumes a very small break between the two shots, so that the car is picked up by the image a little while after it had been left. Moreover, this segment presents a unity of action with no unity of place; therefore, it is a sequence rather than a scene.

16. SCENE
$15-16 = montage with effect.$
A whole "moment" in the story is skipped between the two segments: From the stopped car, we jump to a scene in which the characters are

seated in another car, a cab, as we soon guess. The type of montage contributes to the effect of surprise. A series of shot–reverse shots gives us the substance of the conversation among Pachala, Liliane, and the cab-driver.

17. AUTONOMOUS SHOT
$16–17 = dissolve.$

A single shot shows Michel and his friend Daniel working on the set in the television studio (sequence shot).

18. AUTONOMOUS SHOT
$17–18 = dissolve.$

This autonomous segment is distinct from the preceding one and is separated from it by a punctuation; the shot reveals a new location—the cafeteria where Michel and his friends are having lunch. Like the preceding shot, it is a sequence shot.*

19. EPISODIC SEQUENCE
$18–19 = 0.$

Two succeeding episodes, which are complementary and which acquire meaning only when taken together:

First episode: Phone rings. Juliette's neighbor answers and replies that Juliette is out. Shot of Michel making the call.

Second episode: Phone rings. Liliane answers. Shot of Michel in insert.

One cannot, without ignoring important significations, interpret the two little scenes separately. Michel phones the two girls and invites whichever one is available to spend the evening with him. By means of this double composition, the sequence "echoes" a remark Michel had made a little earlier: "Hold it. I haven't made my choice yet!"

---

* For our purposes a sequence shot need not be long. Any noninterpolated autonomous shot is a sequence shot (compare Chapter 5, Part 5, above).

The episodes are experienced from the point of view of the girls; the shots of Michel are not sufficiently elaborated, or frequent enough, to constitute the second series of an alternate syntagma.

20 A, B, C, D. AUTONOMOUS SHOT

19–20 = 0.

The preceding sequence was focused on the people Michel was talking to over the phone (Juliette's neighbor and Liliane), Michel himself appearing only in inserts (spatially discontinuous diegetic inserts).

In this instance we are confronted with a borderline case such as occurs in linguistics (problem of the limits of the "word," discontinuous signifiers, etc.). We find within an autonomous shot *A* not one insert *B* but three or four inserts *B,* all of them repeating the same theme and separated from each other by returns to the original syntagma. When the quantitative difference between the duration of the image in *A* and the duration of the image in *B* is too great, it becomes impossible to speak of an "alternate syntagma." On the other hand, it would be artificial to call the four occurrences of theme *B* four distinct autonomous segments. I have chosen to consider the four images as four variations of a single insert.* (Vladimir Propp encountered a similar problem in his analysis of the Russian folk tale, with its "triplications").

21. AUTONOMOUS SHOT

19–21 = dissolve.

A long dissolve introduces this admirable sequence shot, with its great lyrical continuity. The lateral traveling shot that follows Juliette and Liliane on their walk along the *grands boulevards* of Paris brings them to a telephone booth (and only then does the music that had provided a rhythmical background to their walking stop). The last visual "element" of this autonomous shot (the telephone) constitutes the point of departure for the following syntagma (phenomenon of overlapping).

* On this problem, see p. 164, footnote.

22. SCENE

21–22 = 0.

The telephone conversation between Michel and his two friends is treated in a scene in the television studio, which is cut into by two inserts of the girls.

The emphasis on the details of the studio atmosphere (shots of the head engineer at the sound monitor) and the very brief references to the girls' faces (never more than a single shot) indicate that this is a scene with inserts, rather than an alternate syntagma.*

23 A, B. AUTONOMOUS SHOT

22–23 = 0.

Two inserts of the faces of Liliane and Juliette in the phone booth (for the reduction of the two shots into a single unit, see the explanation given in connection with shot 20). Discontinuous diegetic inserts.

24. ALTERNATE SYNTAGMA

22–24 = 0.

In this case, on the contrary, we have an alternate syntagma. Pachala in his office is shown at greater length than Michel who is phoning him; in this respect, there is no strict equality between the two "themes." But the shots of Michel are numerous, and two of them are organized sequentially; they function not as inserts but as a series that alternates with a longer series.**

In the cinema, a telephone conversation can be rendered in several ways:

1. Sequence: Its use is rare, for in this case the conversation itself is mutilated.
2. Scene without inserts: Only one of the speakers is shown on the screen (in *Adieu Philippine*, segment 36).
3. Scene without inserts: Within a scene focusing on one of the

---

* See p. 164, footnote.
** See p. 164, footnote.

speakers, we see separate shots of the other speaker (in *Adieu Philippine*, segment 19 or 22).

4. Alternate syntagma: Shots of the two speakers are combined in equal or unequal series (this is the possibility I have chosen in this instance).

We recall that the alternate syntagma is based on the interlacing of two or more series whose alternation on the screen is perceived as signifying a diegetic simultaneity. Does the passage analyzed here correspond to this definition? In one way, no, because we see each of the speakers at the moment he is speaking: The alternation of the images might translate the alternation of the dialogue and not the simultaneity of two actions. This is, indeed, what occurs in certain scenes of conversation where the actors, brought together in the same room, are shown as they speak, but in that case the alternation, which does not break the unity of the scene, has no relevant value.

In the present case, things are different. Pachala and Michel are each situated against a familiar backdrop: Pachala, whose wife we glimpse, is seated in his cluttered, dusty study, while Michel is in the studio, next to the head engineer. The two are engaged in different actions—work in the studio, leisure at home—and it is on this more encompassing level that the simultaneity occurs. It is the simultaneity of two "moments" when Pachala and Michel are brought together by means of a telephone conversation but are still separated by the concrete reality of a situation in daily life.

25. AUTONOMOUS SHOT
    24–25 = *dissolve.*
Single shot of Pachala sitting on the first floor of the Maison du Café (sequence shot).

26. SCENE
    25–26 = *dissolve.*
The same place, a little later. Michel, accompanied by Daniel, one of his television friends, joins Pachala. The three of them discuss an idea for a commercial.

27. AUTONOMOUS SHOT
26–27 = o.

The location has changed. Now we are on the ground floor of the same café. The two girls enter, looking for Michel. The sequence shot follows them as they climb the stairs.

28. SCENE
27–28 = o.

Same place as scene 26. The three men conversing at the moment Liliane and Juliette arrive.

It is not the arrival of the girls (segment 27) that makes me divide this passage into two scenes (26 and 28): The shot that shows them might indeed have been a simple insert, interjected into the midst of a single scene. The criterion here is the presence of a break between syntagmas 26 and 28. Because the conversation is not picked up at the same moment it was dropped, we must assume that several moments have elapsed between the two units of the narrative.

29. SEQUENCE
28–29 = *montage with effect.*

A montage with effect, emphasized by music, introduces this rather long sequence describing the work preparatory to shooting a commercial, and then the actual shooting of the film. Although the place does not change—we are in an appliance store—there is temporal discontinuity: A number of punctuational devices (dissolves) and a reading of the images themselves (weariness of the actors in the little film) lead us to understand that the shooting has occupied a much longer stretch of time than what we experience on the screen.

30. SCENE
29–30 = *dissolve.*

Phone conversation, with inserts of one of the speakers. Pachala's wife answers a call from Michel; the latter is seen only very briefly.

On the other hand, Pachala's study, where Pachala is sleeping on a couch, is described at length, the scene continuing after the phone call.

31 A, B, C, D. AUTONOMOUS SHOT
$$30-31-30 = 0.$$
Displaced diegetic inserts (Michel). For an explanation of this reduction to a single segment, see segment 20.

32. ALTERNATE SYNTAGMA?
$$30-32 = 0.$$
Liliane's room. The two girls are confiding in each other. Liliane tells Juliette that she has gone out secretly with Michel. The alternation in this case occurs between two series, each of which has a different diegetic status: One is actual; the other is past and is *told* by one of the characters.

1. Liliane's room. Beginning of the conversation.
2. Liliane and Michel (flashback).
3. Liliane's room, then her parents' room. Location of the conversation.
4. Liliane and Michel.
5. Return to Liliane's room.

This is an instance of the "alternate" type that is relatively rare, although this segment of *Adieu Philippine* is not its only example. There is an alternation between two series, and the relation between the two situations is chronologically precise (present-past); that is why I associate it provisionally with the alternate syntagma. However, the two series, even when each one is considered as a whole, are not simultaneous; the series "Liliane-Juliette conversation" is subsequent to the series "Liliane-Michel" (alternate flashback). This lack of total simultaneity distinguishes the type analyzed here from the ordinary form of alternate syntagma—without allowing one to confuse it with the parallel syntagma, however, where no chronology is indicated. No doubt, it will be necessary eventually to redefine it as a specific type, whose position in the outline of the syntagmatic categories remains to be determined.*

33. SCENE

32–33 = o.

The identification of a distinct segment here is based on two circumstances:

1. The narrative no longer depends on the alternation of two series (the conversation between the two girls no longer refers directly to Liliane's date with Michel).

2. The location is different, without the narrative having *followed* this displacement (break between the two syntagmas).

* Indeed, this question is part and parcel of a much broader and more difficult problem. The reader will remember that I had, at one point, thought it possible to define *a* syntagmatic type (which I termed "alternate syntagma") *solely on the basis of images in series* and that I had subsequently rejected this solution for a variety of reasons. However, an account of these difficulties—and of their corollary, the *isolation* of two particularly clear alternating types (parallel syntagma and alternate syntagma)—does not resolve the problems created by the fact of the alternation. The latter subsists, and so far I have not been able to account for it in a manner that satisfies me. The solution would seem to assume that a rigorous semiological theory be established in order to account for *two facts* that are both very "pronounced" in films though neither of them has yet been satisfactorily explained: (1) the phenomenon of what one might call the *transformation of the insert* (an autonomous segment with a single insert can easily be "transformed" into an autonomous segment comprising multiple inserts and thus into an *alternate type*—in *Adieu Philippine*, see, for example, segments 12, 20, 22, 24, 30, and 31) and (2) the distinction between *true alternation* (which establishes a narrative "doubling" in the film) and *pseudo alternation* (which may be reduced to a mere visual alternation within a unitary space or else derives simply from the fact that the *filmed subject* itself assumes a vaguely "alternating" aspect within a certain relationship). This distinction has not yet been clarified, but the example of autonomous segments 2, 3, 16, and 68 in *Adieu Philippine* demonstrates that there is a problem. Once they are resolved, these "data" (and perhaps some others I have not presently grasped) will allow one to integrate more satisfactorily the inheritance of the alternate ex-syntagma, whose problems are as yet unsolved, into my "second version" of the chart of large syntagmatic categories.

From this point of view, autonomous segment 32 of *Adieu Philippine* might be thought of as the *transformation of a subjective insert* (for example, the transformation of a sequence of conversation between Juliette and Liliane in which an insert allowing us to "visualize" Liliane's narrative of her secret meeting with Michel would have been interpolated).

Juliette and Liliane are in the kitchen, cooking their dinner. We follow them back into the room, where they eat their meal on the bed.

34. AUTONOMOUS SHOT
33–34 = *dissolve.*

The two girls wake up the next morning (sequence shot).

35. AUTONOMOUS SHOT
34–35 = *dissolve.*

Liliane and Juliette on a department-store escalator. During this long sequence shot, they are discussing a plan to keep Michel from having to leave for military service.

36. SCENE
35–36 = 0.

A little later. Over the phone, Juliette sets a date to meet with Regnier, a friend she thinks is influential, and who will be able, she hopes, to intervene in Michel's favor. We never see or even hear Regnier; the scene is entirely focused on Juliette's facial expressions.

37. SEQUENCE
36–37 = *fade.*

Evening. Michel and Liliane sitting in a car. We see the car drive off. Then, a little later, we see it traveling through Paris.

38. SEQUENCE
37–38 = 0.

The same evening, a nightclub. Juliette dancing with Regnier. Michel arrives with Liliane, and they join the others. Within the sequence, skipped moments are indicated by dissolves.

39. SCENE
38–39 = *dissolve.*

In the washroom of the nightclub, the two girls, fixing their hair, comment on the situation. An insert (segment 40) bisects the scene without, however, breaking the temporal continuity of the corresponding diegetic "moment." Despite the interruption, the two fragments constitute an entity, the second fragment being an exact chronological prolongation of the first.

40. AUTONOMOUS SHOT
$39-40-39 = 0.$

Shot of the nightclub, where Michel and Regnier are sitting opposite each other in silence. Although its relationship to the preceding scene is one of simultaneity, this insert describes an aspect of the story that is foreign to its encompassing syntagma. Therefore, it is a discontinuous diegetic insert.

41. SCENE
$39-41 = 0.$

Outside the nightclub. Brief scene during which Regnier, annoyed at Juliette's attitude, says good-bye and leaves.

42. SCENE
$41-42 = 0.$

Inside the nightclub, a few moments later. Michel and the two girls converse.

43. ALTERNATE SYNTAGMA
$42-43 = fade.$

A number of visual elements, sometimes quite distinct, at other times much less so, are interwoven with dazzling complexity. In the same location (the set in the television studio), three simultaneous diegetic series alternate rapidly on the screen.

1. Sound monitor. The script girl and the director giving incomprehensible orders.

2. Set. Technicians and actors going through a production of the play *Monserrat*.

3. Monitoring screens on which we see the program. If we reflect

that the second series (television-studio set) is itself divided—on the one hand, the cameramen and technicians pushing the cameras and pulling cables; on the other hand, the actors—this will give us an idea of the possibilities of combination in the series: listening booth/actors on the screen; actors on the screen/real actors; real actors/technicians; etc. The finest combination, which one had been expecting throughout the passage, brings together a technician and some actors on the monitoring screen. Michel passes inadvertently through the field; we see him on the screen, in the midst of the actors, which greatly angers the director.

44. SEQUENCE
   43–44 = o.
The next morning, in the studio, Michel is being scolded for his intrusion. Angry, he decides to leave for Corsica with his friend Daniel.

The action has lasted only a fraction longer than the duration of the sequence, but not without a brief ellipsis between the two high points (argument with the studio manager, discussion of vacation plans with Daniel).

45. DESCRIPTIVE SYNTAGMA
   44–45 = o.
From Paris, we move suddenly to Corsica. There is no transition between the shot of the two friends in front of the television studio and the picture of life at the *Club Méditerranée*: men and women in bathing suits, *pareos,* and leis are sunbathing, sitting at the bar, walking around or dancing to aggressive music. Five consecutive shots articulate a descriptive syntagma; their succession on the screen translates a complex of spatial coexistences at a specific moment in chronology.

From this example, we can easily see that this type of montage is not reserved only for the description of objects or motionless people. Motionlessness is not a relevant criterion, for there is no question of evaluating time within the shots. The characters may very well be engaged in some action, as long as the camera does not follow the unfolding of this action or examine its purpose—as long as it merely isolates a crude "slice" of this action that has neither beginning nor ending. One "action"—one moment picked up by the image—yields to another, and there is no continuity between the two. The duration of the action may be partially encompassed within the individual shot, but there is no temporal succession between the shots, whose only intelligible relationship is one of simultaneous presence in space.

Several young people are seated together by the edge of the pool; standing in the crowd, a man is looking around; elsewhere, two boys are walking. Each shot lasts several seconds, but the viewer cannot follow any of these characters in their activities, and he cannot establish any relationship between them other than the fact that they all find themselves at the *Club Méditerranée* on a summer day in 1960.

The last shot of this sequence provides a transition to the next sequence (overlapping). In this instance, we can easily grasp the change from the descriptive mode to the narrative: During this shot, two young men are at first confused with the crowd of other people, but gradually they detach themselves, and we recognize Michel and Daniel, who then begin walking off in a clearly determined direction.

46. SEQUENCE

45–$46 = 0$.

The last shot in the previous syntagma had isolated Michel and Daniel from the undifferentiated group of vacationers. Two shots, forming a sequence, pick them up and follow them briefly. Although we cannot hear it, the dialogue, by its very existence, provides a redundant indication of a change of unit.

47. SCENE

46–$47 = 0$.

Sitting by the edge of the water, Michel and Daniel are talking about the girls at the club.

48. SCENE

47–$48 = 0$.

Same location, several moments later. The break between the two scenes is indicated by a break in the dialogue, as well as by the visual composition of the shots (a boat that had been in the background has by now disappeared).

49. SEQUENCE
48–49 = o.

Arrival of a bus bringing new members to the club. Vacationers dressed in a variety of exotic costumes climb off the bus and are greeted exuberantly by the others. Among the newcomers we see Juliette and Liliane.

50. SCENE
49–50 = *dissolve*.

The four friends (Juliette, Liliane, Michel, and Daniel) walk toward their cabin, talking.

51. SCENE
50–51 = *wipe*.

A little later, by the seaside, Liliane and Juliette tell Michel that Pachala is also in Corsica and that they should go to him to get paid. This brief scene contains only two shots.

52. SCENE
51–52 = o.

A similar scene continues the same theme. The location has changed: The four friends are now by the pool.

53. SCENE
52–53 = *dissolve*.

This new scene, with its very simple composition, lasts longer than the preceding scene. At the bar of the club, Michel is flirting with a girl while Juliette and Liliane are making fun of him.

54. SCENE
53–54 = *dissolve*.

Michel meets the two girls in the showers of the club. Brief argument.

55. SCENE

$54-55 = $ *fade.*

Evening. A party at the club. This episode might have been conveyed in a sequence, if, for example, the director had described several different moments of the evening. He chose to show only one such moment—one, however, that is very characteristic of the party. The dancers are engaged in various noisy games, jumping up and down to the music. When the music stops, we follow one couple to the bar, where Michel speaks briefly to Liliane: They will leave tomorrow with Juliette to look for Pachala. This shows us that a scene can be fairly complex and can render a varied, but *continuous,* complex of successive actions.

56. SEQUENCE

$55-56 = $ o.

Two shots show Michel's car going along the roads of Corsica. Followed distantly in the first shot, it is shown closer up in the second shot.

57. SEQUENCE

$56-57 = $ o.

Evening. The car stops, and the friends set up camp for the night. This sequence describes a succession of different actions, which are not, however, organized into distinct subgroupings, and, therefore, we cannot call it an episodic sequence.

58. EPISODIC SEQUENCE

$57-58 = $ *fade.*

On the other hand, the composition of this sequence in three very brief episodes is perfectly clear:

1. In the middle of the night. Juliette silently leaves the tent she has been sharing with Liliane.
2. Shot of Liliane holding back her tears.
3. Dawn. Juliette moves discreetly away from Michel, next to whom she has been sleeping.

Between each episode and the next, a fade emphasizes the elliptical construction of the passage, which, by means of three short allusions, suggests all the events and emotions of the night.

59. AUTONOMOUS SHOT
58–59 = dissolve.

This traveling shot of the car driving along a mountain road in the blazing morning sun recalls sequence 56, but in this case Rozier has preferred to rely on the continuity of the autonomous shot.

60. SEQUENCE
59–60 = dissolve.

The car stops in front of a beach. The three friends get out to go swimming and to have a picnic, but they are driven back by wasps. The real theme of this episode is the gradual deterioration of Michel's relationships with Juliette on the one hand, and with Liliane, who feels rejected, on the other.

The action is treated in almost all of its diegetic entirety—in other words, almost as in a scene—but the director has skipped the "conversation scene." Shots of the landscape, of various motions (the race toward the sea, departure and arrival of the car) vary the composition and allow the director to skip various nonessential moments.

61. SCENE
60–61 = dissolve.

The car, stopped by the edge of the road. Michel and Juliette go off to fetch water for the radiator.

62. AUTONOMOUS SHOT
61–62 = dissolve.

Single shot of Liliane waiting alone next to the car.

63. SCENE
62–63 = dissolve.

Same location, a little later. Arrival of a picturesque stranger (Hora-

tio), who is also having car trouble, and who decides to wait with
Liliane. Conversation between the two characters.

64. AUTONOMOUS SHOT
$63-64 = $ fade.

Juliette and Michel walking side by side, talking. It may not be entirely useless to explain why I consider this shot to be a sequence shot
rather than an insert. Not only is its length, not to mention the very
definite punctuation that introduces it, sufficient to give it real magnitude, but, above all, the scene that follows it—thanks to several details in the image—is understood as being distinct from the preceding
scene and could in no way be grouped with it in a single syntagma
interrupted by an insert.

65. SCENE
$64-65 = $ o.

Horatio is dancing with Liliane. An interval has elapsed since we left
them in segment 63. It is night now.

66. SCENE
$65-66 = $ fade.

While Horatio and Liliane are dancing, Michel and Juliette return
with a can of water. All four of them climb into Michel's car.

67. SEQUENCE
$66-67 = $ o.

The next day. It is again daylight. A rapid sequence shows Horatio
pushing his car and then jumping inside it as the motor starts. This
very short and allusive action lets us understand that the episode has
been repeated several times.

68. SEQUENCE
$67-68 = $ o.

The four friends are inside the car; Horatio's constant singing irritates the others. Michel simulates another breakdown of the car and then drives off, leaving Horatio on the road. The sequence ends with alternating shots of Horatio left behind and the others driving off, laughing, but it is an alternation that is too subtly suggested to produce a distinct syntagma.

69. SCENE
68–69 = 0.

Michel and the girls board a ship for the peninsula where Pachala is shooting a film. Scene with the ferryman.

70. SCENE
69–70 = 0.

Several moments later, on the boat, a brief dialogue between Liliane and the ferryman.

71. DESCRIPTIVE SYNTAGMA
70–71 = 0.

The change from the narrative to the descriptive mode is felt instantly. The music provides a lyrical thrust to this series of images, whose unfolding it accompanies. The soft-focus shots of the boat moving across the sea, the sky, the yachts all around, and the two girls at the front of the boat do not sketch out a continuous narration so much as a poetic song of the sea's beauty. We do not see the boat progressing toward a specific destination, nor do we see the landscape change; time itself seems suspended until the moment when, simultaneously, the music ends and the image changes, becoming more focused and showing us the boat slipping into a harbor. This last shot actually belongs to the following unit.

72. ALTERNATE SYNTAGMA
71–72 = 0.

The shot of the boat advancing into the port ends with the image of Pachala shooting his film on a hill overlooking the sea.

The two series (Pachala's film, landing of the three protagonists) combine in a single initial shot and then branch out into two interwoven motifs:

1a. Pachala shooting his film
2a. The others seeing him from the boat
3b. Return to Pachala
4b. Michel and the two girls disembarking

73. SEQUENCE
72–73 = *fade*.

Pachala is paying his actors. Michel goes up to him to ask for money. This sequence, with its weak temporal discontinuity, constitutes a distinct unit, both because of its position in the chronology of the narrative and because of the initial presence of strong punctuation.

74. EPISODIC SEQUENCE

The three episodes are separated by fades, a common device in this type of sequence.

1. Evening. Michel, Juliette, and Liliane by the seaside. Juliette wants to speak with Pachala. Michel follows her and then returns to their camp. Extremely condensed, these events are grouped into a single subunit.
2. Michel and Liliane meet secretly by the boat.
3. Later, lying next to the tent, Liliane pretends to be sleeping when Juliette arrives.

There is obviously an intentional symmetry between this sequence and sequence 58: similarity of the signifiers (episodes separated by fades) and similarity of the significates (intimacy between Michel and one of the two girls while the other is alone).

75. SEQUENCE
74–75 = *fade*.

The next morning. The three friends go looking for Pachala near the boat landing.

76. SEQUENCE
Carrying suitcases, Pachala and his team are struggling up a steep
path toward a pass.

77. SCENE
    76–77 = o.
We shift back to the three protagonists, who are at the foot of the
mountain. They decide not to follow Pachala but to meet him farther
on by car.

78. SEQUENCE
    77–78 = o.
Inside the car, headed toward Ajaccio. Desultory conversation.

79. EPISODIC SEQUENCE
    78–79 = *fade.*
This sequence summarizes the progression of the psychological tensions among Michel and the two girls. Three brief scenes, strongly
punctuated with fades, develop the story:
    1. Outside dancing club at night. Michel is dancing with Juliette.
    2. Same location. Liliane is dancing alone, then with Michel.
    3. Gas station, the same evening. The two girls are arguing.

80. SEQUENCE
    79–80 = *fade.*
Next morning in Ajaccio. Michel has just received his induction notice. The camera follows him from a café to a travel agency where he
goes to buy a boat ticket.

81. SCENE
    80–81 = o.
A remarkably continuous scene describes a moment during the night
drive to Calvi. The psychological conflict has been resolved by the
news of Michel's departure.

82. AUTONOMOUS SHOT

$81–82 = fade.$

Single shot: the car driving along a mountain road as the sun is rising. This recalls segment 59.

83. SEQUENCE

$82–83 = 0.$

The car reaches the harbor in Calvi in full daylight. We now view the long and magnificent sequence of Michel boarding the ship and saying good-bye to the girls.

NOTE: This analysis was made from a 16-mm. copy of the film belonging to the *cinématheque* of the UFOLEIS (Paris). Minor differences in detail (due to editing accidents or to deterioration of the print) that were observed in comparisons with other copies of the same origin have not been taken into account. The author also noticed some differences, negligible on the whole, in the print of the Cinématheque Française.

7 Syntagmatic Study of Jacques Rozier's Film *Adieu Philippine*

The semiotics of the cinema is too new an area of investigation to have fostered very many applications. Nevertheless, one part of its general program—the part concerned with elaboration of the system of the large filmic syntagmas—appears to me sufficiently developed to be applied to the image track of an entire film.

The eight syntagmatic types according to which the image track of *Adieu Philippine* has been analyzed constitute a *complete* inventory—if we understand this to mean that each of the "sequences" of Jacques Rozier's film (or of other films, for Rozier's was chosen only as an example*) is linked to one of these fundamental constructions. But that does not imply that all eight types are necessarily present in every film, especially Jacques Rozier's film.

In fact, it is quite rare for a single work to exhaust all the "syntactic" possibilities of cinematographic language. (Similarly, it is unusual for a written text to contain all types of grammatical construction, except perhaps certain texts written with that purpose in mind or texts that are so long that each type has a large statistical probability of occurring in it.)

---

* Among other reasons, simply because I happened to like the film very much.

Since in this case the *text* is a film, there are two further remarks to be made, both of which derive from the difference between cinematographic language and verbal language:

1. The syntagmas considered here are relatively *long* units and are, therefore, less numerous *in the text* than grammatical figures might have been. Nor do they correspond exactly to these figures: There are more grammatical clauses in the average novel than there are "autonomous segments" in the average film.

2. These units in the cinema—less conventionalized than those of grammar—remain closer to stylistic choices, and the director organizes them mainly on the basis of his aesthetic intentions.* Therefore, the absence of certain types of syntagmas in one film should be studied as carefully as their presence in another film; a chart of the occurrences and nonoccurrences of these syntagmas in a particular film might give us indications about the *style* of the film.

On the other hand, considering the level of filmic production as a whole, the eight major types of autonomous segments do not all occur with the same frequency. Each of them has a mean frequency peculiar to itself, by which we are able to characterize it, and which could be calculated according to simple statistical methods with a suitably constituted sample. (In the same way, the so-called independent clause occurs more often in French than the so-called consecutive clause.) It is obvious that the ordinary sequence is more common than the bracket syntagma, that the scene is more common than the alternate syntagma, that the narrative syntagma is more common than the descriptive syntagma, that the sequence shot is more common than the nondiegetic insert, etc. There are, therefore, types that are intrinsically rare and might appear "recherché" if their frequencies were interpreted in stylistic terms—that is, to different degrees, the parallel syntagma, the bracket syntagma, the descriptive and alternate syntagmas (already more common), and, among autonomous shots, the nondiegetic, subjective, and explicative inserts. There are, on the

---

* It is a characteristic peculiar to cinematographic language—and it is one of its most important characteristics—that in it *grammar* and *stylistics* are almost inseparable. On this point, see Chapter 5, pp. 117–19.

contrary, types that are intrinsically common, corresponding stylistically to a "simpler" cinematographic presentation of the plot, to a more transparent language (but one that is only apparently degrammaticized): Thus, in varying degrees, the ordinary sequence, the episodic sequence, the scene, and, among autonomous shots, the sequence shot and the discontinuous diegetic insert.

The *history of cinematographic styles* may also be looked at relevantly from the point of view of this problem of frequency. Syntagmatic orderings that have become relatively rare today were less so in the period of the classical cinema, whose creators were more interested in using the entire "rhetorical" arsenal of cinematographic language. It is quite likely that films like Fritz Lang's *The Damned* and Orson Welles's *Citizen Kane* may offer one or more examples of each of the types and subtypes in the general chart on page 146 (except perhaps the nondiegetic insert, which has become considerably rarer since the cinema began to talk).

From the point of view of semiological theory, this calls for two remarks: (1) The complete system of cinematographic grammar unfolds only over a sufficient period of time (in this respect, it resembles certain of the kinship systems studied by Claude Lévi-Strauss). (2) Each film has its own relationship to cinematographic grammar: In some cases, there is a selection of types; in others, all types are used. These two solutions (with all the historical subvariations of the first) are equally significant of the syntactic-stylistic choices arrived at more or less consciously by the film-maker.

Here now is a list of the syntagmatic types in *Adieu Philippine,* given in the order of their decreasing frequency in the film:

1. Scene
2. Ordinary sequence
3. Autonomous shot (sequence shot or discontinuous diegetic insert)
4. Episodic sequence
5. Alternate syntagma
6. Descriptive syntagma
7. Bracket syntagma

Not occurring are the parallel syntagma and (within the autonomous shots) nondiegetic, subjective, and explicative inserts.

We know that parallel montage is a "figure" dedicated to a rather literal and somewhat insistent symbolism and that today's films use it rather less than yesterday's. *A fortiori,* the same holds for the nondiegetic insert and also, to a certain extent, for the explicative insert. As for the subjective insert, it should be noted that its frequency has been *doubly* affected by modern cinematographic styles: With a Resnais (*Marienbad, La guerre est finie*) or a Fellini (*8½, Juliet of the Spirits*), it has multiplied, whereas in the films of the *cinéma direct* (in the broadest sense of the word), as well as in the fictional films influenced by the *cinéma direct* (those of Godard, for example), it has decreased. *Adieu Philippine* belongs to the second of these tendencies (even as concerns its production).

In Rozier's film, there are more scenes than sequences. Is this not in keeping with a certain "realism"? This story, which moves us from Paris to the roads of Corsica, is mainly a documentary on modern life, with its vacations, its television, its cars, its youth, and how that youth behaves with its parents and its friends, what its flirtations are like, how it loves, and, above all, *how it talks* (and, indeed, for obvious reasons, the scene is, along with the sequence shot, the syntagmatic type that is best suited to conversation).

The relatively high frequency of episodic sequences should be related to the film-maker's constant concern with montage, with the organization of the narrative—a narrative that is suggestive with certain events, insistent with others, and whose apparent freedom and ease of flow are the only visible traces of a successful structure.

The story, which is simple and linear in its total development, nevertheless contains a fair number of passages in which the narrative ramifies, and two distinct series of "telling little facts" appear alternately. This contrapuntal construction is maintained through the alternate syntagmas.

The high frequency of autonomous shots—diegetic inserts or sequence shots—is essential to this narration, which, *in its integrity,* is structured on the contrast between long, continuous shots and complexes of rapid, sudden shots, often in discontinuous relation to each other, in which case the inserts play a role ultimately analogous to that of alternate montage.*

As for the descriptive syntagma and the bracket syntagma, there are few of them in Rozier's film, but the stylistic interpretation of this fact must be circumspect: They are types that are inherently rare, and we know that the style of a particular work is related to its *departures* from certain expected frequencies (that is to say, there is a relationship between the frequency of each "figure" in the work under consideration and its frequency in the general code) more than to its absolute frequencies.

To summarize, it appears that the frequencies, the scarcities, and the absences identifiable in *Adieu Philippine* allow one to confirm and to define further what one's critical intuition has told one about the style of this film, which is so typical of the *cinéma nouveau* (with its apparent freedom of form, its distaste for devices that are too obviously rhetorical, and the apparent "simplicity" and "transparency" of its narrative), and even—within this "new cinema"—of the tendency which might be called the "Godard *cinéma-direct*": importance of the verbal element, therefore of the scene; global "realism"; but also a veritable renaissance of montage under new forms.

One last comment: It will be noted that the autonomous segment, as it is conceived here, is on the average a *shorter* unit than the "sequence" in the nontechnical sense of that term. This is hardly surprising: The autonomous segment is a purely filmic unit because it is defined by the *treatment of the subject,* rather than directly by the subject itself. Everyday language, on the contrary, tends to call a "sequence" any film passage that forms some kind of integrity from the point of view of the plot (i.e., the "parting sequence," the "sequence of the declaration of love," etc.), that is to say, a unit of *scenario.* Now, it is not infrequent for the same unit of scenario to correspond in the film to several different successive cinematographic treatments (a scene followed by a sequence, a sequence cut into by two or three inserts, an alternate syntagma ending in a scene, etc.): Several suc-

* See Chapter 6, page 164, footnote.

cessive *types of montage* may be used to narrate a certain part of the plot, and, in this case, one has several autonomous segments whereby the recapitulation (or global memory) of the story is made to suggest a single "sequence." Many examples of this situation appear in the detailed outline of the autonomous segments of *Adieu Philippine*.

This explains the fact that, on the average, there are more autonomous segments in a film than there are "sequences" (in the nontechnical sense) and that, for example, *Adieu Philippine*—a film of normal length, which has by no means been overedited—should contain eighty-three autonomous segments.

IV THE "MODERN" CINEMA: SOME THEORETICAL PROBLEMS

8 The Modern Cinema and Narrativity

I

A deep, permanent ambiguity underlies the definition of the "modern" cinema. It is often suggested, and sometimes even affirmed, that the "young cinema," or the "new cinema," has developed beyond the stage of the *narrative,* that the modern film is an absolute object, a work to be read in any direction, and that it has thrown off narrativity, the earmark of the classical film. This is the great argument of the "breakdown of narrativity."

In recent years this argument has appeared under a variety of forms in the writings of many film critics. Here are some examples taken from a debate which attempted to produce a synthesis of positions:[1] For René Gilson, it was "nondramatization" (*"dédramatisation"*), which defined a sort of "Antonioni tendency,"[2] which Marcel Martin, in turn, associated with Mizoguchi;[3] for Michel Mardore and Pierre Billard, it was the idea of a more direct approach to reality, a certain type of fundamental realism which would more or less displace the old narrative habits.[4] For others, it was the concept of a cinema of improvisation, suggested by *"cinéma verité," "cinéma direct,"* and similar approaches (Michel Mardore);[5] for Marcel Martin, it was a "film-maker's cinema," which has taken the place of the "scriptwriter's cinema."[6] Or it was a cinema of the "shot," replacing the old, directly narrative cinema, where one galloped from shot to shot (Michel Mardore).[7] Or, finally, it was a cinema of freedom, open to multiple readings, a cinema of "contemplation" and "objectivity," which rejected the rigid, authoritarian concatenations of the classical film, and rejected the theater, substituting *"mise en présence"* for *"mise en scène"** (Marcel Martin).[8]

And we know that, for Pier Paolo Pasolini,[9] who has reflected with great precision on these problems, the triumphant emergence of the "cinema of poetry" simultaneously compromises the spectacle and the narrative.

Finally, for all of these critics, the recent period has witnessed the birth of a free cinema, a cinema permanently liberated from the supposedly syntactic rules of "cinematographic language."

In this account of partially overlapping positions—admittedly a very incomplete account, of which I have given only samples—one recognizes the updated echo of the famous analyses of André Bazin, Roger Leenhardt, Francois Truffaut, and Alexandre Astruc: rejection of the movie spectacle in favor of a "language cinema" (*cinéma langage*—Truffaut), rejection of the too impeccable "quality" production (Truffaut again), rejection of the too evident "signs" that do violence to the ambiguity of reality (Bazin), rejection of the pseudo-syntactic arsenal dear to the old theoreticians (Leenhardt), rejection of the cinema of pure plot, as well as the movie spectacle, in favor of a cinema of "writing" (*cinéma d'écriture*), a docile and flexible means of expression (Astruc).

My purpose in this text is not to take up arms against any one of these analyses—especially since each one of them contains, to my mind, a great deal of truth—but rather to confront, by means of a successive (and never total) questioning of these different positions, a *great libertarian myth,* which is not fully expressed in any one of the analyses, but which underlies them all and actuates them all (ex-

---

* *Mise en scène* is a theatrical, and by extension, filmic term for the staging and production of a play, or the creation of sets, and the production of a film. *Mise en présence* (literally, "placing in presence") suggests a more direct cinematographic approach, a cinema without sets.—TRANSLATOR.

cept for the ideas of Pier Paolo Pasolini, which, since they raise different though related problems, will be examined separately).

Let me be clear: These analyses I am about to question have the goal and the effect of supporting films that I like, films that I still view without boredom. They are deeply linked to the gradual rise and eventual triumph—at least for large segments of the cultivated population—of the only cinema that is alive today.* To ignore Jean-Luc Godard or Alain Resnais in 1966 is practically to exclude oneself from the cinema, just as one would place oneself outside of literature if one refused to take Robbe-Grillet or Michel Butor seriously in 1966. One might speculate—without as yet being able to account for it structurally—that, in every period and for every art, the *living word,* as diversified as it may be is nevertheless to be found in a single locus. And, even if this locus can at first be recognized only by the glimmerings it radiates—glimmerings that become larger and more intense as we approach their source—it is doubtless this prime evidence, as it is first experienced in the emotional upheaval produced by *Pierrot le fou* or in the profound boredom induced by *The Count of Monte Cristo,* that must guide our reflection, since the only possible goal of this reflection is to reduce the distance, initially enormous, commonplace, and distressful, that separated the emotion or the conviction from its clarification, the language of film from its metalanguage. Moreover, one must not forget that a critic is never altogether a theoretician, but that he is always something of a militant and that

---

* Perhaps there are altogether only two cinemas left that can interest us: the living cinema to which this article is devoted, and the old cinema of *genres,* usually American (westerns, thrillers, burlesque comedies, etc.)—that cinema that is so unintellectual and yet so intelligent, and is, alas, slowly disappearing today, although it lingers on along the paths of nostalgia and complicity, and quite often in the form of quotes in the living cinema (Humphrey Bogart in *Breathless,* the gangster film in *Band of Outsiders,* etc.). This genre cinema was a great cinema, a cinema without problems, where one was never bored. The succession—to the extent that it is not taken up by the living cinema—will, one fears, be assumed by a cinema burdened with ideologies and dubious good will (*One Potato Two Potato, David and Lisa,* etc.): intellectual films, replete with honorable intentions, based on the idea that art can reach the "human" by direct means, whereas it can only attain it after a specific detour—at any rate in late cultural periods like our own.

his purpose is not only to analyze films, but also to support the cinema he likes; to this extent one can say that whatever serves the living cinema is good.

Nevertheless one will indeed one day have to undertake the theoretical analysis of this cinema I support, and it is on that level that I situate the arguments I will now raise against, if not all the points suggested by the critics favorable to the new cinema, at least to that blindly anti-narrative myth which too often underlies them.

II

First remark: Everyone agrees in recognizing the new cinema as defined by the fact that it has "gone beyond" or "rejected" or "broken down" something; but the identity of that something—whether spectacle, narrative, theater, "syntax," inflexible signification, "devices" of the script writer, etc.—varies considerably from critic to critic, as I tried to show in the brief summary of their ideas at the beginning of this text.

DEATH OF THE "SPECTACLE"?   The concept of the spectacle has a certain appeal, but it is not the expression of any rigorous thought. One may take it in its sociological sense: "spectacle" equals social rite consisting in a human gathering oriented toward a predominantly visual event. In this case, I do not see how the modern film is in any way less of a spectacle than the traditional film, and so the implied revolution remains confined to the vocabulary of the critical metalanguage and does not affect the film objects for which it is supposed to account. Did not the spectators, rare as they were, who were able to see *Paris nous appartient*, foregather at an appointed hour at an institutional place; did they not pay for their seats and tip the usher? In these terms, in truth, it is not very difficult to remind the reader, in the face of various enthusiastic excesses, that the cinema will remain a spectacle until one generalizes forms of film distribution, commercialization, and viewing that are so unusual that the method of "imaginary leaps" (*écarts imaginaires*—invoked entirely too often, as

Proust, speaking of the variations of the heart, reminds us) will hardly let us conjure up a valid notion of them from what we presently know. To say that the modern cinema is no longer a spectacle is to indulge in the luxury of a change that is in fact not a change. One may also take the concept of "spectacle" in a more psychological acceptation: A spectacle is any essentially visual event that presents itself to us in the mode of externality and by which we are constituted witnesses. But if this is so, what purer spectacle is there than *A Woman is a Woman*—a musical comedy simultaneously undermined and nourished by the infinitely varied effects of self-parody, and still a musical comedy?

There is no doubt that nonvisual (and particularly verbal) signifiers are more important than ever in the modern cinema, that—above all—they have ceased to be ashamed of themselves (as in the period when silent movies were coming to an end: René Clair's *Sous les toits de Paris,* Charlie Chaplin's *Modern Times*), or, on the contrary, they have ceased to be entirely shameless (as in the ordinary dialogue in French films, which more or less closely always derives from boulevard theater). But although the modern cinema may talk better than the old cinema, it does not talk more, and the image has in no way lost its importance. However one may take it, it is not the concept of the "spectacle" that will allow us to isolate the specific contribution of the new cinema. The recent great films are perhaps better spectacles, but they remain spectacles.

But, one often hears in answer, they are no longer *pure* spectacles. So be it! But in that case the question is simply to define what they possess in addition to their spectacular nature; therefore the concept of the spectacle itself can hardly be of much help in the question that concerns us.

DEATH OF THE "THEATER?" Is it therefore the *theater* from which the young cinema has been freed? That isn't the case either. For, before continuing, one would have to ask: What theater, and what cinema? There has always been a bad cinema copied from a bad theater: It already existed in the age of the silent films and despite the silence ("art films," etc.); since the advent of the talking film, we have had the "psychological comedy" and the "dramatic comedy"—not to be confused with the American comedy—and they are still with us. To mention only the French cinema—which is, admittedly, particularly favored in this respect—how many hundreds of films have we not seen produced according to the genre's implicit recipe, the cake mix of popular entertainment!*

If it is true that the modern cinema has to a large extent freed itself from all this, it has managed while doing so to avoid *boulevard*** entertainment, rather than the theater, and the great films of the past were able to avoid it just as well: Murnau, Stroheim, and Flaherty to be sure; but also, in a very different way, Eisenstein.

Is it, on the contrary, the good theater and the good cinema one is thinking of? But, then, how can one forget that some of the greatest film-makers of the past (Eisenstein) and the present (Welles, Bergman, Visconti) were men of the theater, in the full sense of the term? How can one forget all that an Alain Resnais or an Agnès Varda owe to the so-called theater of distance (*théâtre de la distanciation*), as Jean Carta has so clearly revealed?[10] How can one forget that everything of importance in the theater of today is as far removed from the practices of "elaborate intrigue" as are the films of Milos Forman, Jacques Rozier, or Jean Rouch? And, if one looks at the question

---

* Here is the recipe for the (French) "psychological comedy" (or "dramatic comedy"):

1. One part *social*: juvenile delinquency; a doctor's struggle between conscience and professional secrecy; the problems of prostitution (plague of society), etc.

2. One part *psychological truth*: real, telling little details, of the kind no one invents . . . subtle observation of human behavior . . . little things that seem insignificant but turn out to have deep implications.

3. A dash of *brilliant writing*: scintillating dialogue.

4. A few *acting numbers*: knockout performances ("astonishing presence of Mrs. E. F. and Mr. P. F.").

5. A touch of the nude: just enough. Above all, no vulgarity. "Charming young actress; she dresses (and undresses) delightfully."

** The *boulevard* theater in Paris is a theater of melodrama and (usually marital) comedy, characterized by startling dramatic turns ("Madame, I am your son") and by a very fast-moving, witty, and brilliant (though perishable) dialogue.—TRANSLATOR.

from a wider perspective, if, following the lead of certain theoreticians of the cinema (Balázs),[11] or of the theater (Lessing),* one takes the position that the theater is opposed to the epic (or to the novel, that secular epic) as a fiction caught in *action,* and in its circumstantial thrust is in contrast to that same fiction related in words that are not those of the protagonists, one will indeed have to conclude that the cinema, although an art very different from the theater, is nevertheless not on the point—unless its nature changes radically—of breaking the very apparent and basic bond that links it to the theater.** No more than the distinction between the "spectacle" and the "nonspectacle," will the distinction between the "theater" and the "nontheater" allow us to establish our preferences in theory, so that we can understand more clearly why we like what we like, or what is new about the new cinema.

THE CINEMA OF IMPROVISATION?   Is the answer, then, that the new cinema is a cinema of improvisation? But there are numerous modern films that fall outside of this definition, from *Knife in the Water* to *Jules and Jim,* passing through the works of Orson Welles, Jacques Demy, Alain Resnais, etc. It is true that, when he proposed the formula, Michel Mardore was careful to apply it only to one tendency of the modern cinema, but the idea is current and one often hears it expressed in a much more vague and general way. Really, it

* In the beginning of *Hamburgische Dramaturgie* (in a passage devoted to the problem of the adaptation of novels to the theater). The novelist describes psychological contents, whereas the dramatist must "bring them to life under the eyes of the spectator, and develop them without interruption within an illusory continuity." (Note that in the cinema the "illusory continuity" occurs within each "scene" but is broken between scenes; and this phenomenon, incidentally, has obvious parallels in the theater). In respect to this kind of problem, it is difficult to see how the cinema can ever become *truly* "non-theatrical."
** Above and beyond all one's opinions for or against "filmed theater," one cannot but give credit to Marcel Pagnol for perpetually underlining this fundamental bond—even when it is formulated in terms whose every detail one cannot agree with (namely, the idea that the theater and the cinema are two forms, among other forms, of "dramatic art"). See ch. 1 of *César* (Editions de Provence, 1966, a book of memoirs), published separately under the title "Cinématurgie de Paris" in *Cahiers du cinéma,* no. 173, Dec. 1965 (special issue on Pagnol and Sacha Guitry), pp. 39–54. Passage referred to: pp. 43–44.

corresponds only—and even then with some reservations—on the one hand to Jean-Luc Godard (but the man, we know, has a touch of genius, and genius is always something else; moreover, although it improvises with great felicity, the "individual cinema"—"cinévidu"— is a demanding task-master), and on the other hand to a number of tendencies related to the *cinéma direct* in its broadest sense,* tendencies that, except for a few brilliant exceptions, consist largely in presenting the audience with formless fragments that in other times would have been considered the intermediary genetic stages of a work-in-progress, as Claude Lévi-Strauss once remarked.¹² The indiscrimination of the *cinéma direct* is too often the by-product of laziness or of haste; as Bernard Pingaud notes,¹³ too often it renounces the prestigious aspects of art, or simply of the finished work, without acquiring (at best) any more truth than a good documentary possesses. It is not enough to say that the ordinary direct film is not perfect, for it has really not even been finished.** And it is not just the history of the cinema, but the most basic nature of the aesthetic object itself, that will have to change profoundly before a work of art is able to absorb large sections of untransformed reality into its own purpose, and before it can hope to contain truths other than the only one, transposed and reformulated, that its initial procedures have not placed out of reach. The good films of the *cinéma direct* are good because they are good films. If "improvisation" means a spontaneity of decision and execution acquired by means of the long, slow apprenticeship of real mastery—the great surgeon, over an open abdomen, also "improvises"—or, if it is a stroke of genius, or both together, then most of the great directors have been, in part at least, improvisers. If, on the contrary, improvisation is the locus where laziness and the de-

* *Cinéma direct* itself (Ruspoli), and *cinéma verité* (*Chronique d'un été*, by Jean Rouch), but also the "candid camera" film; the National Film Board of Canada tendency; aspects of the so-called New York school, or of the British "free cinema"; the American feature-documentaries (Leacock, the Maysles brothers); tendencies of the television (Klein), etc.

** Although he spoke of a cinema of "improvisation," Michel Mardore is not in full agreement with the *cinéma direct; his position,* it would seem, is very much like my own. But it is the concept of the cinema of improvisation itself that seems unclear to me.

sire to produce clash and neutralize each other, this simply defines a kind of bad film that belongs as much to the past as to the present. In one case or the other, the distinction between the improvised and the nonimprovised can give us no real definition of the modern cinema.

THE CINEMA OF "NONDRAMATIZATION?"   Is "nondramatization" the answer then? Antonioni? "Dead" spaces? But there are no real dead spaces in a film, since a film is a manufactured object; only in life are there "dead spaces." A moment can be dull, "dead," only in relation to an interest: The fifteen-minute wait before a decisive interview, because the person I am to see is late, is indeed a kind of "dead space," since it is not what I am attending to at the time. But such moments arise only because the occurrences of life are not shaped by one's own will; they do not obey the urge to satisfy the affective arabesque, which is considered most fulfilling (to repeat one of Étienne Souriau's formulations[14]). Filmed by an Antonionian, my fifteen-minute wait would no longer appear as "dead space," since for the while it would have become the very intent of the film—which is always constructed—so that, for those fifteen minutes, the whole life of the film would be contained in the "dead space." The only real dead spaces in the cinema are the boring passages in films—the dull moments—since, while externally disappointing the viewer's attention, which becomes dormant, it produces internally the very conditions responsible for the "dead spaces" in life. It is on the level of cutting and montage—that is, before the film exists—that the destiny of the "dead spaces" is determined: Those the film-maker experiences as such are banished from the film, and we will never see them—for, unlike life in this respect, film must make its choices or cease to exist at all. Thus, all the "moments" that the film-maker has included in his film were alive to him. Antonioni's cinema is simply a new—and a profoundly original—appreciation of what is or is not a "dull moment" in life, and it is not based on a mere aesthetics of space that is filmically "dead." Innovation is an ideological rather than a cinematographic matter, and Antonioni is "modern" far more because of the human substance of his films than because of their "language." He excels in showing us the diffuse significance of those moments of everyday life that are considered insignificant; integrated within the film, the dull moment is reborn to our perception. And surely the most important thing about Antonioni—and about the best films of the *cinéma direct*—is that he was able to gather together within the skein of a more subtle dramaturgy all those *lost significations* of which our days are made. Even more: that he was able to prevent them from being entirely lost, without, however, marshaling them— that is to say, depriving their significates of that shimmering indecision without which they would no longer be lost significations; that he was able to preserve them without "finding" them.* Thus, "non-dramatization"—a useful but risky term—is nothing other than a new form of dramaturgy, and that is why I liked *Il Grido* and *L'Avventura*. Remove "drama," and there is no fiction, no diegesis, and therefore no film. Or only a documentary, a "film exposé." The only real boundary—too often one forgets it—is the one between "film" as the word is currently used (meaning the fiction film, whether realistic or not), and all the special genres that begin by rejecting (that is to say, very much beyond the new dramaturgies, whether Antonionian or Godardian) the principle of the narrative itself: newsreels, promotional films, scientific films, etc. In short, "documentaries" in the widest sense. Many of the average quality "direct" films are really simply fairly decent documentaries, as Philippe Hadiquet rightly calls them.[15]

A FUNDAMENTAL REALISM? Perhaps, then, the new cinema should be defined as a more direct approach to the real, a sort of fundamental realism, or "objectivity?" First, there is an ambiguity that must be resolved: If by these concepts one implies some kind of primordial power, an ability to reveal everything, which the cinema has always

---

* Example: the goatherd on the island in *L'Avventura,* who seemed so incredibly true to life. (What had he done? What, exactly, did he know?) Or the interview with Gabillon in *Chronique d'un été.* (To what extent did he miss his militant past? How did he accept his relative compromise with *bourgeoisie?*)

contained but which it recognized only after a long time, is simply to revert to a mythology that Jean Mitry has rightly criticized,[16] a mythology that conceals behind phenomenological trappings an essential realism whose consequence is the revival, on the level of the "natural meaning of things," of the terroristic inflexibility of signification—which, on the other hand, one is fighting in the name of ambiguity; these are the most questionable aspects of André Bazin's and Roger Munier's theories. It should be noted incidentally that Michel Mardore and Pierre Billard do not conceive of the notion of "realism" in that sense; nor does Marcel Martin, despite some of his expressions that are to my mind unfortunate, such as, especially, "objectivity" and "mise en présence"—a film is never objective, and "mise en présence" (presenting) cannot replace "mise en scène" (producing), of which it is only another form. The author of L'Immortelle, at the time of his great "subjectivist" period, pointed out, indeed, that the cinema is the most subjective of the arts, because of the simple fact that any "shooting" of film automatically implies a choice of angle;[17] and the true lesson of phenomenology, we know, is by no means in the unilateral triumph of cosmophania,* but in the obstinate affirmation of a definite interchange between things that are and the person for whom they are, in the ineluctable "adverse spectacle" Valery speaks of, and that is already entirely contained in the expression "there is"—the elementary form of existence as well as of the cinema, since it implies that there is something (that something exists) and that someone exists for that thing to be there. "There is" actualizes both the filmed object and the filming of the object.

The real modern inheritor of the cosmophanic myths is not the young cinema as a whole, but rather a certain crazy optimism that has sprung up around the cinéma verité: the belief in a kind of innocence of the image, which is somehow mysteriously exempt from connotation, as well as—even as it lends itself to the discursive patterns that the slightest dislocation of the camera already introduces—

---

* Cosmophania (cosmophanie) is a coined word derived from the Greek κοσμος (cosmos) and φαινειν (to show). Thus, it indicates the faculty to present the world in its entirety, to show "everything."—TRANSLATOR.

from the enormous weight of implication that burdens the word:[18] a
desperate myth of some kind of iconic adamism, to speak in Barthesian terms. In the enormous ideological inflation characterizing
the few beautiful and the many botched works of the *cinéma vérité,*
one might recognize a wayward, sad, and obstinate sister of the semiological approach—at least if the latter is considered in its least technical aspects, and in its deepest affective foundation. The prevailing
wind today is one of distrust for language, and words are being ques-
tioned everywhere. Created in order to question the world, speech itself has now become the object of questions; fashioned as a tool for
deriving accounts from things, it is being asked now to account for
itself. In this no-man's-land of suspicion and noble neurosis, the
"general semantics" of American scholars has developed an unexpected optimism (namely, that the purification of language will pu-
rify human relations), whereas "logical positivism" has surrendered
to an active, relativistic, and somewhat limited pessimism (that the
true discourse is only a true discourse; the word contains no other
truth than that which is contained in its correct sociolinguistic usage).
The *cinéma vérité,* on the contrary, attempts to avoid these difficulties by supposedly rejecting coherent discourse and the use of iconic
attestation; even the speech of the (film) heroes is supposed to be un-
shaped, nascent—it is part of the image, as if it were being swept
along some vast circuit of visual innocence (the proliferation of interviews in the *cinéma-verité* films has no other source). It is a pathetic attempt.*

* Those readers who have only seen *Lonely Boy, Les Inconnus de la terre,
Les Maîtres-fous,* and a few other films of this quality that have been com-
mercially distributed will perhaps find that I am too severe. But they should
not forget all those more specialized films that present us with, variously, ten
games of American football (a riot of zoom shots and illegible pan shots, the
savage yells of the coach and his "boys," etc.), fifteen interviews on the
psychosexual problems of Quebec coeds (stammerings, emotional exhibitionism,
etc.), a large number of documentary reports on assorted boxers, actors, automobile racers, producers, and colonial plantation owners, etc. (that is, pure and
simple journalism), twenty psychodrama studies of mental patients, peasants,
drug addicts, students, natives of Central Africa, and, in general, of anyone
who has "problems." One realizes that this type of cinema hesitates between
two types of ideology: that of image objectivity, which I have just described
and which is a sort of curious behaviorism; and another kind, more disturbing,

The fact remains nevertheless—and it is immediately apparent at the viewing of certain films—that the best works of the new cinema, among which one finds films of the *cinéma-direct* variety, often present their viewers with *a certain type of truth* that, indeed, one finds less frequently in the great works of the past—a truth that is extremely difficult to define but that, somehow, one places instinctively. It is the exactness of an attitude, of the inflection of a voice, of a gesture, of a tone. It is, for example, the marvelous, almost danced scene in *Pierrot le fou* among the pine trees by the beach (*"Ma ligne de chance . . . Ta ligne de hanches . . ."* "My life line . . . Your hip line . . ."): a highly "unrealistic" scene nevertheless, since it is a piece of choreography, a reference to American musical comedy—we are a long way from the simple-minded "realism" of the cinematographic "culturist" tradition, "realism" for film societies. No other film passage, however—unless perhaps, to a lesser extent, the silent seduction scene during the parade in Stroheim's *Wedding*

---

which is the vulgarized and eclectic product of various methods of revelation or of therapeutics used in modern psychosociology (psychodrama, group dynamics, brainstorming, in-depth interviews, psychotherapy, etc.). One simply forgets that these methods, unless they are handled in a controlled, technical way, can only lead to two results: Either the subjects remain caught in their original positions, retaining all their "blocks" and speaking only conversational platitudes, or else they are traumatized by the indecent and irresponsible indiscretion that is all that remains of these methods when they are taken out of the hands of the specialists, and one then witnesses, not the revelation of some latent content, but a series of agitated, muddled expressions (the subjects ranting at themselves or at each other, crying, chattering, etc.), which almost make one nostalgic for the old methods of education based on "manners." It is incidentally significant that, of all the modern methods, the only one that is relatively neglected by the *cinéma vérite* is precisely the one that is most like a technique, one in which the specialist's performance obeys precise operatory rules and does not aim to express some truth or impression so much as to provoke a predictable and controlled result: actual psychoanalysis (I add *actual* to distinguish it from the various "cinematographic contributions" that operate on the principle of intrusion without the safeguard of an orderly procedure—that is to say, the manipulation of speech that is not constantly spurred by the concern for efficiency and the expression of immediate truth, for it is this refusal to give speech a strict, codified status that renders the caricatures of psychoanalysis so haphazard). In short, with the cinema that pretends to be the cinema of reality it would appear that the most essential division is the one contrasting the *cinéma-direct* tendency (ideology of external objectivity) to the *cinéma vérité* tendency (ideology of the saving intervention).

March—had portrayed with an accuracy as fundamentally direct, as superbly careless of the external probabilities of time and place, the mute corporeal agreements that love produces and by which it is produced, the ambience of gestures and smiles, the thousand minor acceptances of a docile receptiveness that is no mere obedience and that mold the woman's sunny face in the succeeding directions her lover's ballet of active, amused, and moving tenderness describes around it, impelling it. One finds evidence of the accuracy of this approach not only in all the Godard films, in all the Truffaut and some of the Antonioni films, but also in a considerable number of modern films, from *L'As de pique* to Jacques Rozier's *Adieu Philippine,* passing through *Saturday Night and Sunday Morning* and various films by Losey, Olmi, Rossi, De Seta, Makabeyev, etc. One might even say that these instances—whose truth remains to be defined[19]—are, for all their fragility, the most precious conquests of the cinema that, since 1966, we have called "modern." It is surely not some principle of objectivity, some faultless realism, that can define this modern cinema, but rather the liability to certain truths, or to certain *accuracies,* that make the young cinema more adult and the traditional cinema occasionally very youthful. The films of the past, even the most beautiful,* are generally a little "above themselves," like those precocious adolescents who, among their parents' guests, speak a trifle loudly, though not foolishly.

THE ORDERED CINEMA.   To observe that such accuracies have become possible, however—even though the directors of the past were not, on the whole, less intelligent or less sensitive than those of today; less cultivated, perhaps, but that explanation is inadequate—is to reexamine that new and subtler dramaturgy that admits more objective details, details of the kind that the traditional plot film sacrificed or overwhelmed. Exactness of tone—a priceless conquest that renders a whole area of the cinema obsolete—might well be, in turn, only a consequence.

* See passages of Murnau's *Dawn* (the first appearance of the city woman), Sjöstrom's *Wind* (certain of Lillian Gish's expressions), or Stroheim's *Greed* (the character of Marcus), etc. And, naturally, certain passages of Eisenstein (except in *Potemkin*) and of Pudovkin (except perhaps *Storm over Asia*).

Furthermore one must not forget that this new "realism" does not characterize all of the modern cinema, since, alongside this tendency but distinct from it, in a contrast that is gradually becoming clearer, there has arisen a whole cinema of *controlled diction*, a generalized recitative approach: The cinema of Alain Resnais, with which one can associate, in varying degrees, aspects of the films of Agnès Varda, Chris Marker, Armand Gatti, and Henri Colpi.[20] In this case the protocol of image and text is a great deal more exacting; it is as if the inherent realistic potential of the filmic vehicle, formerly the property of the convention of a moderate degree of discretely theatrical realism (for example, the Carné-Prévert films), had now divided itself between a "cinema of passion" (in the sense that one speaks of "passionate love," as René Gilson correctly notes),[21] a cinema of exuberance and discovery (and it is this cinema that is occasionally able to capture those so direct truths I have just spoken of; we know the interest Godard has shown for Jean Rouch's experiments) and, on the other hand, a cinema of premeditation and indirection, wonderfully expressed by Alain Resnais and his successive script-writers—a cinema that believes only in reconstructed truths;* a cinema (perhaps more

---

* Most critics blasted Agnès Varda's film, *Le Bonheur*. That was the result of a kind of misunderstanding. I did not like the film either, but to attack it for its lack of realism is, to my mind, a serious misconstruction. Certainly, the workers' way of life, as the film presents it, is quite fantastic. But it had to be so. For the film is a philosophical tale, such as the eighteenth century enjoyed, or rather it is a militant utopia in the style of the nineteenth century (but unfortunately lacking in a more lucid account of the actual social factors—and especially the class factors—that enter into the problem considered). It is also, in one way, an act of courage. For, although it is true that a few persons in the social environment where films are produced dream of a world in which love would be truly free, a world both animal and completely human, where the body's carelessness would also be a generosity, a sympathy and a perfect *society* of women and men, a world in which that irresponsible, disrupting, clinging monster of *sentimentalism*, as it has come to be since the death of paganism, will be tamed—although it is true that a futurism of the passions nourishes some of the conversations in Paris's Left Bank, the fact is that, aside from Pierre Kast in *La Morte-saison, Le Bel âge,* and *La Brûlure des mille soleils,* no one besides Agnès Varda had gathered these scattered ideas into such a boldly provocative form. These human relationships of a new type, these multiple love affairs openly conducted away from such pettinesses of bourgeois adultery as the sincere but futile sufferings of jealous, exclusive emotions, are all presented in the *actual* mode, as if they existed, as if they were already

Brechtian than it is aware of) that orders with meticulous patience a whole series of insistent, composed signs, not without making certain that their scrupulously unusual disposition will ensure a problematical and uncertain, although inevitably worked-at, deciphering; a cinema that hesitates between ambiguity and riddle (in *Muriel,* did Alphonse actually send a letter of explanation to Helène twenty years earlier, at the time of the missed rendez-vous? Was there really a last year at Marienbad? Was the amnesiac in *Une aussi longue absence* the husband or not? etc.); a cinema of tense uncertainty that, rather than presenting the aporias of meaning in a form intended to imitate their appearance in daily experience, deliberately constructs a labyrinthine model suggesting some bizarre modernistic ritual within which the spectator will lose himself, but according to an itinerary traced in advance.* One could say that Alain Resnais and Jean-Luc

---

existing. Hence the lack of realism. But is that not also the very definition of utopia (i.e., the optative translated into the present of the indicative)? For that matter, these free relationships are already practiced more or less in some "artistic" circles; but if Agnès Varda had placed the action of her film in such a setting, the story—which would then be realistic—would have lost all the power of its militant impact. For what the film means to say is that workers, too, could live like that. In short, the misunderstanding derives from the fact that the film was viewed as if one would see a Godard film as a typical example of the ordered cinema. I repeat: I did not like the film, not at all in fact. This was for reasons pertaining to the enactment of the utopia in its details. But who would maintain that there was not a certain amount of courage and beauty in the fact that a modern woman can speak of such unusual things, and therefore how can one fail to sympathize with the sincerity of her attempt?

* In normal life, "ambiguity" (despite its etymology) is only rarely a choice between two (or more) precise solutions. It is usually a semantic indetermination within a given field, the very questioning of which contains no discrete units. Similarly, in *Pierrot le fou,* when Ferdinand who is beginning to be tortured decides to say "She is at the Signe de la Marquise," this semi-betrayal indicates an ill-defined agglomeration of motives, which cannot be innumerated and which are, for that matter, liable to coexist at the same point along the chain of meaning: fear of torture, uncertainty as to what it is the two men in blue shirts want, the suspicion that Marianne is their accomplice and is betraying him, resentment that she had never answered his earlier questions, transcendental resignation, and a feeling of the abrupt reversal of desired conditions (as at the moment of the final suicide), etc.—Is Jean-Luc Godard an "excessive romantic," as Bernard Dort suggested in an article in *Les Temps modernes?* Certainly. But he is also, in a special way, one of the first "realists" of the French cinema.

Godard represent the two great poles of modern film: meticulously indirect realism as opposed to a generously abandoned realism (and, as for "truth," we find it on one side as on the other); in the first instance, the triumph of *"mimesis"* and of the reconstruction of the model, and, in the second instance, a luxuriating avatar of *"poiesis,"* to restate some Barthesian concepts. The film of the past, always more or less "realistic," but always more or less simplified, was located *this side of the dividing point,** and surely one of the characteristics of the modern film is this redistribution of the cinematographic field through one of those great binary openings whose importance in certain language phenomena is well known.

A FILM-MAKER'S CINEMA? What about the concept of a "film-maker's cinema" as distinct from the old "script-writer's cinema"? Can it provide that criterion of cinematographic modernity that must exist somewhere, since we experience its consequences but find it so difficult to define? There is no doubt that today's cinema is very often a "cinema cinema," while the old cinema was so frequently the ulterior and secondary illustration of a previously worked-out story; Godard's films are, once more, the best examples; criticism like Michel Cournot's even derives the conditions of its existence from this fact. *But,* it was already the filmed object that had appealed to us in the great films of the past (*Nosferatu, Le Maudit, Nanook of the North*), and not its pretext in the scenario. *But,* all of Alain Resnais's films are initially "script-writer's films": The systematic way in which this director, refusing to imagine his works alone, seeks out, at the stage of the scenario, various collaborators of sufficient weight to have their own perception of things, leaves us in no doubt as to his opinions on the importance of the precinematographic level that the film stratifies and builds around. *But,* Antonioni's films derive their interest from a

---

* In the old cinema, there were of course nonrealistic, marvelous, and fantastic films. But they constituted a distinctly marginal area, at least since the 1935–40 period; and Alain Resnais is not their descendant. The ordered cinema is one of the two branches emerging out of a sort of common realistic trunk that, between 1940 and 1950 approximately, had become on the whole a dominant trend in relation to the various "fantastic" tendencies.

whole reflection on the problems of the couple and of solitude, a reflection implying experiences, conversations, and mental and emotional journeyings—that is to say, a whole body of essentially extracinematographic phenomena. *But,* the films of Godard himself bear witness to a narrative *inventiveness,* which is a sensitivity, a fantasy, an observation prior to being a cinema. This "prior" does not automatically imply chronological priority, but it certainly implies an essential hierarchy. It is quite probable that Godard is one of those men for whom inspiration can only be fired during the actual shooting, men who are able to make films through constant reflection (even if it is not ordered) about the cinema,[22] and who are able to create only in the borderland of a poetry that is also an essay on poetry (the reader surely recognizes here one of the most striking features of modern literature). But even if, for a director like Godard, the cinema, mentally present before existing, becomes the necessary catalyst for filmic creation—in the same way that the idea of the "book" is always present in the minds of modern writers, even when the book they are writing is hardly begun—the fact remains that what Godard presents us with, by means of the intercession (necessary for him) of the *consciousness of making a work of the cinema,* is ultimately a narrative that has managed to retain in its net a great amount of the afilmic world: love, politics, gangsterism, contemporary society, the sea, Paris, a lyrical appreciation of woman that is somehow compatible with the obscurely archetypal, Delilah-like shadow of her forever possible betrayal, etc. In a Godard film there is always a story.* How-

---

* "I do not see why the fact that one does not tell a story should be more modern than anything else," Eric Rohmer remarked very rightly in "L'Ancien et le nouveau" (previously quoted interview), p. 37. There are certain similarities between the *nouveau roman* [the French "new novel"] and the new cinema, but I am not sure whether this general resemblance is as profound as one is sometimes confusedly tempted to declare. At the very least one should point out that the new novel develops to a much greater extent phenomena as yet barely present in the cinema ("breakdown of the narrative," etc). Too often one forgets that between the novel and the cinema as such there exists a considerable difference of ages: The novel is almost an old man, and the cinema is a young man who has only just reached his majority. The problem is complicated, of course, by the fact that the "new novelists" and the "new cinema" directors are roughly of the same age and are influenced by the same

ever "broken up" and unfamiliar the story may be—instead of being caricaturally linear—this fact never changes; indeed, Godard is one of the most prolific of modern French scenario-writers (this remains true even when, as is often the case with Godard, the scenario is born in the midst of the shooting and is, in a way, only the consequence of the film). To exclude the dimension of the scenario from the modern cinema, or to belittle it, is like saying that the only scenarios are those that are like the scripts of Aurenche and Bost.

A CINEMA OF THE SHOT?   Is the modern cinema therefore a cinema of the "shot," as distinguished from the old cinema, which was more concerned with racing from shot to shot, straight to the sequence? But if that is the case, what is one to say about what Jean Mitry calls the expressionist tendency—German expressionism itself, the last films of Eisenstein, etc.—a tendency no one will deny is an old one, that nevertheless usually gave precedence to plastic connotations at the expense of rhythmic connotations—painting cinema and not music cinema—and that was grounded to a large extent on the hope of inducing a horizontal reading of the film that would consider each image at length? And what, on the other hand, is one to say about the *great renaissance of montage,* which, after a period dominated by the "sequence shot," is now re-emerging as one of the most striking characteristics of the new cinema? Is not the "message" in *Muriel*—that impression of a kind of vast existential failure—mainly suggested, as Bernard Pingaud[23] observes, communicated through the continual breaks of rapid montage? Is not *Salvatore Giuliano* a montage film from end to end? As for the youthful dynamism of Claude Lelouch's *Une Fille des fusils,* is it not derived as much as from the story of the film as from the wonderful exuberance of its montage? And what of the importance of stopped photographs—frozen images, confessions of montage—in *Jules and Jim,* and in many Godard films? And what about the interrupting titles—deliberate breaks in the nar-

---

currents of thought. The fact is, however, that, when someone says, as one occasionally hears, that the cinema is "far ahead of literature," one must conclude he must never have read anything at all.

rative flow, also confessions of montage—in *Cleo from 2 to 7* and in *Vivre sa vie*? And the counterpoint of Hiroshima and Nevers in *Hiroshima mon amour*, a counterpoint that, despite its modern accent, seems to emerge straight from the editing table of a Balàzs, an Arnheim, a Pudovkin, or a Timochenko? And all the film "collages," one sees . . .

A CINEMA OF POETRY? There remains, finally, the notion, recently suggested by Pier Paolo Pasolini, of a distinction between the "cinema of prose" and the "cinema of poetry." As attractive as it may seem, the idea is nevertheless basically fragile. For the concepts of "prose" and "poetry" are too linked to the use of the verbal language to be easily carried over to the cinema. Or else, if one takes "poetry" in its broadest sense—as the immediate presence of the world, the sense of things, the inner quickness beneath the surface of externality—one will have to recognize that the cinematographic enterprise, whether successful or not, is *always* initially poetic. But if one considers poetry in its technical sense—the use of verbal idiom according to some orderly procedure, with supplementary restrictions added to those of the language, a second code capping the first—one encounters a difficulty which hardly seems surmountable: The absence of a first unitary and complete code in the cinema, that is, the absence of a specifically cinematographic idiom. Pasolini is aware of this problem; indeed he outlines it with great precision.[24] But he believes that, all things considered, it can be circumvented. I believe, on the contrary, that this is impossible, and later I will show why.[25] Furthermore, to these obstacles one must add still another: The concept of "prose," in whatever sense it is given, has no plausible equivalent in the cinema; and if a prose does exist in the lexical domain, it is only in distinction to poetry and because a long rhetorical tradition has divided into two a domain that is *initially literary* (for prose, properly speaking, is literary prose, that of a Chateaubriand or of a Stendhal, and not that which Monsieur Jourdain discovered; prose is already the artistic use of language and is already distinct from utilitarian language; it creates objects that have their own value, and

at which the thrust of language ceases). As for the cinema, it is *never* used for daily communication; it always creates works. The distinction between poetry and prose has meaning only within a broader distinction, one that separates *literature* from the simple use of idiom as a tool. And it is this primary distinction that is lacking in the cinema, so that no film can pertain to prose in the strict sense, nor, strictly, to poetry.

So much for the linguistic implications of Pasolini's theory—at least for the time being, for I will return to them later; let us examine his thesis in the light of the history of the cinema. If there is any single trend running through all of this history, it is indeed the one that leads from the poem-cinema to the novel-cinema—that is to say, in a certain way from the "cinema of poetry" to the "cinema of prose," and not the other way around. Pasolini tends to confuse poetic *accents*—which are not rare in the modern cinema—with poetic *structures;* he tends also to compare the most beautiful contemporary films to the dullest traditional movies, and he does not consider the very early films. Obviously there is more poetry in *À Double tour, Lola, Shoot the Piano Player, The Knack, Pour la Suite du monde,* or *8½,* than in *Le Président, Un Grand patron, Volpone,* or *Dernier atout.* But is it not simply that the substance and form of each one of the first-mentioned films are more poetic and less radically vulgar than the form and substance of each of the older films; and is one quite sure that the language of the first differs fundamentally from that of the second group? Can one be sufficiently certain that the "free indirect subjectivity" of which Pasolini speaks represents a procedure *precise* enough for one to see in it the beginnings of a *technical language of poetry* for the cinema?[26] And is it not, in the final analysis, confused with that inevitable subjective coloration of the filmic object by its filming perception—which is a characteristic of all cinema—so that the only real difference would finally be that of poetic and prose perceptions, which can only be clarified by the analysis of each film and does not, in the cinema, necessarily coincide with the existence of general restrictions peculiar to any "poetry" distinguished from "prose"? Furthermore, if one extends the matter further back, is it not, among the films that seem the most outmoded today—but not always rightly—that one encounters the most coherent and systematic attempts to construct a film as one structures a poem? What about Pudovkin's "lyrical montage," which Jean Mitry has so well analyzed?[27] What about the coronation scene in *Ivan the Terrible,* or the procession before Vakulintchuk and the scenes of mist in *Potemkin?* What about Abel Gance in *Napoleon* and *La Roue?* And the attempts of the "pure cinema" to substitute a cinema of *themes* for the story-cinema? And Jean Epstein's enthusiastic analyses of the poetic value of the close-up shot? And the use of slow motion in the dormitory scene in *Zero for Conduct?* And all the systems of montage mentioned earlier, whose aim was to formalize the various filmic counterpoints, to solidify the thematic "depth" in the normative prescriptions of a formal syntagmatic system? And the accelerated filming in the scene with the black coach in *Nosferatu?* And the incredible aerial traveling shot in the beginning of Murnau's *Faustus?* They are all, indeed, instances of those "grammatical elements as poetic functions"[28] that Pasolini tends to identify with the new cinema. In truth, though today's cinema is at times rich in poetic resonances, though the bad films of every period by definition exclude the so-called poetry "of things" and the poetry of their organization, the fact remains that the only attempts that have been undertaken toward not only a poetic cinema but also a cinema as organized poetic *idiom*—since this is what Pasolini is talking about—were, precisely, in the old cinema.* And the fact is that, since its birth, the cinema has practically never ceased to evolve in the direction of an ideal (*technically* prosaic) flexibility and a freedom that are entirely

---

* To my mind these attempts have culminated in a failure which, on the level of general theory, cannot be overcome by the few magnificent but isolated successes. A film may be a *poetic novel,* it cannot be a poem (except in the case of purely thematic, non-story-telling short films, like Ruttmann's *Berlin* or Sucksdorff's *Rhythm of a City.* In a poem there is no fable, and nothing intrudes between the author and the reader. The novelist draws up a world; the poet speaks of the world. The fiction film still seems to me to be closer to the novel than to the poem. And, finally, the period in which one believed that a film could be a poem is that of the old cinema rather than that of the new cinema.

novelesque, as is shown, in different ways, by the analyses of François-Régis Bastide (the cinema as a modern sociological substitute for the traditional novel), André Bazin and the filmologist critics (the cinema pertains to the novel rather than to the theater), Jean Mitry (progressive victory of narrative montage over the "lyrical," "intellectual," and "constructive" types of montage), and Edgar Morin (withdrawal of the archetypal, naïve imagination peculiar to many of the first films to the advantage of a more sophisticated use of the powers of the fabulous within the framework of the relatively late "realistic" film's verisimilitude). More generally, one will observe that the so-called fantastic cinema, which in certain early periods came very close to merging with one of the mainstreams of the cinema as a whole (German-Swedish expressionism from 1910 to 1930, the fantastic films of the period 1930–35, such as *Frankenstein, The Invisible Man,* and *King Kong*), eventually became a *genre,* and a rather special genre at that, which even in part overlaps what the French call the *cinéma-bis:* horror films, grade-B Italian movies, sadistic Japanese films, Soviet fantasy films, British terror films, etc. As a corollary, the so-called realistic film, which has long been contrasted to the fantastic film or to the film of the marvelous as if they were the two great poles of the cinema (and this is simply the famous theme: "Lumière *vs Méliès*"), has taken over almost the whole of modern film.

Pasolini also defines the new cinema as the *noticeable presence of the camera;*[29] whereas, in traditional films, on the contrary, the camera tried to make its presence unfelt, to make itself invisible before the spectacle it was presenting. But, while it is true that this analysis may apply to certain films of the not-so-distant past—the classical American comedy, for example, and in general all the films related to what Bazin called "classical editing" (*"découpage classique"*), which was made to appear invisible—it cannot describe the various tendencies of the very early cinema whose aesthetics, on the contrary, were based on the aggressive presence of the camera: montage in Eisenstein, Pudovkin, or Abel Gance, camera movements in the expressionist or *Kammerspiel* films, the optical distortions and unusual angles in the films of the French "avant-garde," Dreyer's close-ups in *The Passion of Joan of Arc*—in a word, the aesthetics that theoreticians like Epstein, Eisenstein, Balàzs, Arnheim, or Spottiswoode had in mind when they insisted constantly on the specific enriching that the filmed object derives from the filming. And conversely, within the modern cinema there is a tendency one might call "objectivist"—Rohmer, some aspects of Antonioni, of De Seta, and of the *cinéma direct,* etc.—and that carefully "erases" any camera effects; thus, on this point I am in agreement with Eric Rohmer.[30]

III

Spectacle and nonspectacle, theater and nontheater, improvised and controlled cinema, dramatization and nondramatization, basic realism and contrivance, film-maker's cinema and script-writer's cinema, shot cinema and sequence cinema, prose cinema and poetic cinema, the camera-in-presence and the invisible camera: None of these distinctions seems to me to account for the specific character of the modern cinema. In each one of these conceptual pairs, the feature claimed as "modern" is too often found in the films of yesterday and too often is lacking in the films of today. Each one of these antitheses was proposed with implicit reference to certain films of the past and to certain modern films—and to that extent therefore remains partially true—but with no effort sufficient to account for the greatest possible number of historically known circumstances. Of course such an attempt is no simple one and is hardly likely to be fully satisfied in the few pages that follow. But it is not forbidden to try; one accepts in advance the inevitable incompleteness of the results . . .

I note, first, that if all of the conceptual pairs examined above are insufficient, they are so perhaps all for the same reason. They are so many partial expressions of a same underlying idea: That in the past the cinema was entirely narrative and no longer is so today, or is so at least to a much lesser extent. I believe on the contrary that the modern film is more narrative, and more satisfyingly so, and that the main contribution of the new cinema is to have enriched the filmic narrative.

More or less associated with this idea of a presumed "breakdown" or weakening of narrativity is, among many critics, the notion of a breakdown of the "grammar" or "syntax" of the cinema. I would say, on the contrary, that the cinema has *never* had either a grammar or a syntax in the precise linguistic sense of these terms (some theoreticians believed that it did, but that is another matter), rather, it has always obeyed, and today still obeys, a certain number of fundamental semiological laws that pertain to the most profound necessities of the transmission of any information—semiological laws that are extremely difficult to isolate, but whose models are to be sought in general linguistics, or general semiotics, and not in the grammar or normative rhetorics of specific languages. The whole muddle of the latter approach derives from the fact that one looks for "language" among the various highly derived and specific (and consequently very removed from cinematographic reality) idiomatic manifestations, without reflecting that the filmic laws are most probably located far beyond the place one usually expects to find them—that is to say, on a much deeper level, a level in some ways prior to the differentiation of verbal language (with all its idioms) from other human semiotic systems.

We are told that "cinematographic syntax" no longer exists, that it was suited to the silent film, but that the living film wants nothing to do with such a burden. But the *syntagmatic* articulations—rather than being actually syntactic articulations, for, as Ferdinand de Saussure observed, syntax is only one part of the syntagmatic category[31] —are like Monsieur Jourdain's prose. Every discourse must be governed by them, willingly or not, or else it becomes unintelligible. The occasionally excessive reactions of some of the devotees of the young cinema can be explained and excused by the corresponding excesses of a "syntax" that, during the period of *"ciné langue"*[32] and even later, was considered to be as strict as the grammar of a verbal language. But the new, more flexible, forms of the cinema are governed just as much by the great fundamental figures without which no information would be possible; a discourse of some length is always, in one way or another, divisible. The study of "cinematographic language" became a burden only when it tried to be normative. Today it no longer pretends to govern films; its aim is only to study them; it no longer pretends to precede them, but it admits to following them. Similarly, in the domain of verbal language, the most elaborate linguistic theory cannot influence the future evolution of our languages. And we know the extent of the gap between the linguist and the normative "grammarian," which was illustrated in 1963 by the exchange, published in *Arts,* between Etiemble and Martinet.* Even the most "advanced" films still pertain to a semiological approach, though in order to apprehend new objects, the latter may have to become more flexible, as I will show in several examples further on.

In short, two very different things are meant by "rules" of the cinema: On one hand, there is a corpus of prescriptions derived from a *normative aesthetics* that can reasonably be considered outdated or uselessly restrictive;** on the other hand, there are a certain number of structural configurations that are in actual fact laws and whose details are constantly evolving. When one says that the films of the "new wave," for example, have completely "dismantled the narrative," or that they have "entirely displaced syntax," one is really taking a very limited view of the problems involved; one is considering "narrative" and "syntax" in a very narrow way, and thus one is unwittingly giving credit to the devotees of the aesthetics one is fighting against (for it is the latter who restrict the meaning of "narrative" and "syntax" to the order of a purely ideological or commercial codification, with no relation to the codified structures peculiar to the filmic vehicle as a whole). It is precisely to the extent that they react

---

* Of the two, the linguist was André Martinet.
** Another source of misunderstanding: The new cinema has displaced—and very rightly so—a number of "rules," such as the prohibition against the 180-degree angle shot or the taboo against going from an establishing shot to a close-up with no change of axis, or against the actor looking at the camera, etc. But these rules have nothing to do with the semiotics of the cinema: They are miserable little "devices," the laughable orders of an underling, and as early as 1951 Jean Cocteau was lampooning them in his *Entretiens autour du cinématograph* [*Cocteau on the Film,* New York, 1954]. To push them aside—as they must be—is by no means to "push syntax aside."

against such prejudices that the innovations of the young cinema are interesting; but, in doing so, far from demonstrating the nonexistence of "syntax," they are really discovering new syntactic regions while remaining (at least as long as they are intelligible, as is the case almost always) entirely submissive to the functional requirements of filmic discourse. *Alphaville* and *Last Year at Marienbad* are still, from one end to the other, diegetic films, and they were still conceived in relation to the requirements of narrative fiction, despite their undoubted originality, their editing, and their montage. *Impossible constructions do exist in the cinema.* Thus, any progression of a hero along a precise itinerary excludes the descriptive syntagma; an autonomous shot cannot begin in Moscow and end in Paris (at least in the present state of cinematographic techniques); a nondiegetic image must in one way or another be linked to a diegetic image, or it will not appear to be nondiegetic, etc.[33] But such orderings have never been seriously tried by film-makers, unless perhaps—and even then one would have to examine the matter more closely—by some extreme avant-gardist who had deliberately abandoned the effort to make himself understood (and, then, usually in cinematographic "genres" initially foreign to the narrative fiction film). And the reason that the other film-makers never attempt to construct such combinations, or even to imagine that they might exist, is precisely because the main figures of cinematographic intelligibility inhabit their minds to a much greater extent than they are aware of. Similarly, the most original writer does not attempt to fashion an entirely new language.

IV

That is why we must now stop looking at the history of the cinema and take a more semiological and technical approach, and from this vantage point return to the critique of the Pasolinian theories, which, more than any other attempt at defining filmic modernity, try to define their subject precisely and go beyond the stage of general impressions.

THE "IM-SEGNI" OR ICONIC ANALOGY?   At first glance, our author says, there is nothing in the cinema corresponding to what *idiom* is for the writer. That is to say, there is no codified instance prior to the actual aesthetic undertaking. Fine. Nevertheless, Pasolini continues, one must assume that there is something in the cinema that, in one way or another, assumes the same role as language in literature, since the constant fact is that the cinema is not an "abortion," that it is able to communicate.[34] It is at this point, I believe, that the more questionable statements begin: An artistic semiotic system, such as the cinema, can function perfectly well without the assistance of an initial codified *language*. The cinema is in the same position as figurative painting in Claude Lévi-Strauss's analysis in *The Raw and the Cooked:* The first level of articulation is replaced by the "natural" —that is, the cultural signification that perception invests in the objects represented in the picture (or on the screen).

Literature requires language, because the *sound* produced by the vocal organs possesses no intrinsic meaning. Therefore it has to be *articulated* to acquire meaning, which is withheld from "inarticulate shouts," and the two articulations that constitute language—that of the phonemes and that of the monemes, in André Martinet's terminology—are nothing other than the inevitable creative instances of literal signification (i.e., denotated signification), lacking which the poet would have nothing on which to project the interplay of connotations. But the film-maker does not work with vocal sound initially deprived of meaning. His raw material is the image—that is to say, the photographic duplication of a real spectacle, which always and already has a meaning.* Consequently, this codified, or at least codifiable, language, which Pasolini postulates and which he defines as an indefinite, labile, but virtually organizable body of "im-segni"

---

* Except, of course, for dialogues. In respect to them, the film-maker is approximately in the same position as the writer (keeping in mind the difference between the oral and the written). As for "real noises," they raise essentially the same problems as do images, transposed to the auditive dimension. One must not confuse *sonorous* and *phonic:* A sound of the world has its own precise meaning (the locomotive's whistle, etc.); a phonic sound acquires precise meaning only by means of the linguistic articulations.

(image signs) existing prior to the cinema, is to my mind a dubious, burdensome artifact. Simple iconic analogy, photographic resemblance, replaces it quite advantageously. Indeed, film "communicates," but that is not a mystery whose elucidation justifies the introduction into theory of an additional instance openly presented by Pasolini as being hypothetical and adventurous[35]—it is, much more simply, because the dullest and least connoted photograph of an automobile will have "automobile" for its meaning and thus will yield to the film-maker a significate, which a verbal language could attain only by means of its two articulations (that of its phonemes (/o/, /t/, /m , /b/, etc.) and that of its monemes (distinguished within the language "automobile" from "train," "wagon," "airplane," etc.) The cinema arrives at the same results *with no code other than that of perception with its psychosociological and cultural conditionings,* in short with no *language-like* code.

These "im-segni," which, incidentally, Pasolini analyzes very skillfully, do, I am persuaded, exist, and they play the major role in our comprehension of the particular images of particular films—but not within the deepest mechanism of filmic intellection. How is one to understand films, Pasolini asks, without somehow possessing a knowledge of the symbolic values of these visual images: dream images, images of the memory, of emotional experience, images of daily life with their whole load of implicit extensions for each society and each period? Certainly, the total understanding of a given film would be impossible if we did not carry within us that obscure but quite real dictionary of "im-segni" Pasolini talks about; if, to take a single example, we did not know that Jean-Claude Brialy's car in *Les Cousins* was a sports car, with all that this implies in twentieth-century France, the diegetic period of the film. But all the same we would know, because we would *see* it, that it is a car, and that would be enough for us to grasp the *denoted* meaning of the passage. Let no one object that an Eskimo with no experience of industrial civilization might not even be able to recognize the car! For what the Eskimo would be lacking in would not be the ability to translate, but a specific acculturation; it would not be his language of "im-segni" that would be deficient but his *perception* as an aggregate of psycho-social integrations. A manufactured object—a car—as soon as it exists in the world, becomes an object of perception like all other objects of perception, and a child in our society has no more trouble identifying a truck than he does a cat.*

* As the reader can see, this passage devoted to the ideas of Pier Paolo Paso-lini—which was written early in 1966—is a mixture of approval and argument. The reasons for this double attitude, which has not in the meantime been modified, are clearer to me today, to the extent that my own concept of photo-graphic and phonographic *analogy,* and of its role in the semiotics of the cin-ema, has become subtler and more clearly defined (on this point see Chapter 5). Pasolini's "im-segni"—that is to say, the first organized and organizable body of significations that, in the cinema, precedes "cinematographic language" itself— these "im-segni" are therefore the elements of various codes we would now call "cultural"; Pasolini had in mind particularly, as this discussion shows, the *icon-ological* and *iconographic* connotations peculiar to each sociocultural group and lacking which the images themselves would have no meaning. I am not in disagreement with Pasolini as to the existence of such instances; simply, what I am criticizing is the peculiarly Pasolinian idea that these codifications *already* pertain to language, that they are somehow of the same nature as "cinemato-graphic language," whose first level they would constitute, so that the film-maker *as such* would always be constrained to handle (or partially to invent) two languages simultaneously: that of the "im-segni" and that of the cinema. Therefore, what seemed to me to be "doubtful" and a "burdensome artifact," and an "additional instance openly presented by Pasolini himself as being some-thing adventurous and hypothetical," is not the "im-segno" itself, but its un-justified elevation to the level of language (and, furthermore, of already cinemat-ographic language, with the consequence that the code of the "im-segni" would be to the film-maker as the code of language is to the writer. That is indeed why I insist on the *perceptual* and *cultural* status of these "im-segni," to distin-guish it from the language character of the properly cinematographic codes (which today I would classify as "specialized codes"; see above, pp. 112–13). Thus, when Pasolini uses the example of the image of the wheels of a train speeding amid a cloud of smoke and asserts that it is, in our period, a fixed and codified figure ("Le Cinéma de poesie," previously quoted, p. 56), I am per-sonally struck by the fact that the image belongs to the iconography and icon-ology of our society much more than to cinematographic language. And that is why I insist so much on the idea that, for a *properly cinematographic semiotics,* the first level of organization (i.e., the one that is to the film-maker as language is to the writer) is not made up of "im-segni" but of visual and auditory analo-gies: If the novel's reader is able to recognize a "dog" in the story it is thanks to the linguistic unit "dog," and if the film-viewer recognizes a dog within the film's story that is thanks to the image's visual analogy with a real dog. This does not prevent, for a more general semiotics, many of the phenomena that Pasolini designates as "im-segni" from being reintroduced *as analogies and within analogies* (see above, p. 113), for it is the peculiarity of certain codes (nonspecialized codes) to be invisible to the decipherer of the most literal

From the presumed existence of a primary language of "im-segni" (which is codifiable, but never really codified), Pasolini deduces the idea that the film-maker is obliged to invent a language *first* (i.e., the attempt to isolate clearly the "im-segni"), and then an art—whereas the writer, who already possesses the language, can allow himself to invent only on the aesthetic plane. It is in that *first* that all the misunderstanding lies. If it is true that *cinematic invention* is inevitably a mixture of artistic inspiration and language-like fashioning, the fact remains that the film-maker is always foremost an artist and that it is through his endeavors to order the things of reality differently,

---

visual and auditory information. In other words, when very broadly cultural codifications occur in films—as they do frequently, especially when one thinks of the contents of individual films—they are often present *in the image itself* (or in the sound itself)—that is to say, within the "analogy," or at a point that, in relationship to the total economy of the filmic significations, is distinct from that occupied by the codifications that constitute what one calls "cinematographic language." The image of the wheels of the train derives from society, not from the cinema; when it appears on the screen it is identified by visual analogy with the real wheels of a train, and it is thanks to this resemblance that the film is able to carry all the additional significations associated with this image in culture. But if the image is ordered along with other images in an alternate montage, as in Abel Gance's *La Roue, another kind* of codification emerges, one that is specifically cinematographic and is no longer broadly cultural, and is superimposed over the visual analogy and not merged with it. Similarly, one must point out that cultural codifications, when they occur in films, often appear on the level of the actual filmed "objects," whereas cinematographic codifications mainly affect the disposition of the *objects once they are filmed:* That is why I stated earlier (Chapter 5) that the specifically cinematographic paradigms have as their frames of reference the "large segments" of the film.

There remains, of course, a problem, and that is that cinematographic language itself, in as much as it is a body of orderings, must certainly be influenced by various sociocultural codifications: Just as the "filmed object" retains the meaning it had outside of the film, the types of filmic ordering must in one way or another refer to given patterns of intelligibility within society. Thus, parallel montage is a peculiarly cinematographic figure, but it is inconceivable that it could legitimately exist in the cinema in a society that had no *prior* notation (in its language, its writings, its "logic," etc.) of the symbolic and intelligible value of certain very general *types of relationship* such as alternation, parallelism, antithesis, etc. However, what is peculiar to the cinema is the over-all system that governs the various orderings in relation to each other—that is to say, the relationship of the relations or the paradigm of the syntagmas. On the level of the filmed objects, on the contrary, there is no governing system specific to cinematographic language (there are *several* over-all systems of these "objects," peculiar to different individual films, but that is another matter).

through his aesthetic intentions and his strivings for connotation, that he is occasionally able to bequeath some eventually conventional form liable to become a "fact of language." If filmic denotation today is rich and diverse, as indeed it is, that is only as a result of the strivings for connotation in the past.*

THE RENEWAL OF "CINEMATOGRAPHIC SYNTAX":   We know that image structures, such as the parallel syntagma, the alternate syntagma, the bracket syntagma, inserts, episodic sequences, etc., which I have analyzed elsewhere—and still other image structures, such as the *flashback* (i.e., succession as the signifier for precession) for example, or the *flash forward* (immediate succession as the signifier for distant succession), etc.—are among those figures of connotation that have, in time, also become intelligible patterns of denotation. Now, what is important to note is that most of these semiological figures have not fallen out of use at all but are, on the contrary, in current use in the modern cinema. Not, of course, that the stock of figures has remained unchanged from Griffith to our times. In the cinema, too, there is a diachrony. It would be easier to pick out procedures that have aged: the nondiegetic metaphor (except as renewed by Godard, as we will see in an example further on), slow-motion, accelerated motion, the use of the iris diaphragm (except for nostalgic and humorous "quotation": *Shoot the Piano Player*), the excessive reliance on "punctuation" (except in the instance of a deliberate renewal of this technique: the first sequence in *Une Femme mariée*), the use of shot/reverse-shot in its mechanical form imitated from ping-pong** (but the scene in the Paris apartment with the white walls, in *Pierrot*

---

* I will not further develop this point, at least not here, for it has been sufficiently outlined in another part of this book (Chapter 5, part 4). Also, I will not analyze any of the figures of connotation that have become intelligible figures of denotation, since that forms the subject of the passage on the large syntagmatic category of the image track (Chapter 5, part 5). I have therefore deleted—hence this note at this place—about two pages of the original version of this text in the form of a separate article, which began after the words " . . . the strivings for connotation in the past." The passage was devoted to the above questions.

** The comparison is Jean Mitry's.

le fou, with Anna Karina's love song, is handled in a more flexible form of shot/reverse-shot), etc. Despite these normal evolutions, one should think twice before asserting that cinematographic syntax has been "completely thrown overboard." The license of poetic inspiration must not be confused with some impossible license on the level of the deeper articulations, which, even if they are partially arbitrary and are furthermore in a constant state of evolution, nevertheless guarantee, within given synchronic conditions, the correct transmission of information. Only the isolated and unexpressed thought—if such a thing exists—can (perhaps) be removed from such a law. From the moment that *saying* occurs (i.e., the desire to communicate, concern for the public, etc.), a certain number of semiological restrictions appear, which characterize the expression of thought rather than thought itself, that is, if the two things are not identical. Thus, as linguists have observed, the sentence is *first* of all a unit of speech, not of thought, reality, or perception.

Rather than some cataclysmic "breakdown" of filmic syntax, we are witnessing with the new cinema a vast and complex trend of renewal and enrichment, which is expressed by three parallel developments: (1) Certain figures* are for the time being more or less abandoned (example: slow motion or accelerated motion filming); (2) others are maintained, but as more flexible variations, which must not prevent one from recognizing the permanence of a deeper semiological mechanism (examples: the shot/reverse-shot, the scene, the sequence, alternate montage, etc.); (3) finally, new figures evolve, increasing the cinema's possibilities of expression. Let us consider the last point.

So far, I have identified, from the origins of the cinema to the present, only a limited number (eight) of large *basic* syntagmatic types. Now, there is a passage in Godard's *Pierrot le fou* that cannot be reduced to any of these models, or to any variation of these mod-

* I am not using the word *figure* in the sense of a "figure of style" (or of speech)—that is to say, as a means of connotation—but in a much broader sense: as any characteristic and recognizable syntagmatic configuration. This use of the word is justified by the confusion, peculiar to the cinema, between connotative and denotative patterns.

els. It is the moment when the two protagonists hurriedly leave the white-walled Paris apartment by sliding down a drain pipe, and flee in a red 404 Peugeot along the banks of the Seine. This "sequence," which is in fact not a sequence, freely alternates shots taken from the sidewalk in front of the building (the last few feet of the descent along the drainpipe, the race into the 404 parked in front of the building, the car taking off, and the brief appearance of the dwarf with his transistor radio, etc.) with other images that, from the diegetic point of view, occur several minutes later in another location, since we now see the 404 driving rapidly along the banks of the river. The passage thus yields several unusual repetitions: From the banks of the river we go back to the drainpipe; the entrance of the car at the foot of the building is itself shown two or three times with slight variations in the position and in the movements of the characters (variations that remind us rather of a construction dear to Robbe-Grillet: *Le Voyeur, La Maison de rendez-vous*).

Therefore, in this syntagma, time does not function according to a vectorial scheme—a scheme that corresponds to the simplest and most common narrative procedure; it cannot be a linear narrative syntagma (i.e., scene, ordinary sequence, or episodic sequence). Nor is it an alternate syntagma, for the alternating images do not refer to simultaneous events but to clearly succeeding events (the shots of the roadway along the river obviously come later); nor does the alternating of the images indicate an alternating of events (i.e., "alternative" variation of the alternate syntagma), since the protagonists have not made several trips back and forth between the building and the river bank; still less does it correspond to a counterpoint of pure connotation, with a momentary absence of the significate of temporal denotation (i.e., parallel syntagma), for the events shown follow a precise chronological order, and only one order, on the level of the significate (diegesis): first entering the car and second driving along the river. And the passage is not a descriptive syntagma either, since it presents us with the evidence of temporal consecution, and not just that of spatial coexistence. Any "frequentative" modality is likewise excluded, since the passage in no way indicates a customary or repeti-

tive action, but quite clearly a single succession of unique occurrences. Nor is it an example of the bracket syntagma, for in this
instance the film obviously shows a singular event in its own terms
and not in terms of some other event (that is, there is not the slightest
attempt at categorization). Last, it is not an autonomous shot, since it
contains several images corresponding to a single unit of the diegesis.
It is in fact a kind of dislocated sequence, highly expressive of the
mad rush, the fever, and the randomness of existence (clearly identifiable significates of denotation). In the midst of the frenzy of the
hasty departure (significate of the denotation), it presents as equal
possibilities—which implies a sort of self-confession of narrativity, an
awareness of its own fablic nature—several *slightly* different variations of a frantic escape, sufficiently similar to each other nevertheless
for the event that really did occur (and which we will never know)
to take its place among a class of quite clearly outlined occurrences.
One is reminded of certain of Marcel Proust's observations, for, faced
with the different circumstances of life, Proust had an acute and accurate sense of other psychologically possible or likely occurrences but
claimed he was incapable of predicting in advance which one would
actually be realized. (We might remark that this Proustian distinction corresponds fairly well to a typology that anyone can observe in
his own experience: There are indeed, from this point of view, two
types of mind or two forms of intelligence, and the one able to pre-
dict the possible outcome to "emerge" often lacks penetration and
psychological acuteness in the imaginative description of the different
variants that, in the given context, are just as probable as the possibility that is realized.) In the passage we are considering, Jean-Luc
Godard would seem to belong to the second type, since he is able to
suggest with a great deal of truth, but without determining the outcome, several possibilities at the same time. So he gives us a sort of
potential sequence—an undetermined sequence—that represents a
new type of syntagma, a novel form of the "logic of montage," *but
that remains entirely a figure of narrativity* (i.e., two protagonists,
different events, places, times, one diegesis, etc.—in the same way
that in the same film the shots of the Renoir paintings constitute a

revitalization of the old nondiegetic metaphor, considerably aged, by the way, since the days of Eisenstein and the symbolically moving statues of *October.*

There would be many other examples to examine: The still photograph, which had been little used up to now and to which Rudolf Arnheim gave only a very modest place in his montage chart* is now, with the modern cinema, experiencing its first real flowering: the examples of Jeanne Moreau's face in *Jules and Jim,* the sequence "I bet you can't do everything I can do" in *A Woman is a Woman,* and, finally *La Jetée* or *Salut les Cubains* (entirely composed of still photographs). The use of the off-screen voice in various modern films is especially rich: Occasionally it is the voice of an anonymous commentator—much less the incarnation of the author than of narrativity itself, as Albert Laffay observed in another context[36]—occasionally it is that of the film's protagonist addressing himself directly to the audience—a new form of aside: Belmondo's voice in *Pierrot le fou,* the first sequence in *Marienbad.* To these two examples one must add the on-screen voice in dialogued scenes and the frequent use of written titles (in Godard, Agnès Varda, and others), and also the on-screen voice itself when it assumes the recitative mode and acquires a sovereign density that pulls it away from the image and transforms it from within into a kind of off-screen voice, thus to some extent subtracting it from the diegesis (*Hiroshima mon amour, La Pointe courte,* etc.). Thus the film is able to play on five levels of speaking: five possible ranges, five "personae." One could write a whole study of the voice in a Godard or Resnais film on the problem of "Who is speaking?" And one could write another study on the revitalization of what used to be called "subjective images" in Fellini (*8½, Juliet of the Spirits*), Resnais (*Marienbad*) or Robbe-Grillet (*L'Immortelle*).

"SYNTAX" IS NOT STEREOTYPE: Thus "syntax," still as poorly named as ever, is nevertheless alive and well. But many misunderstandings derive from the fact that "syntax" is often confused with *stereotype* (or cliché). An original film is commonly presumed to

* *Film as Art,* Berkeley, 1957, p. 131.

"turn cinematographic grammar upside down"; conversely, cinematographic grammar is credited only with mediocre films. That is to confuse the language process with the aesthetic (or stylistic) process. Between art and language there are complex semiological relationships;
art is not actually language; it always exists in one way or another *beyond* language, or *beside* it, and that is why dolts are not the only
ones to respect grammar. We know to what account Flaubert turned
the imperfect tense; this "account" of course was not already inscribed
in the French language, but the imperfect was (and still is), and linguistically Flaubert's imperfect is in no way different from the imperfect of a lock-picker (which is the one syntacticians analyze): It is a
codified morphosyntactic unit. Similarly, the use of shot/reverse-shot,
however novel and interesting some of its recent appearances may be,
nevertheless still represents a banal figure since it always induces us
to reconstruct the unity of a diegetic space despite (and thanks to)
the bipartition of the screen space.

Let us return to Pasolini. He believes that "cinematographic grammar" has not been able to form a real grammar, but rather a "stylistic
grammar," that is to say a hybrid system between art and language:
It is never, he says,[37] anything more than a dictionary of conventions,
conventions that have the "peculiarity of being stylistic rather than
grammatical." This analysis, which despite its great ingenuity I cannot accept, calls for two remarks: (1) It shows that Pasolini himself
must not *really* believe in the hypothesis of an underlying and already codified cinematographic stratum of "im-segni" prior to the
film-maker's artistic endeavor, since he now states that the first filmic
codification is stylistic, thus overlapping on my own view that it is the
striving for connotation that in the cinema has ultimately produced
the enrichment and codifying of denotation; and (2) on the other
hand, the misunderstanding surfaces again when Pasolini gives us an
example of the "stylistic conventions." He cites the common, conventionalized image of the wheels of a train spinning at full speed within
a cloud of smoke.[38] This is not, he says, a grammatical fact; it is obviously a "styleme." I don't argue with this. But such an image has
nothing to do with "cinematographic syntax." For the latter implies

a certain number of *filmic constructions* and not just a certain number of *filmed objects*. The image of the wheels of the train refers neither to some "by-passing of syntax," nor, on the other hand, to some fixed, conventionalized syntactic expression; it constitutes a fact that is foreign to syntax, a specific visual element—having its own "form" and its own "content"—liable to being filmed.

Any properly filmic syntagmatic fact implies the conjunction of at least two visual elements, occurring in two images (montage) or in the same image (camera movement or, even, static implication). To say that the image of the wheels of the train is a fact *of style* is correct but insufficient; it is a cliché, a stereotype. And it can be so only because it is a singular fact. Grammar has never dictated the content of thought that each sentence should have; it merely regulates the general organization of the sentences. *A grammatical fact can be neither a cliché nor a novelty,* unless it is so at the moment of its first historical occurrence; it exists beyond the level where the antithesis cliché/novelty even begins to have a meaning—that is to say, it remains confined to the stage of the initial idiom and not to that of the secondary language of art. The present of the indicative, as used by Robbe-Grillet, is still a vulgar present of the indicative, entirely "banal," and yet no one accuses it of being a cliché. And no one accuses Malherbe of triteness for using the objective predicate, or Victor Hugo for using the relative clause, or Baudelaire for the conjunction of two adjectives. The image of the wheels of the train is in no way the filmic equivalent to these examples; rather it would correspond to Malherbe's metaphorical comparison of a young girl to a rose, which is a *singular* construction (formal and semantic) and must accordingly be judged according to the categories of originality and triteness. As long as one considers such examples, one will have the elements not of a "stylistic grammar" of the cinema, but of a *pure rhetoric* that has nothing grammatical, and not very much cinematographic, about it, for the image of the wheels of the train (and similar images) most commonly represent *cultural stereotypes,* which if they are picked up—or even partially varied—by the cinema are picked up and varied by other forms of expression as well. There is a grammar of the cinema (or, to be exact, there is a large syntagmatic category of the fiction film); but its location lies elsewhere: In the scene, in the sequence, in the different syntagmas, in the other "types" I have mentioned only too briefly, in the structured, signifying, and stabilized syntagmatic orderings, which are never clichés, and were novelties only once, but which make up the scattered and disconnected elements of a code of filmic intelligibility ("analogy" and dialogue constituting the rest), the stammering equivalent of a real syntax, and not of a list of singular contents or forms.

Cinematographic grammar does not consist in prescribing what should be filmed. Alternate montage, for example, simply determines that the alternating of images will signify the simultaneity of the corresponding referents, but it says nothing about what is to enter those images. The distinction between a mechanical and stereotyped "grammar" and a free, agrammatical originality—a distinction that seems to underlie so many discussions of the modern cinema—is profoundly questionable. For a grammar, since by definition it is composed *only* of stereotypes, cannot be stereotyped, and a certain free creative originality is necessarily "grammatical" in one respect or another from the moment its message becomes intelligible.*

* I want to avoid a confusion that crops up frequently in this type of discussion. The analysis developed in this section is not in any way intended to distinguish between "form" in films (which would be a general category, beyond the subdivisions of the original and the banal), and "content" (which would always be singular, therefore, depending on the case, original or banal). The distinction between "form" and "content" must be absolutely rejected, I believe; the only solution that seems satisfactory to me is the one advanced by the linguist Louis Hjelmslev, which places the *facts of the significate* (content) to one side, and the *facts of the signifier* (which is erroneously considered to be the constituent of "form" and which, in Hjelmslevian terminology, constitutes "expression") to the other side, with each member possessing its own form and substance. (For the possible application of these concepts to cinematographic analysis, see Chapter 8 of this volume.) The purpose of this discussion was to distinguish between constructions *specific to cinematographic language in general* and constructions that occur in particular films. Both have their signifier and their significate (which is to say, in ordinary language, their "form" and their "content"), and these signifiers and significates each have their own form and their own substance (form, in this case, is taken in the sense that seems to me to be the correct one). In other words, I want to insist on the presence of a specific level of "figures" that by definition, relate to the filmic vehicle itself—and these are the figures that actually define "cinematographic

Recently, certain linguists have turned their attention to the problem of "purely semantic" anomalies (sentences that appear to be grammatically correct, but whose message doesn't "come through"). Example: "The Batavian brassiere woke up suddenly with a too apparently postprandial rictus." But, in cases like this, it is once more from the misunderstanding of certain structural requirements of dis-

---

language"—and to distinguish it from another semiological level, which is, incidentally, *doubly* contrasted to the first in that it is both *less general* (since it concerns particular films) and *more general* (since it incorporates systems that are very broadly cultural and that extend beyond the cinema itself). On this second level one can speak of the "originality" or "triteness" of individual films (or film passages, or film "auteurs," etc.) according to whether the cultural systems have been integrated as they are into the film (i.e., stereotypes), or whether on the contrary the film-maker has rejected them, displaced them, "faked" them, revitalized them, etc.

Nevertheless it is true that "cinematographic language" itself is liable to be judged in terms of originality or banality. This derives from certain of its characteristics I have already mentioned: It does not really constitute a language system; it is not a pure "grammar," but an indiscernible mixture of grammar and rhetoric; it is more readily influenced by the individual creations of film-makers than written verbal languages are by the individual creations of writers. A true verbal language—German or French—is never in itself original or banal (or, if it is, it is so in a completely different way and one that is foreign to this analysis: as when one compares one verbal language to other verbal languages). In the domain of the cinema, on the contrary, it is much easier to find words that can be characterized as being more or less original *on the level of the language itself* and not only on the level of their style (example: the "potential sequence" in Jean-Luc Godard's film analyzed earlier). If one uses Roland Barthes's triple distinction between *langue, écriture,* and *style* (language system, "writing," and style) in *Le Degré zéro de l'écriture* (*Writing Degree Zero*), one will notice that "cinematographic language" resembles "writing" most in that it represents a distinct instance of individual styles, but that it is, however, not confused with a language system (nevertheless there remains a difference between the cinema and the domain of the verbal: In the latter, "writing" is distinct from language, which exists; in the cinema, it is distinct from what might be called a language, if that language existed. It is precisely the peculiarity of the cinema that what serves it as a language is, in fact, a "writing,"—that is to say, something that is not a style, but is less radically distinct from a style than a language is.

Despite this reservation, one must still be cautious, when speaking of "originality" or "banality" in the cinema, not to handle these concepts *in the same way*, or on the same level, according to whether one is considering individual films, or more or less original aspects of the general language of films. Thus, a film that would borrow only what was most banal from cinematographic language could nevertheless be an original work, whereas a film in which all the particular constructions would be banal would necessarily be a banal work.

course that the unintelligibility of the message derives. It is not, to be sure, a matter of the *grammatical structure* itself (at least in the usual meaning of the term), but of the *semantic structures* (that is to say, again grammatical, in some way) of the French language [or in the case of this translation, of the English language—TRANSLATOR] (A. J. Greimas)—or then, depending on the linguistic school, it is a question of certain actually grammatical "subrules" (Jean Dubois) that are sufficiently fine to be generally omitted from "official" grammars, but the ignorance of which results in sentences possessing *various degrees of agrammaticism* (Noam Chomsky). Thus the verb "to wake up" is semantically compatible within the same minimum statement only with an animate subject or one metaphorically assimilated to an animate subject ("The dog wakes up," "Hope was awakened"); it could not have for subject the term for a nonpersonified item of clothing (brassiere in my example). The adjective *postprandial* is used only with substantives belonging to the category of coenesthesis (sensations of *fullness, heaviness, acidity, sleepiness,* etc.) and consequently excludes (except in a specially indicative context) a substantive like *rictus.* Etc. Now, remember that "cinematographic grammar" is not a "real grammar" in the usual sense of the word, but simply a body of partially codified semantic implications (or fine grammatical rules).

One of the most striking characteristics of modern films is that they are in most cases highly understandable: In this respect they differ from various experimental films, with their avalanche of gratuitous and anarchic images against a background of heterogeneous percussions, capped by some overblown avant-gardist text. On the contrary, the "emancipated" stories that the best modern films are occasionally able to tell us find, in order to make themselves understood, very direct paths, and they mobilize a sufficient number of true accents, of memories peculiar yet common to everyone (and become so many analogical systems in the intellection of the film) for even the slightly experienced spectator to understand them more rapidly than he would understand the conventional narratives of commercial production, whose advertised—and very real—conformism does not exclude (but on the contrary multiplies) various clumsily announced and yet improbable contortions of the scenario, contortions that are never immediately apparent to the mind because they differ too much from the "figures" of common existence.

To contrast grammar and originality is, therefore, to contaminate two different problems. On the one hand there are, in the cinema, "texts" that are original and others that are less so. On the other hand there is "cinematographic grammar," with the ambiguous status of its connotation that has become a means of denotation, a discovery that has become a vehicle—a status that is precisely responsible for the confusion I have been trying to clarify.

For it is indeed true that filmic denotation—that is to say, the communication of the literal meaning of the story—*could* always be guaranteed outside of any codification thanks to perceptual analogy alone (or, again, by dialogue—a code, but not a cinematographic one). One can imagine an hour-and-a-half-long film composed of a single shot whose angle would be constantly horizontal and frontal, with no camera movement at all, and no optical effect (dissolve, etc.), with no temporal ellipsis, no lighting other than one that would be uniformly flat, and no voices besides those that would be strictly diegetic (on-screen voices), etc. But such a film would hardly resemble the cinema —it would be more like a play (and an exceptionally linear one at that) recorded by the camera. Even films like Hitchcock's *Rope* or Jean Rouch's *Gare du Nord* would seem like truculent semiological orgies next to this imaginary film. But the point is that such a film is possible, whereas nothing similar is imaginable, *mutatis mutandis*, in a book. The fact is that even the most "colorless" prose, a zero-degree of "writing"—if such a thing exists—would still retain the code of its language (whose function in the cinema is guaranteed by perceptual analogy that allows one if necessary to economize on any language-like codification). However, semiological description must address itself to the real cinema, not to an imaginary cinema. Now, *from the moment that the cinema encountered narrativity*—an encounter whose consequences are, if not infinite, at least not finished—it appears that it has superimposed over the analogical message a second complex of codified constructions, something "beyond" the image, something that has only gradually been mastered (thanks to Griffith, mainly), and that, though it was originally intended to render the story more living (to avoid a monotonous, continuous iconic flow, in short, to connote), has nevertheless ended by multiplying the modes of denotation, and thus *articulating* the most literal message of the films we know.

V

Examples of the great "syntactic" flexibility and richness of the modern cinema should be gathered, and more extensively analyzed; one should show with greater detail than I have done that all these new conquests are made in relation to the diegesis, and that the new cinema, far from having abandoned the narrative, gives us narratives that are more diversified, more ramified, and more complex. I do not have the space here to bring this analysis, which I have only just begun, to its proper conclusion. My intention was simply to emphasize how strange it is to hear people speak, and not without insisting sometimes, about the "breakdown of the narrative" at a time when a new generation of cinematographic narrators has come to the fore, when we have been able to see films like *Il Grido, L'Avventura, 8½, Hiroshima mon amour, Muriel, Jules and Jim*; at a time when it appears that the author of *Breathless* and *Pierrot le fou** is only beginning his career, and though this film-maker does not appeal to everyone, he has managed nevertheless to impose himself on the general attention, and it seems difficult not to recognize in him a richness of invention and a power to develop and change, in which it is astonishing that not everyone can see—under the pretext that its forms have been renewed—the specific temper that characterizes the great tellers of tales.

* The films mentioned in this text have been chosen among those that had already been produced and distributed in the beginning of 1966, when this article was written.

9 Mirror Construction in Fellini's *8 ½*

Like those paintings that show a second painting within, or those novels written about a novel, *8½* with its "film within the film" belongs to the category of works of art that are divided and doubled, thus reflecting on themselves. To define the structure peculiar to this type of work the term *"construction en abŷme"* (literally, "inescutcheon construction"), borrowed from the language of heraldic science,* has been proposed,[1] and indeed it lends itself quite well to that structure permitting all the effects of a mirror. [At the risk of losing some of the accuracy of the original term, the translator has preferred to substitute the term "mirror construction," which is less unfamiliar, certainly less awkward-sounding, and therefore perhaps more suggestive than "inescutcheon construction." The image is that of a double mirror, reflecting itself.]

In a very interesting study devoted to Fellini's film, Alain Virmaux[2] has shown that, although mirror construction in the cinematographic domain is not an invention of Fellini's, since it is found already in various earlier films—*La Fête à Henriette*, by Jeanson and Duvivier, René Clair's *Le Silence est d'or*, Bergman's *The Devil's*

---

* In heraldry the term "inescutcheon" refers to a smaller shield placed at the center of a larger shield, and reproducing it in every detail, but on a smaller scale.—TRANSLATOR.

*Wanton**—the author of *8½* is nevertheless the first to construct his *whole* film, and to order *all* his elements, according to the repeating mirror image. In fact the precursors of *8½* only partially deserve to be called "mirror-construction" works, because in them the "film within the film" was only a marginal or picturesque device (*Le Silence est d'or*), at times a simple "trick" of the script-writer's (*La Fête à Henriette*), at best a fragmentary construction (*The Devil's Wanton*) lending perspective to only part of the film's substance, the rest being presented directly, and not through reflection. Moreover, Alain Virmaux,[3] Raymond Bellour,[4] Christian Jacotey,[5] and Pierre Kast[6] have all emphasized the fact that the content of the entire film, and its deepest thematic structure, are inseparable from its reflecting construction: The character of the director, Guido, Fellini's representative in the film, resembles his creator like a twin, with his narcissistic complacency, his immense sincerity, his disorderly existence, his inability to make a choice, his persistent hope in some kind of "salvation" that will suddenly resolve all his problems, his erotic and religious obsessions, his open desire to "put everything" into the film (just as Fellini puts all of himself into his films, and especially into *8½*, which is like a pause in his career, a general viewing of the past, an aesthetic and effective summing up).** As Pierre Kast observes, the criticisms one might address to the style of the film, or to the style of Fellini's work in general (that it is confused, disparate, complacent, has no real conclusion) are already present in the film, whether they are expressed by Guido himself or by his scenario-writer, Daumier, his inseparable companion, a companion Guido curses but whom he needs as he needs his bad conscience; thus, again it is the mirror construction alone that has allowed Fellini to integrate into his film a whole series of ambiguous reflections on whatever his own film might be accused of.

---

 * One might add Roger Leenhardt's *Le Rendez-vous de minuit*, in which the "film within the film" already played a more central and complex role.
 ** As Alain Virmaux observes, the title *8½* designates the film less in terms of its own characteristics than in terms of a sort of retrospective reference to all of Fellini's previous work. [Since it was, literally, his eighth-and-a-half film. —TRANSLATOR.]

There is however a point that, I believe, has never been emphasized as much as it deserves to be: For, if 8½ differs from other films
that are doubled in on themselves, it is not only because this "doubling in" is more systematic or more central, but also and above all
because it functions differently. For 8½, one should be careful to realize, is a film that is *doubly doubled*—and, when one speaks of it as
having a mirror construction, it is really a double mirror construction
one should be talking about.* It is not only a film about the cinema,
it is a film about a film that is presumably itself about the cinema; it
is not only a film about a director, but a film about a director who is
reflecting himself onto his film. It is one thing in a film to show us a
second film whose subject has no relationship, or very little relationship, to the subject of the first film (*Le Silence est d'or*); it is entirely another matter to tell us in a film about *that very film* being
made. It is one thing to present us with a character who is a director
and who recalls only slightly, and only in some parts of the film, the
maker of the real film (*The Devil's Wanton*); it is another matter for
the director to make his hero into a director who is thinking of making
a very similar film. And, if it is true that the autobiographical and
"Fellinian" richness of 8½ is inseparable from its mirror construction,
it is nevertheless only explained in its opulent, baroque entirety by
the self-reflecting of that construction.

Guido's problems, it has been said, are those of Fellini reflecting on
his art: Was it enough, then, for Guido to be a film-maker, like Fellini? The similarity would have remained very general. But Guido is

---

* One might also say—it is essentially a question of vocabulary—that the expression "mirror construction" refers *only* to those works defined here as
"doubly self-reflecting," and not to the majority of cases where a film appears
within a film or a book within a book or a play within a play. A shield is not
said to be "inescutcheon" everytime it contains some other shield, but only
when the other shield is, except in size, identical to the first. [Metz is, of course,
referring to the heraldic term "construction en abŷme," which I have changed
to "mirror construction." A double mirror reflects itself into infinity—and this
captures something of the suggestiveness of "en abîme," "abîme" meaning
"abyss" or "chasm"—each reflection being identical to, though one degree
smaller, than what it reflects.—TRANSLATOR.] If one agrees to this acceptation,
one will have to say the *Le Silence est d'or* contains nothing resembling mirror
construction, and that in *The Devil's Wanton* or in *Le Rendez-vous de minuit*,
mirror construction remains partial and fragmentary.

a director reflecting on his art, and by a curious irony these two successive reflections end by canceling each other out to a certain extent,
so that 8½ is finally a film of perfect coincidence; extremely complex,
its structure nonetheless attains a lucid simplicity, an immediate legi-
bility. It is because Guido is thinking of his film, and reflecting on
himself, that he merges—at least temporarily*—with Fellini; it is because the film that Guido wanted to make would have been a study
of himself, a film-maker's summing up, that it becomes confused with
the film that Fellini has made.** The ordinary interplay of reflection
would never have yielded such a wealth of echoes and relationships
between Fellini and his character had it not been reflected by the reflecting of that character himself; film-maker and reflecting film-
maker, Guido is doubly close to the man who brought him to life,
doubly his creator's double.

It is even in the concrete details of its handling that the device of
"the film within a film" diverges here from its more common use. For
we never see the film that Guido is to make; we do not even see extracts from it, and thus any distance between the film Guido dreamt
of making and the film Fellini made is abolished: Fellini's film is
composed of all that Guido would have liked to have put into his
film—and that is precisely why Guido's film is never shown separately. The reader can judge for himself the extent of the difference between this structure and the structure in *Le Rendez-vous de
minuit,* for example, where large extracts of the "film within the
film" are explicitly shown at several specific points in the first film,
which suffices to create a distance between the two films. In 8½ we
do not *even* see Guido shooting his film or working on it—and here it

* Taken as a whole, the relationships between Guido and Fellini are obviously more complex; among other things, Guido's character is not entirely
identical to Fellini's. However, I am not concerned with psychology here, but
simply with identity (in the sense that one speaks of identity cards). *For the
duration of the film,* Guido fully represents the person of Fellini.

** Must I point out that I am speaking here of the film Guido dreamed of
making, not the film that outside pressures (his producer, etc.) might perhaps
have imposed on him had he finally decided to start filming? For Fellini's film,
although it tells us only very little about the exact state of his working plans,
or the intentions of his producers, is on the other hand extremely precise about
Guido's deepest wishes concerning his film.

differs from *The Devil's Wanton,* for example; we see him, simply, in the period when the film is being prepared, living or dreaming, accumulating in the very stream of his own chaotic existence all the material that, without ever succeeding, he would like to place in his film and that Fellini is able to put into *his* film. It is, therefore, because the "film within the film" never appears separately within the first film that it can coincide with it so completely.

All that we see of this film Guido is dreaming about are the screen tests of the actresses; but it is here that the *tripling* of the film most clearly manifests itself. Guido has an actress to play the role of his wife in the film; the latter is played, in *8½,* by Anouk Aimée; and she in turn can only be an incarnation—very much interpreted, it goes without saying—of the problems Fellini encounters in his own life.*
It is during the sequence of the screen tests that a character in *8½,* watching the private screening and thinking of Guido, whispers, "Why, that's his own life," making a reflection that one can only reflect on by applying it to Fellini himself.

It is therefore not enough to speak of a "film within the film": *8½* is the film of *8½* being made; the *"film in the film" is, in this case, the film itself.* And of all the literary or cinematographic antecedents that have been mentioned in connection with Fellini's work, by far the most convincing—as critics have often pointed out,[7] but perhaps without ever entirely explaining why—is André Gide's *Paludes,* since it is about a novelist writing *Paludes.***

* If one reflects that the actress in the screen test was herself played, in Fellini's film, by another actress—and that, at the other end of the chain, Fellini's wife (Giulietta Masina) is also an actress—one will become positively dizzy. More seriously, one can observe that, following *8½,* Fellini shot *Juliet of the Spirits,* which is, as we know, a sort of feminine version of the preceding film; the woman's role is played by Giulietta Masina. This confirms the tripling process that appears in the screen-test sequence in *8½.*
** One thinks of course also of *Les Caves du Vatican* and *Les Faux-monnayeurs.* Alain Virmaux, Raymond Bellour, Pierre Kast, and Max Milner (articles already quoted) have all emphasized the Gidian aspects of Fellini's work. Alain Virmaux quotes this sentence from Gide's *Journal* (1899–1939): "J'aime assez qu'en une oeuvre d'art on retrouve ainsi transposé à l'échelle des personnages, *le sujêt même* de cette oeuvre." ("I rather like the idea that in a work of art one finds, transposed in this way to the scale of the characters, *the very subject* of the work.") I have underlined *"le sujêt même"* ("the very sub-

This triple-action construction gives the ending of the film, which has been variously interpreted, its true meaning. The version Fellini finally retained* contains not one but three successive denouements. In a first resolution, Guido abandons his film because it would have been confused, disorderly, too close to his life to become a work; because it would have been reduced to a disparate series of echoes and resonances; because it would have carried no central message capable of unifying it; and finally, and above all, because it would not have changed his life. That is the meaning of Guido's symbolic suicide at the end of his stormy press conference, as well as of the last words of Daumier. In a second movement—the allegory of the fantastic rondo —the abandonment of the film returns Guido to his life, as he sees all those who have peopled it parading in front of him; he asks his wife to accept things as they are; he has given up, at the same time he has given up his film, that rather messianic hope of a "salvation" that would suddenly bring order to all the elements of his chaos and thus modify their profound meaning and lend them the perspective of the future. But it is at this moment that Guido—who is no longer a director but is again a man like other men—once more takes up his director's megaphone to direct the audience of his memories. Therefore the film will be made; it will have no central message, and it will not alter life, since it will be made out of the very confusion of life; but out of that very confusion *it will be made*. Notice that this second phase of the film's resolution heralds not only the existence of 8½ itself, but also the principle of its creation: It will be a film woven from the life of its author and possessing the disorder of his life. Things, however, do not stop there: Having organized his fantastic dance, Guido, holding his wife by her hand, *himself now enters the circle*. Is this merely the symbol of that complacent tenderness—Fellini's as well—that ties Guido to his own memories and to his own

---

ject"): Gide, one sees, was thinking less of ordinary "doubling in" than of the peculiar variety of "doubling in" I am discussing in these few pages. Similarly, one should remember that Gide was one of those who have used the term *"construction en abŷme."*

* Fellini had first planned another resolution. See Camilla Cederna, 8½ *de Fellini: Histoire d'un film* (Paris: Julliard, 1963).

dreams, and of which he has accused himself (not without some complacency and some tenderness) in earlier sequences? Are we not at last witnessing the final casting off of this great vehicle of a film, which, like a rocket freed from its various supports, will be able to soar on its true flight? Having entered the circle, Guido has also come to order; this author who dreamed of making 8½ is now one of the characters of 8½; he can give his hand to the maid, the producer, the cardinal, his mistress; he no longer needs his megaphone, for it is now Fellini's film that will commence. No longer is Guido at the center of the magic circle; now it is only the small child dressed in white, and blowing his pipe, the ultimate, and first, inspirer of the whole fantasy —Guido as a child has become the symbol of Fellini as a child, since, in any case, *the place of the director, which is now empty,* can only be occupied by a character external to the action of the film: by Fellini himself.

And so Fellini's film begins. And though one is right to underline the paradoxical and startling thing about 8½—that it is a powerfully creative meditation on the inability to create—the fact remains that this theme takes us back, beyond any possible affectation on Fellini's part, to a situation more fundamental and less paradoxical than it is occasionally said to be. Out of all the confusion we have witnessed in the film, an admirably constructed film and one that is as little confused as possible will, it is true, be born; but is this not simply because the last stage of creation—that voluntary awakening that *stops* the undefined course of things in order to *establish* the work—can never be described in the created work, which owes its creation only to that ultimate step back, to that infinitesimal yet gigantic instant that is all that separates Guido from Fellini?

10 The *Saying* and the *Said:* Toward the Decline of a Plausibility in the Cinema?

Very often in the cinema it is the *saying* that determines absolutely what is *said.* Not, to be sure, in the general inevitable sense, in which it always and everywhere determines it, but—in this art, which more than any other is linked to industry and to public fashion—in a more cruel, less healthy way: A tacit, generalized convention demands that the actual choice of film as means of expression, as a form of saying, limits from the very beginning the field of the sayable, and automatically results in the preferential adoption of certain subjects. There are, in the full sense of the term, *film subjects* (whereas one cannot speak of "book subjects" in the same way), and even certain *contents,* to the detriment of others, are reputed to be "cinematographic." An implicit and pessimistic correlation suggests that the cinema cannot say everything: Thus one often thinks of the film as if it were still—in every meaning of the word—silent.

The principal merit of the various "new cinemas" that have sprung up around the world in recent years is perhaps that they have tried to reverse the terms of this imprisoning quandary: Today, in vital films, the said often governs the saying. The "new" film-maker does not look for a film subject; he has something to say, and so he says it in film. Occasionally he also says it simultaneously in a book he is writing; or perhaps his film itself is a book, either his own, or the book of one of his friends'—or even a book that one of his friends likes especially. Indeed, for the art of the screen, to gain a little more freedom from the restrictions of what is sayable in film is to break down a little more the relative and too long maintained isolation of what one calls "cinematographic culture." The mad hope that the cinema would be able to say everything (the hope that inspired Alexandre Astruc to quip that he would make a film of Descartes's *Discours de la Méthode*) is still far from being realized—very far even from a more modest degree of realization than the goal Astruc provocatively suggested. Nevertheless, in the newer accents, which are more real and more diversified than those of the great films of the past, of the best recent films, the cinema is beginning to accept the challenge of that hope.

Film and the Three Censorships

This nascent liberation is taking place on two levels. The first is directly political and economic; the second is specifically *ideological,* and therefore ethical.

The mutilation of the contents of films is frequently the pure and simple result of political censorship, or of the censorship of "moral standards," in short of *censorship* proper. More frequently still, it is the result of commercial censorship: the self-censorship of the production for the sake of its commercial requirements; this is consequently a true *economic* censorship. It has this in common with the first type, that it is a censorship by institutions, and indeed the concept of "institutional censorship" would adequately describe both kinds. (If the second is self-censorship that is simply because the censoring institution and the censored institution are temporarily merged: Consider, for example, the Hayes Code). Institutional censorship, we know, is harsher on the film than on the book, the painting, or the piece of music, so that in the cinema the problems of content are linked to *external permission* much more directly than in the other arts.

As for the third censorship, *ideological* and moral (or immoral?) *censorship,* it does not derive from institutions, but from the excessive internalizing of institutions among certain film-makers, who, once and for all, have stopped trying (or have never tried) to break out of the narrow circle of recommended topics for films.

According to the precise levels on which they intervene in the process that leading from the idea to the film, these three censorships are ordered into a "natural" and very effectively restrictive gradation: Censorship proper mutilates distribution; economic censorship mutilates production; and ideological censorship mutilates invention.

If, as is the case, one frequently observes a very marked discrepancy between the contents of films that have actually been shot and what the cinema as a whole could say; if the modern spectator is in more than one instance a person who loves the cinema a great deal but rarely feels this way about any individual film—this is quite often the result of the two institutional censorships. From this point of view, the blossoming of "new cinemas" in Poland, Czechoslovakia, Brazil, Spain, West Germany, and other countries are all truly political victories, won against the inheritors of Stalinism or the rigidities of reaction. As for the common attempts among the "young directors" of all nations *to modify the profession*—reduced teams, smaller budgets, the use of friends, 16mm. techniques, "parallel" distribution, cooperative or subscription financing, etc.—they constitute, to the extent that they are successful, a victory over economic censorship.

There remains the actual ideological aspect of the problem; it is linked to the political and economic aspects, simultaneously as cause and consequence: The initial successes of the new schools are noticeably beginning to clean the ideological atmosphere of the cinema as a whole; conversely the struggles of which these initial successes are the fruit would never even have been undertaken had they not, in the minds of those who conducted them, been preceded by the idea or the image of what a more *emancipated* cinema could be.

The problem of the ideology of films nevertheless possesses a certain degree of autonomy; although it is both the cause and the consequence of the forms in which the *cinematographic institution* is clothed, the ideology of films is not actually that institution itself, nor its direct, mechanical reflection. Certain already old films, produced long before the first instances of liberation in the cinematographic profession, possessed a profoundly modern accent and are an authentic part of the "new" cinema. Moreover, and above all, it is not rare that ideological censorship alone is able to make many subjects disappear from the screens, *and many ways of treating those subjects,* which institutional censorship would not have repressed: If the history of the cinema up to 1965 has not shown a single character of a forty-five-year-old German yielding the impression of truth one derives from the son of the old architect in Jean-Marie Straub's *Nicht Versöhnt,* that is not the result of any institutional censorship but of an insidious *restriction of filmic possibilities* that is nothing other than the cinematographic aspect of the Plausible, which now remains to be studied more closely.

The Plausible (First Approach)

We know that Aristotle defined the Plausible (τό εἰχός) as the unity of that which is possible in the eyes of common opinion; and thus it is distinguished from the unity of that which is possible in the eyes of knowledgeable people (this second "possible" being presumably identical to the true possible, the *real possible*). The *arts of representation*—and the cinema is one of them, which, whether "realistic" or "fantastic," is always figurative and almost always fictional—do not represent all that is possible—all the possibles—but only the plausible possibles. The post-Aristotelian tradition—consider for example the concepts of credibility, seemliness, and propriety in the classical French writers of the seventeenth century—has extended this idea by adding to it a second variety of Plausibility, which is not entirely different from the first and not entirely absent from the thought of the Greek philosopher: Everything that conforms to the laws of an established genre is plausible. In the one case as in the other (i.e., common opinion, rules of the genre), it is in relation to *discourses,* discourses that have already been pronounced, that the Plausible is defined, and thus it appears as the effect of a *corpus:* The laws of a genre are derived from earlier examples of that genre—that is to say, from a series of discourses (unless they have been explicitly set forth in a special discourse, poetic art or other); and common opinion is simply an innumerable and scattered discourse since, in final analysis, it is composed of what people say. Thus, from its inception, the Plausible is a reduction of the possible; it is an *arbitrary* and *cultural* restriction of real possibles; it is, in fact, censorship: Among all the possibilities of figurative fiction, only those authorized by previous discourse will be "chosen."

For the classical French writers of the seventeenth century, it was plausible and reasonable (in the common opinion of the spectators at the royal court and in town—or their secret desires or hopes, for with the Plausible one is never far from the Desirable, just as with the Agreed-upon one is never far from the Proper) that Pyrrhus should appear to be a moderate and courteous prince, and not the rough warrior that in fact it had been his fate to be. It was plausible, too (in the laws of the comic "genre") that a character in a comedy should possess a single, official vice—avarice, preciosity—and that all the grotesque misadventures that inevitably befall him should be the direct consequence of that vice and that their relationship to it should be as the clear and joyous relationship of predicated manifestations to their immutable essence.

Cinematographic Plausibility

For a long time there existed—and there still exists today, though to a lesser extent, and that is already a great deal—a *cinematographic plausibility.* The cinema had its genres, which could not be mixed: the western, the gangster film, the opportunistic "dramatic comedy" in the French style, etc. We know that the western had to wait fifty years before turning to even such mildly subversive topics as weariness, discouragement, or old age: For half a century the young hero, healthy and invincible, was the only type of plausible man in the western (as concerns the protagonist at least); moreover he was the only type accepted by the legend of the West, which, in this instance, provided the precedent. In the last sequence of John Ford's *The Man Who Shot Liberty Valance*, the journalist indeed says, tearing up the pages on which his associate had written down the old senator's true story: "In the West, when the legend is more beautiful than the truth, we print the legend."

But there is more to the matter. It was the cinema as a whole that functioned—and that too often still functions—like a vast genre, an immense cultural province (province nonetheless), with its list of permissible specific contents, its catalogue of filmable subjects and suitable moods. In 1959 the critic Gilbert Cohen-Séat[1] observed that the contents of films could be classified under four main headings: the *marvelous* (with its brutal, therefore pleasurable, sense of uprooting), the *familiar* (with its "telling little details" humorously pointed out, but, as the author emphasized, "removed from the sphere of controversial problems, from sensitive topics"), the *heroic* (which satisfied an impulse of generosity that the spectator does not discharge in ordinary life) and, finally, the *dramatic* (which addresses itself directly to the affective tensions of the average spectator, but in a demagogic way—as the spectator himself would apprehend them—and never placing them in a broader perspective by which the public, even if it had not initially recognized these tensions, would eventually have the opportunity to resolve or to outgrow them. Thus, every film made for the average salesgirl, for example, only further imprisons her in her average, vainly tragic, or arbitrarily inhibiting salesgirl's problems: What should you do when a nice young man you like asks you for a date, but under conditions that make his intentions appear somewhat less than "uninvolved," etc.? (What the average insipid film will never tell you, because that would run counter to the common opinion of salesgirls as well as to the laws of films made for salesgirls, is that, for example—among the ten other ways of stating a pseudo-problem that has been shaped into an impasse, and is *therefore dramatically plausible*—the "involved" intentions of the nice young man, at least to the extent that they indicate the reality of a desire, that is to say, something other than indifference, are "involved" only in a certain sense—but to revitalize this sense would be to deflate the dramatic, and therefore to betray the plausibility peculiar to the genre; in this way the Plausible simply increases the alienations of each spectator).

Let us return to Gilbert Cohen-Séat's four types of filmic contents; if it is indeed the peculiarity of the richest and newest films (even if they were made in 1920) to slip through the mesh of this formidable four-way partition of the cinematographic *sayable,* how can one deny that this set of categories (or some similar classification, more perfected if necessary, but whose establishment would raise no great difficulties) more or less accounts for the majority of ordinary productions—that is to say, nine films out of ten.

In 1946, in the first issue of the review *Les Temps Modernes,*[2] Roger Leenhardt observed that the traditional cinema, aside from its formal aesthetic inventions, and considering only the level of the "content" itself, had come up with very little in fifty years: vast, simple landscapes (the desert, the sea, snow scenes, etc., but not subtle or complex landscapes like those around Aix-en-Provence, for example); the large city, crowds, the machine; the child and the animal; the great, elementary emotions (terror, violence, love, etc., but not emotions of another kind, such as those really occurring in our highly developed societies). The traditional cinema, the author concluded, has *taught* us few things, unless you consider that it has taught us the cinema itself as a new form of expression. Leenhardt's classification is obviously quite different from Gilbert Cohen-Séat's, yet both agree in ascertaining the existence of a restriction of the *said* specifically linked to the adoption of the film as a form of *saying*—in other words, a restriction at the very heart of that cinematographic Plausibility that only a few remarkable films of yesterday and today manage to avoid, and that, partially successful in their demands, the various schools of the "young cinema" as a whole have also managed to avoid.

Thus, behind the institutional censorship of films, around it, beside it—*beneath* it, but larger than it—the censorship of the Plausible functions as a second barrier, as a filter that is invisible but is more insidious than the openly acknowledged censorships: it bears on *all* subjects, whereas institutional censorship is concentrated around only a few political and "moral" aspects; it controls—and that is the worst thing about it—not exactly the subjects themselves, but the way the subjects are handled, that is to say, *the very content of films,* for the subject is not the content, it is only an initial, very general, characterization of that content.

To borrow the structuralist terminology of the linguist Louis Hjelmslev, one might say that the institutional censorships in the cinema regulate the *substance of the content,* or the subjects that correspond to nothing other than a classification (simultaneously brutal and vague, although quite real on its level) of the principal "things" a film can talk about: The "politically advanced" film or the film that is too "daring" is censored, while the "romance" or the "historical" movie is not, etc.—whereas the censorship of plausibility addresses itself to the *form of the content,* that is to say, to the manner in which the film speaks about whatever it is telling (and not just to that which it is speaking about) or, in final analysis, what it is *saying,* the real nature of its content. And that is why the restriction of plausibility affects virtually all films, through their subjects. In his Copenhagen lecture of 1953,[3] Louis Hjelmslev spoke indeed (in connection with the language of words) about the very large role that what is called ideology plays in the forming of content. The institutional censorships have never prohibited anyone from portraying an adolescent on the screen (i.e., level of the "subject" equals substance of the content); the reason one has had to wait for works that are relatively late in the history of the cinema and that are still very rare, like *Dernières vacances* (Roger Leenhardt), *Masculine-Feminine* (Jean-Luc Godard), *Loves of a Blond* (Milos Forman), or *Le Père Nöel a les yeux bleus* (Jean Eustache), to encounter adolescents in film who, in the specifics of how they were shown (i.e., the so-called level of the "tenor" equaling true content equaling form of the content), at last seem *convincing*—which is what one means when one says "real"—is because film for a long time remained hermetically sealed in a tradition of the *filmically plausible adolescent,* which tradition was itself subdivided into seven or eight main types of acceptable adolescents; they are, in their approximate order of historical appearance: (1) the heroic and overemotional "beau" of the silent movies; (2) the "nice young man" of the insipid, optimistic "dramatic comedy"; (3) the stammering, pimply teen-ager who provokes laughter; (4) the misfit with his heart in the right place (Carné's *Les Tricheurs*); (5) the dreadful juvenile delinquent, etc.

Content and Expression; Form and Substance

To distinguish between "form" and "tenor" in the cinema—or between "form" and "content"—makes it impossible to analyze either the film, the form, or the tenor. One will have to come around to seeing that, just as the film-maker's means of *expression* have both their own *substantial* qualities (that the image is not sound, that the non-linguistic sound is not speech) and their own *formal* organization (camera movements, cuts, splices, the image/speech relationship, use of the voice, etc.), the *content* of films also possesses its own substantial properties (it is one thing to speak of love, and another to speak of war)* and its own formal organization: It is one thing to speak of

* Of course to mention "love" and "war" as two distinct themes already implies a rudimentary organization and therefore an incipient forming of content. But that is another matter: In examining the relationships between form and substance in their widest range, one comes to see necessarily that one refers to the other *ad infinitem,* and all depends on what *level of analysis* one is placed. Thus, distinctions like a "romance," a "war film," etc. would really refer to the form of the content, for the person studying, for example, the thematic distribution of films produced in a certain country during a certain period. But for the person analyzing a specific film, whose subject is already determined, this subject will function somewhat like an initially amorphous underlying level of content-substance, which will receive a form (form of the content) by virtue of the approach peculiar to a film-maker whose "war film" would be different from all other war films. This approach in turn (if one agrees to give this term to the succession of main "war sequences" in the film under examination) will yield instances of substances to the person analyzing each one of its sequences in order to study their internal structure more closely, etc.

But the level we are considering is that of the film and not that of the *group of films* (i.e., production of one country, or of one director, production of a period, etc. nor of the *part of the film* (episode, sequence, shot, etc.). It is on this level that the subject functions as the substance of the content, and the approach (true content) as the form of the content. (*Continued*)

love in *Sissi impératrice* [or *Love Story*—TRANSLATOR] and another to speak of love in *Senso*. Except in the scholarly rhetoric of schools and colleges, form has never been distinct from content ("content" is anyway meaningless); it has always been contrasted to substance, or to matter. As for the content—that is, the contained—form is not what it is contrasted to (since, to be intelligible, it must have some form itself), but obviously it distinguishes itself from the *containing*, that is to say, from expression—a purely methodological distinction (like the preceding one), which does not imply real separation but amounts simply to a recognition that every object of language (including film) has an aspect that is manifest and an aspect that manifests. This distinction, which is the distinction between the significate and the signifier, is used to differentiate between what can always be seen and what must always be looked for.

It is for these reasons that the first successes of modern cinema against the institutional censorships, successes that have value already in themselves, have implications that go beyond merely themselves: They allow one to hope that not only the subjects of films but also the reality of their content (the form of their content), will gradually become freer, more diversified, and more mature.

The Possibilities of Reality and the Possibilities of Discourse

The Plausible, I said, is *cultural* and *arbitrary*: I mean that the line of division between the possibilities it excludes and those it retains (and even promotes, socially) varies considerably according to the country, the period, the art, and the genre. Thus the plausible film gangster in America wears a trenchcoat and a fedora, whereas in France (except in cases of imitation of the American cinema) he has the natural traits of a Robert Dallan—his appearance less neat, short back-combed hair, and a strong "gutter-accent." (Similarly, the

---

More generally, one will observe that the distinction between form and substance, like all concepts having some depth, has the peculiarity of being simultaneously relative and absolute: relative *amid* the diversity of cases to which it applies, absolute *within* each one of them, therefore in some way absolute itself.

plausible woman in French literature of the eighteenth century was nimble and healthy, whereas in 1830 she was virtuous and languishing).

But such variations affect the content, and not the status, of the Plausible—which resides in the very existence of a line of division, in the actual act of the restriction of possibilities. Always and everywhere the work that is bogged down in pure Plausibility is a closed work, and it adds no new possibility to the "corpus" of previous works in the same genre and in the same civilization: The Plausible is the reiteration of discourse. Everywhere and always, the work that is partially freed from the Plausible is an open work, a work that, here and there, enacts or re-enacts one of the possibilities of life (if it is a "realistic" work) or of the imagination (if it is a "fantastic" or "nonrealistic" work), whose previous exclusion through the plausibility of earlier works had succeeded in losing it from memory. For it is never directly through the observation of real life (in realistic works) nor directly through the exploration of real imagination (nonrealistic works) that the content of the work is determined in the creative act; it is always to a great extent in relationship to earlier works in the same art: The director who intends to film life, or to film fantasy, always does so, to a much greater extent than he is aware of, in relation to other films—if only by the fact that what he will produce will not be, in the end, a section of life, or a body of fantasies, but a film. Since the film-maker shoots films, to some degree he often shoots the films of other people, believing that he is shooting his own. To tear oneself away, even partially, from an attraction so profoundly rooted in the very fact of culture, in the shape of *fields,* requires unusual strength of mind. Books reflect each other; so do paintings, and so do films.

The "easiest" possibilities, those most readily enacted by life, or in dreams, are extremely difficult to translate into fictional discourse: They must be transplanted, made to live in a world that is not the one in which they grew easily. Everything occurs as if the *real* possibilities, those of life and those of dreams, could only be admitted into discourse long after they had occurred, and then only singly, by degrees, so to speak; as if each one—far from benefiting from some easiness due to its frequent occurrence in another sphere—had, on the contrary, to be reconquered with great effort, at its root, and rather than being positively lifted out of the universe, it had to be contradictorily torn away from its very absence in prior discourse. To things that have not yet been *said* (however common their occurrence outside of "writing") there adheres an enormous weight that must be raised by whoever wants to say them first. The sayer's task is double therefore: In addition to the always considerable labor of saying things, he must also somehow say their exclusion from other sayings. The small, twisted tree, which is a common thing in Africa, becomes a rarity in Monaco where it is raised with constant care. Similarly, the "leftist" student one encounters every day in the Latin Quarter in Paris, but who was for a long time excluded from cinematographic plausibility and thus from the screen, has been obliged, in order to reappear, to wait for the diligence and talent of the author of *La Guerre est finie;* then the student was hailed as a wonderful new presence, as something never before seen, *and therefore as truth* (or, truth in art)—while those who applauded him had never ceased crossing his fellows in the street.

For a film heroine to exhibit, for even a fraction of a second, a gesture or an intonation that is true implies the success of a most difficult enterprise on the part of the film-maker; it is something that occurs once in a year, producing a shock in the viewer, and each time it occurs it renders forty films, retroactively devoted to the pure Plausible, obsolete in a single stroke.

Relative Plausibility;
Absolute Plausibility?

The Plausible and its opposite, the true, can only be defined in a manner both relative and absolute. An absolute criterion alone is not enough: There is no work entirely grounded in the Plausible (even the most conventional films can give us, for the duration of a few shots, a glimpse of something else), nor is there any work entirely free from all the plausibilities (it would have to be made by a super-man). It is equally obvious that the truths of today can become the plausibilities of tomorrow: The impression of truth, of a sudden lib-eration, corresponds to those privileged moments when the Plausible is burst open by some new point, or when a new possibility makes its appearance in the film; but once established, this possibility in turn becomes a fact of discourse and of "writing," and hence the germ at least of a new Plausibility: thus, for example, the "young Czech" approach to film, the small tender-ironic notations that, in a single stroke, greatly enriched what was sayable on the screen, has become in turn a form of saying and now runs the danger of no longer teach-ing us anything.

And yet, a purely relative definition of the Plausible—a relativistic definition—would also be inadequate: For each time that filmic plausibility yields a point there occurs at that point and at that mo-ment something like an absolute, irreversible increase of the sum of the filmable contents—and it is thus, in large part, that from one truth made plausible to another truth made plausible the cinema (an art younger and more naïve than its brothers, and in which, all things being equal, there remains more to be conquered) in the course of its development has gradually taken on more and more, and has said it more and more subtly.

The "truth" in artistic discourse is not directly connected to non-written truth (or "the truth of life"), but rather, passes by way of interior comparisons (explicit or not) into the field of art; it can, therefore, only be relative. But it is absolutely relative, for a new con-quest, which perhaps will die in the freshness of its truth, will at least definitively enrich the Plausible: and this, itself—no matter that it is continually reborn, each of its deaths is directly felt as an absolute moment of truth.

A Second Definition of the Plausible

But it should be understood that I have defined up to now, not the Plausible itself, but the conditions that make the Plausible possible, or, to put it differently, the stage that exists immediately prior to the Plausible. Indeed, this phenomenon of the restriction of possibilities occurring with the passage into "writing" is nothing other, in the end, than *convention* (or the "banal" or the "stereotyped"), that is to say: *that which permits the Plausible.*

Placed before the fact of convention (arbitrary and alienating restriction of possibilities), cultures have a choice between two main attitudes as different from each other as health is from sickness, or, perhaps, as the moral is from the immoral. The first attitude involves a sort of good conscience that is both lucid and primitive (see Hitchcock, for example), that proclaims and assumes convention, and that presents the work for what it is—that is to say, as the product of a controlled genre intended to be viewed as a performance of discourse in relation to the other works of the same "genre": Thus the language of the work refuses to encompass the underhanded devices designed to give the illusion that it could be translated into the terms of reality —it *rejects Plausibility,* in the full sense of the word, since it renounces the attempt to *appear true.* Works of this variety afford their spectators (who know the rules of the game) some of the most intense "aesthetic" enjoyment there is: The enjoyment of complicity, or of competence, of microtechniques, and of comparisons within a closed field. At its peak, the western gave cinephiles many of these pleasures. It was a kind of cinema that was extraordinarily healthy. This has been pointed out, but pointed out badly: For its health was not derived from the fact that it portrayed healthy things (heroism, the simple, frugal life, etc.), but that it portrayed them in a healthy way. It was like a ballet of stock figures and scrupulous rituals, a protocol in which surprising variations themselves were only ingenious and as yet unrealized combinations of a limited and pre-established number of basic elements. The classical western was healthy not because it spoke of horses and wide open spaces, but because it was frank. It belonged to the category of the *great controlled genres,* those genres that, plausible or not in the details of their peripatetics, in any case never seem to be true, for they never pretend to be anything other than discourses—the fairy tale, the epic, the myth, the oriental theater, etc., as well as large portions of Classicism.

The plausible work, on the contrary, lives out its conventions—and even its very nature as a fiction—in bad conscience (but, as we know, in good faith): It attempts to persuade itself, and to persuade the public, that the conventions that force it to restrict its possibilities are not laws of discourse or rules of "writing"—are not in fact conventions at all—and that their effect, observable in the content of the work, is in reality the effect of the nature of things and derives from the intrinsic character of the subject represented. The plausible work believes itself to be, and wants us to believe it to be, directly translatable into terms of reality. It is then that the Plausible attains its full use: Its function is to *make real*. The Plausible—rather than the conventional, for the latter is itself more or less plausible according to the case (thus the convention of the gangster film is more plausible than that of the classical western—is therefore that suspicious arsenal of devices and "tricks" whose purpose is to naturalize discourse and to hide control, even at the risk of being changed into actual signs in the eyes of the analyst, since their function is to be located always at the same place as one or another of the conventional points in the film, thus disguising it to the majority of the audience while drawing it to the attention of a minority. In this sense the Plausible, which is in principle the naturalization of the conventional rather than the conventional itself, nevertheless cannot but contain the conventional in its definition—and that is why, in this essay, I have approached it from the point of view of the restriction of possibilities; for it is only where the Plausible intervenes that naturalization occurs: There is no Plausibility, there are only plausible conventions. A convention that has not been made plausible is what it is: an implausible convention. The overturning of a specific convention is neither plausible nor implausible—it is simply true in the discourse, at the moment of its occurrence. The Plausible (the word says it sufficiently) is something that is not the true but does not seem too distant from the true: It is (uniquely) that which resembles the true without actually being the true. (I am not, of course, referring to the nonartistic meanings of the word "plausible." In everyday usage, "plausible" indicates a degree of logical possibility somewhere between the "possible" and the "probable": "Your explanation seems plausible to me." But this is an entirely different matter.)*

The "dramatic comedy" in the French style is the prime example of cinematographic plausibility, for each one of the conventions of this genre is scrupulously justified by a turn (if necessary, one that is specially produced for the occasion) in the "natural logic of the plot" or of the "psychology of the characters." The entire crooked arsenal of the transparent innuendoes and heavy-handed subtleties of French wit—especially in matters of the "heart," that is to say, of the body—is called upon to give a semblance of truth to the narrative. Does the producer demand a "happy ending" (a rule of the genre)? One will then see the unfaithful wife suddenly realize that her lover is even more worthless than her husband, and so she goes back to the latter ("the logic of feelings"). Does the genre (and common opinion) call for a few shots of "nudity"? In that case one will witness a conversation between husband and wife after an evening at the theater; in the foreground, the bedroom where the husband is undoing his tie in front of a mirror; in the background, the bathroom where the wife is undressing behind the half-open door: This opening, which is only natural since the couple is conversing, makes it

*"Plausible" and the term that Metz uses in French, *Vraisemblable,* do not entirely coincide. *Vraisemblable* is commonly used to indicate simple likelihood: *"Il est vraisemblable qu'il ne viendra pas demain."* ("It is likely he won't come tomorrow".) Hence Metz's parenthetical observation about the "nonartistic meanings of the word." *Plausible* may often have a negative connotation in English, when it implies a quality of speciousness, which *vraisemblable,* except in ironic comment, does not have. Finally, *vraisemblable* contains the two words *vrai* (true) and *semblable* (seeming like) that allow Metz to pun "The Plausible (*Le Vraisemblable*) . . . is that which resembles (*ressemble*) the true (*le vrai*) without actually being the true (*le vrai*)." Etymologically, *verisimilitude* would be a closer translation for *vraisemblable* than *plausible,* or *plausibility,* but it does not have the flexibility of the latter term. Incidentally, "plausible" has an etymological suggestiveness not inappropriate in this context, since it is derived from the Latin *plaudere,* to clap hands, which is also the root for *applause* (how common opinion signifies its acceptance and *approval.*) —TRANSLATOR.

plausible both that the heroine's semi-nudity be visible (dictate of the genre) and that it be not too visible (dictate of censorship and therefore of the genre also). Thus the film-maker kills two birds with one stone and has the additional merit of having given us a true picture of the bedtime ritual of a bourgeois Parisian couple (an example of "observation of human behavior," hence the film-maker's good faith). Does convention require—simultaneously and contradictorily, as is quite often the case—that the hero have a respectable and peaceful occupation (doctor, architect, etc.) but that there be a certain amount of violence in the film? No problem! The architect will be attacked in the street by a young hoodlum; the doctor, in charge of a clinic, will speak harsh words to a young intern who has been struggling desperately to perform his duties, but is short-tempered and in poor control of himself, etc. Each aspect of the protocol peculiar to the genre or to the common expectation of the spectators is thus turned around and, with utmost seriousness, disguised as one of those occurrences arising from freely observed experience. We are a long way indeed from the healthy good conscience—and the shameless bad faith—of the classical western, in which the most implausible and hastily assembled pretext (the hero accidentally bumps into the meanest outlaw of the country, who just happened to be in the saloon at the time, etc.) was sufficient to trigger—I mean to trigger in the *work*—the liturgical six-shooter show-down, worked out to a fraction of a second, which the viewer, with an artless and naughty cheerfulness, had been waiting for since the beginning of the film.

The Plausible and the New Cinema

There are two ways, then, and only two ways, to avoid the Plausible, which is the painful (and, might one say, "bourgeois?") phase of art. One can avoid it, so to speak, either before or after it occurs; the *true* genre films avoid it, and so do the *truly* new films; the moment in which one avoids it is always a moment of truth: In the first case it is the truth of a code that is freely assumed (within which, and thereby, it becomes possible to say many things), and in the second case it is the occurrence in discourse of a new possibility, which invests the corresponding point with a shameful conventionality.

It is no accident therefore that the champions of the "young cinema," the very ones who are attempting to broaden the field of the filmic sayable by reclaiming portions of it from exclusion from the cinematographic Plausible, often exhibit—as much in their spoken or written remarks as in frequent quotations and references within their own films—a nostalgic, amused, knowing, and infinitely appreciative sympathy for the true genre films (westerns, ganster films, musical comedies, etc.), films—most of them American, for it is doubtful whether there have been true genres in the cinema other than the American genres—that nevertheless would seem to represent a position contrary to the one that those who protect and extend their memory are striving for. Indeed, are not those films, those products of industry, the height of the manufactured, the triumph of a certain Hollywood machinery, the epitome of convention, whereas the young film-makers dream only of a free personal expression?

Yet—though they are not always clearly aware of it (for, in this as in other cases, ideology often lags behind practice)—what many film-makers of the new generation, through a romantic ideology of individual creation, are working at with a diligence and a talent that have already borne fruit, is the reduction, or the progressive relaxation, of the cinematographic Plausible with its corollary, the gradual enrichment of the filmic sayable (experienced as the "desire to say everything"). The enemy, whom they detest and whom they never mention, is—through and beyond the institutional censorships they rightly attack—the Plausible, that damp, intimate face of alienation, that unconfessed mutilation of the saying and the said; the Plausible, whose empire has extended, up to now, to almost every film produced, but which has not yet been able to annex, for reasons that are various yet ultimately similar, the genre films the young film-makers esteem and in which they find something like a mysterious secret of the cinema, and the new films, like those of the past that have nourished these film-makers, or those they want to make, or occasionally those they do make.

Notes

1

1. A Laffay, "L'évocation du monde au cinéma," in *Temps modernes,*
   1946. Reprinted in Laffay's *Logique du cinéma* (Paris, 1964), pp.
   15–30.
2. A. Bazin. See especially vol. II (*Le Cinéma et les autres arts,* 1959)
   of Bazin's *Qu'est-ce que le cinéma?* Paris: Éditions du Cerf, 1959),
   on the problem of adaptations, of filmed theater, of films about art,
   etc. [A condensed English-language version of the four volumes of
   Qu'est-ce que le cinéma? has been compiled and translated by Hugh
   Gray in *What Is Cinema?* (University of California Press, 1967)—
   Translator.]
3. R. Barthes, in *Communications,* no. 4, 1964 (special issue: "Recherches sémiologiques"), pp. 40–51.
4. *Ibid.,* p. 47.
5. E. Morin, *Le Cinéma ou L'homme imaginaire.* Paris: Éditions de
   Minuit, 1956, p. 123.
6. *Ibid.,* p. 122.
7. Albert Michotte van den Berck, "Le caractère de 'réalité' des projections cinématographiques," *Revue internationale de filmologie,* vol. I,
   no. 3–4, Oct. 1948, pp. 249–61.
8. *Ibid.,* pp. 257–58. What Albert Michotte van den Berck has defined
   is, of course, the "stereocinetic" effect whose importance in the cinema
   was underscored by Cesare Musatti in his article "Les Phénomènes
   stéréocinétiques et les effets stéréoscopiques du cinéma normal"
   (*Revue international de filmologie,* no. 29, Jan.-March 1957).
9. A. Michotte van den Berck, *op. cit.,* pp. 258–59.
10. "Ontologie de l'image photographique," in *Problèmes de la peinture*

(a collection of essays by different authors, published in 1945). Reprinted in *Qu'est ce que le cinéma*, vol. I, pp. 10–19. Translated into English under the title "The Ontology of the Photographic Image," in *What is Cinema?*

11. J. Leirens, *Le Cinéma et le temps*, Paris: Éditions du Cerf, 1954.
12. In *Esprit*, 1937.
13. J. Giraudoux, in "Théâtre et film," preface to *Le Film de la Duchesse de Langeais* (Paris, 1942). Reprinted separately in Marcel Lapierre's *Anthologie du cinéma* (Paris, 1946), pp. 297–302. Passage mentioned: p. 298.
14. Leirens, *Le Cinéma et le temps, passim.* and especially p. 28.
15. *Ibid.*, p. 113, in relation to film stars.
16. H. Wallon, *Revue internationale de filmologie*, no. 13, April-June 1953.
17. Michotte van den Berck, p. 256.
18. Wallon, "L'Acte perceptif et le cinéma."
19. Jean Giraudoux, "Théâtre et film," p. 299.
20. Mitry, *Esthétique et psychologie du cinéma* (Éditions Universitaires, Paris, 1963), vol. I, pp. 182–92.
21. *Ibid.*, p. 183.
22. Arnheim, *Film als Kunst* (Berlin: Rohwolt, 1932), p. 40. [Selections from this book have been reprinted in English in *Film as Art* (University of California Press, 1960)—TRANSLATOR.]
23. *Ibid.*, p. 39.
24. *Ibid.*, p. 40.
25. Bazin, "Ontologie de l'image photographique," in *Problèmes de la peinture* (collected works, 1945). Reprinted in *Qu'est-ce que le cinéma* (Éditions du Cerf, 1958.) Vol. I, pp. 10–19.

2

1. This text was written in the fall of 1966. The surge of interest, acknowledged in the first sentence of the essay, has not declined since; see, for example, the *Seminaire international sur les méthodes d'analyse du récit* (*International Seminar on the Methods of Analysis of the Narrative*) (Urbino, Italy, July 1967).
2. Gerard Genette has been interested in this problem of description and its relationship to narration; with greater detail, he reaches conclusions similar to those expressed here. See *Figures* (Paris, 1966) and also "Frontières du récit" in *Communications*, no. 8, 1966 (special issue "L'Analyse structurale du récit"), pp. 152–63, and especially pp. 156–59.
3. Albert Laffay, "Le Récit, le monde et le cinéma" (*Temps modernes*, May-June 1947); reprinted in *Logique du cinéma*, pp. 51–90. On the point under consideration, see especially pp. 81–82.

4. In "Problems of Denotation in the Fiction Film" (Chapter 5 of this volume) and also, somewhat differently, in "The Cinema: Language or Language System?" (Chapter 3 of this volume).

5. *Projêt de recherche collective sur le langage gestuel* (with A. Julien Greimas), 1966, mimeo; and also the article "Langage gestuel" in *Supplément scientifique à la Grande Encyclopédie Larousse*, 1968. Texts not reprinted in this selection.

3

1. *Cahiers du cinéma*, no. 94, April 1959. The interview was conducted by F. Hoveyda and J. Rivette.

2. J. Carta has analyzed Eisenstein's early conversion to montage. See "L'Humanisme commence au langage," in *Esprit*, June 1960, pp. 1113–32, and especially pp. 1114–16.

3. Pudovkin, in *Cinéa-Ciné pour tous*, Jan. 1, 1924. Reprinted in Pierre Lherminier's selection, *L'Art du cinéma* (Paris, 1960), pp. 189–200.

4. *Ibid.*, p. 190 in Lherminier's book.

5. R. Micha, "Le Cinéma, art du montage?" in *Critique*, Aug.-Sept. 1951, no. 51–52, pp. 710–24. For the idea I am discussing, see pp. 723–24.

6. See particularly the comparison between Griffith and Dickens in "Dickens, Griffith and the Film Today," Eisenstein's contribution to *Amerikanskaya Kinematografyia: D. U. Griffit* (Moscow, 1944). Reprinted in Jay Leyda's edition of *Film Form* combined with *The Film Sense* (New York: Harcourt, Brace, and Meridian, 1957), pp. 195–255.

7. R. A. Fowler, "Les débuts d'O. Welles à Hollywood," in *Revue du cinéma*, second series, no. 3, Dec. 1946, p. 13.

8. The concept is used here in a broadened sense derived from J. Kurylowicz, "Linguistique et théorie du signe," in *Journal de psychologie normale et pathologique*, vol. 42, 1949, p. 175. Besides, the idea of subordinating morphology to syntax, which is dear to this author, points in the same direction.

9. See Claude Lévi-Strauss, "La Notion de structure en ethnologie," paper delivered at the symposium on Social Structure, New York, 1952. Reprinted in *Structural Anthropology*.

10. Roland Barthes, "L'Activité structuraliste," in *Lettres nouvelles*, Feb., 1963, pp. 71–81.

11. Vol. III of *Qu'est-ce que le cinéma?* (*Cinéma et Sociologie*, 1961), pp. 172–73 (in a passage of the article "La Cybernetique d'André Cayette," which was originally published in *Cahiers du cinéma*, no. 36, 1954). [This article was not included in Hugh Gray's selection.—TRANSLATOR.]

12. Barthes, in *Arguments,* no. 27–28, 3d and 4th quarters, 1962, pp. 118–20.
13. A. Moles, "Poésie expérimentale, poétique et art permutationnel," in *Arguments,* no. 27–28, pp. 93–97.
14. Roland Barthes's expression.
15. See the next section, "From *Ciné Langue* to Cinema Language," for the over-all historical development.
16. The impression of reality is a factor common to both the realistic and fantastic film content. Many film theoreticians had felt this, suggested it, half said it before Edgar Morin established it solidly in *Le Cinéma ou L'homme imaginaire.* See Chapter 1 of this book.
17. In his manifesto on the montage of attractions (*Lef,* May 1923, Moscow). This idea was further developed by Eisenstein in *Notes of a Film Director,* R. Yurenev, translated by X. Danko, (Foreign Language Publications, Moscow, 1958).
18. Which Eisenstein's personal remarks (*passim.*) reflect, as do the works of Jay Leyda, B. Amengual, Jean Mitry, and others on Eisenstein.
19. G. Cohen-Séat, *Essai sur les principes d'une philosophie du cinéma,* rev. ed. (Paris: Presses Universitaires de France, 1958), p. 13.
20. Bazin speaks of them everywhere. His basic writing on the subject is "L'Evolution du langage cinématographique" (a synthesis of three earlier articles) in *Qu'est-ce que le cinéma?,* vol. I (*Ontologie et langage,* 1958). This essay is included in *What is Cinema? op. cit.* ("The Evolution of the Language of Cinema"), pp. 23–40.
21. These terms of Dziga Vertov's summarize perfectly the concept of "montage or bust." The first (*ciné phrase, film sentence*) is found in "Kinoki-Pereverot," the manifesto of the "Soviet Tronkh" (Vertov's "Group of the Three") which was published in *Lef* (Mayakovsky's review), May-June 1923 (the same issue that published Eisenstein's manifesto), reprinted in French in *Cahiers du cinéma,* no. 144 (June 1963) and 146 (Aug. 1963). The passage quoted is from p. 33 of *Cahiers* no. 144. The second term (*"ciné langue"*) is found in *Ciné-oeil* (Moscow, 1924) and is reprinted in M. Lapierre's *Anthologie du cinéma, op. cit.,* pp. 207–9.
22. Leenhardt, "Ambiguité du cinéma," lecture delivered on Sept. 2, 1957, and reprinted in *Cahiers du cinéma,* no. 100, Oct. 1959, pp. 27–38.
23. Jean Renoir, in *Radio-cinéma-télévision* (Nov. 22, 1959), *Cahiers du cinéma,* no. 100, Oct. 1959, and in many "remarks" elsewhere. What is more remarkable, he said the same thing as early as 1938, in *Point* (Dec. issue).
24. Astruc, manifesto published in *L'Écran français,* March 30, 1948.
25. Astruc, in *Ciné-Digest,* no. 1, 1949.

26. Marcel Martin, *Le Langage cinématographique,* Paris, 1955.

27. *Ibid.,* pp. 236–37.

28. Merleau-Ponty, lecture at the IDHEC (Institut des Hautes Études Cinématographiques), March 13, 1945. Published in *Sens et non-sens.*

29. *Ibid.*

30. Cohen-Séat, *Essai sur les principes* . . . , p. 128.

31. *Ibid.,* p. 119.

32. Especially Edgar Morin, *Le cinéma ou L'homme imaginaire, op. cit.,* pp. 55–90 (i.e., all of ch. 3).

33. F. Ricci, "Le Cinéma entre l'imagination et la réalité," in *Revue internationale de Filmologie,* no. 2, Sept.-Oct. 1947, pp. 161–63.

34. The concept and the terminology are from Edgar Morin, *op. cit.*

35. Morin, in "Le Rôle du cinéma," *Esprit,* vol. 38, June 1960, pp. 1069–79. For the point considered here, see p. 1071.

36. See especially L. Sceve, "Cinéma et méthode" in *Revue internationale de filmologie,* no. 1 (July-Aug. 1947), no. 2 (Sept.-Oct. 1947) and no. 3–4 (Oct. 1948). For the point considered: no. 2, pp. 172–74.

37. D. Dreyfus, "Cinéma et langage," in *Diogene,* no. 35, July-Sept. 1961.

38. Béla Balázs's expression (cf. further).

39. The passage was published (in a French translation) in P. Lherminier's anthology *L'Art du cinéma, op. cit.* See p. 208, for the idea I am discussing. Lherminier's text is based on the German edition of 1949, *Der Film* (Vienna, Globus Verlag), in which the author gathered together and condensed *Der Geist des Films* and *Der sichtbare Mensch oder die Kultur des Films.* [A selection of Balázs's main theoretical writings has been published in English: *Theory of the Film,* translated by Edith Bone (London, 1953)—TRANSLATOR.]

40. See F. R. Bastide, "Le Roman à l'echafaud," *Esprit,* vol. 28, June 1960, pp. 1133–41. For the point considered here: p. 1139.

41. This phenomenon has been well analyzed by F. Chevassu, in *Le Langage cinématographique* (Ligue Française de l'Enseignement, Paris, 1962), pp. 36–37.

42. Bazin, "Le Ces Pagnol," in *Qu'est-ce que le cinéma?, op. cit.,* vol. II, pp. 119–25. (This text is not included in Gray's selection.)

43. M. Pagnol's first manifesto: 1930. Second manifesto: 1933.

44. From Pagnol's second manifesto, "Cinématurgie de Paris," *Les Cahiers du film,* Dec. 15, 1933.

45. This was noted by R. Leenhardt in "Ambiguité du cinéma" (*op. cit.*). See *Cahiers du cinéma,* no. 100, p. 28.

46. Arnoux, in an article later included in *Du muet au parlant* (New edition, 1946). My reference is to P. Lherminier's selection (*op. cit.*) in which it appears with no references.

47. In *Zhizn Iskusstva* (Leningrad), no. 32, Aug. 5, 1928.
48. Souriau was speaking about "new film techniques" (Cinemascope, etc.) for the symposium on film effects in relation to new techniques (*Symposium sur les effêts de film en fonction de techniques nouvelles,* of the Second International Congress on Film, Paris, Feb. 1955). Reprinted in *Revue internationale de Filmologie,* no. 20–24 (1955), pp. 92–95. The above passage refers to p. 94.
49. Here and there the work has been begun: by B. Pingaud and J. Ricardou on Alain Resnais (*Premier plan,* no. 18, Oct. 1961); J. Carta on Resnais, Agnès Varda, and Chris Marker (*Esprit,* June 1960); and R. Bellour on the same film-makers (*Artsept,* no. 1, quarter, 1963).
50. Bazin, in "L'Avant-garde nouvelle" (*Festival du film maudit,* limited edition published in 1949 on the occasion of this same festival), reprinted in *Cahiers du cinéma,* no. 10, March, 1952, pp. 16–17.
51. De Saussure, *Course in General Linguistics,* translated by Wade Baskin (New York, 1959), p. 9.
52. *Ibid.,* p. 16.
53. C. Lévi-Strauss, "Structural Analysis in Linguistics and Anthropology," *Word,* Aug. 1945. Reprinted in *Structural Anthology* (New York, 1963).
54. De Saussure, *Course . . . , op. cit.,* p. 17.
55. In a text not included in this book, I have dwelt on the problem of the "articulations" in relation to non-linguistic semiotics: "Les sémiotiques, ou sémies. À propos de travaux de Louis Hjelmslev et d'André Martinet," *Communications,* no. 7, 1966.
56. See "On the Impression of Reality in the Cinema" (Chapter 1 of this book).
57. R. Jakobson, "On Linguistic Aspects of Translation," in *On Translation,* R. A. Brower, ed. (Harvard Studies in Comparative Literature, 1959).
58. "Arbitraire linguistique et double articulation," in *Cahiers F. de Saussure,* 15, 1957, pp. 105–16. Reprinted in *La Linguistique synchronique* (Paris, 1965), pp. 21–35. Passage mentioned: pp. 26–27.
59. J. Vendrys, ed., in *Le Langage, introduction linguistique à l'histoire,* Renaissance du livre, 1921.
60. See further on, "Cinema and Literature" (pp. 75–84).
61. E. Benveniste, "La Phrase nominale," *Bulletin de la Société de Linguistique de Paris,* vol. XLVI, 1950. Reprinted in *Problèmes de linguistique générale* (Gallimard, Paris, 1966), pp. 151–67.
62. Jakobson, "Results of the Conference of Anthropologists and Linguists," in *Supplement to International Journal of American Linguistics,* vol. 19, no. 2, April 1953.
63. E. Buyssens, *Les Langages et le discours,* Office de publicité, Brussels, 1943, ch. II, paragraph A, pp. 8–12.

64. A. Martinet, *Elements of General Linguistics,* translated by Elisabeth Palmer (London: Faber and Faber, 1960), p. 118.

65. From this point of view, Jean Mitry's book (*Esthétique et psychologie du cinéma,* vol. 1) represents considerable progress on many earlier works on the theory of the cinema.

66. De Saussure, p. 137.

67. L. Hjelmslev, "Stratification in Language," *Word,* 10, 1954. Reprinted in French in *Essais linguistiques* (Copenhagen, 1959). For the taxeme, see pp. 40 and 58 of the *Essais.* . . .

68. G. Guillaume, "Observation et explication dans les sciences du langage," in *Études philosophiques,* 1958, pp. 446–62. Passage under consideration: pp. 446–47.

69. C. Bally, "Sur la Motivation des signes linguistiques," in *Bulletin de la Société de Linguistique de Paris,* 1940, vol. XLI, pp. 75 ff., and specifically p. 87.

70. S. Ullman, pp. 341–43 of *Journal de psychologie normale et pathologique,* 1958 ("Orientations nouvelles en Semantique"). See also *Précis de semantique française,* Bern, 1952, *passim.*

71. Already noted by Roland Barthes in "Les Unités traumatiques au cinéma," *Revue internationale de filmologie,* no. 34, July-Sept. 1960.

72. Notably by M. Martin, *Langage cinématographique,* pp. 152–54.

73. I have already spoken about filmic intellection elsewhere. In addition, pages 194–200 of Edgar Morin's book (*Le cinéma ou L'homme imaginaire*) are very enlightening on this question.

74. See pp. 40–42 of this book.

75. Gilbert Cohen-Séat, *Essai sur les principes* . . . , pp. 145–46.

76. C.f. Étienne Souriau's famous distinction between the representational and the nonrepresentational arts, also with a remark in the same vein in connection with the cinema and its poetry in D. Dreyfus, "Cinéma et langage" and in connection with the cinema, as early as 1927, L. Landry, "Formation de la sensibilité," *L'Art cinématographique,* no. 2, p. 60.

77. The terms are used in Hjelmslev's sense. See all of the last part of *Prolemomena to a Theory of Language,* Indiana University Publications in Anthropology and Linguistics, 1953 (the English translation of a work originally published in Danish in 1943).

78. See Jean Mitry, *Esthétique et psychologie du cinéma,* "Le Mot et l'image," pp. 65–104 of vol. 1.

79. Mikel Dufrenne, *Phénoménologie de l'expérience esthétique* Paris: Presses Universitaires de France, 1953, vol. 1 (*L'objêt esthétique*), pp. 240 ff.

80. De Saussure, *Course* . . . , p. 66.

81. E. Buyssens, *Les Langages et le discours,* ch. 5, pp. 44–48.

82. See Roland Barthes's diagram at the end of *Mythologies* (Paris, 1957), p. 222.

83. J. Vendryes, "Langage oral et langage par gestes," *Journal de psychologie normale et pathologique,* vol. XLII, 1950, pp. 7–33; passage referred to on p. 22.

84. E. Buyssens, *Les Langages et le discours,* ch. IV, paragraph A, pp. 34–42.

85. C. Lévi-Strauss, "The Structural Study of Myths," *Myth, a Symposium.* Reprinted in *Structural Anthropology* (New York, 1963).

86. V. Propp, *Morphology of the Folktale* (Mouton and Co., 1958). Each one of the "functions" the folktale is divided into is characterized by an abstract substantive (prohibition, transgression, pursuit, etc. . . .); each of the abstract substantives corresponds to the substantiation of a sentence predicate as Walter Porzig, for example, has shown ("Die Leistung der Abstrakta in der Sprache," *Blatter fur deutsche Philosophie* IV, 1930, pp. 66–67).

87. Barthes, *Mythologie, op. cit.,* pp. 215–17 ("Le Mythe est une parole").

88. "Entretien avec Roland Barthes," an interview with Barthes conducted by M. Delahaye and J. Rivette for *Cahiers du cinéma,* no. 147, Sept. 1963, pp. 22–31. Passage referred to: pp. 23–24 ("Macrosemantique").

89. G. Mounin, "Les systèmes de communication non-linguistiques et leur place dans la vie du vingtième siecle," *Bulletin de la Société de Linguistique de Paris,* vol. LIV, 1959 (the entire article).

90. R. Jakobson, "Closing Statements: Linguistics and Poetics," *Style and Language,* Th. A. Seboek, ed. (MIT Press, 1960), pp. 352–53.

91. Mounin, "Les Systèmes de communications non-linguistiques . . ." *op. cit.*

92. *Ibid.,* p. 187.

93. Jean Fourquet, "La Notion du verbe," *Journal de psychologie normale et pathologique,* 1950, pp. 74–98. Louis Hjelmslev, "Le Verbe et la phrase nominale," *Mélanges de philologie, de litérature et d'histoire offerts à J. Marouzeau,* 1948, pp. 253–81, reprinted in *Essais linguistique (op. cit.),* pp. 165–91. (The verb as "clause connecting," p. 190). Émile Benveniste, "La Phrase nominale," *Bulletin de la Société de Linguistique de Paris,* vol. XLVI, 1950; reprinted in *Problèmes de linguistique generale (op. cit.),* pp. 151–67. (The double "verbal function:" cohesive and assertive; the verb as "predicate of reality.") André Martinet, "La Construction ergative," *Journal de psychologie normale et pathologique,* July–Sept. 1958; reprinted in *La Linguistique synchronique* (Paris, 1965), pp. 206–22. (The concept of the "predicate of existence," in connection with Basque syntax.)

94. A. Martinet, *Elements of General Linguistics,* p. 23.

95. É. Benveniste, *Les Langages* . . . ch. III, paragraph C, pp. 30–33 ("Parole, discours, langue").

96. Eric Buyssens's term.

97. "Principes de bibliographie et de documentation," a study by Claude Brémond summarized by Gilbert Cohen-Séat in *Problèmes actuels du cinéma et de l'information visuelle* (Paris, 1959), vol. 2, pp. 79–88. Passage referred to: p. 79.
98. This is Gilbert Cohen-Séat's famous distinction; see *Essais sur les principes* . . . , p. 54.

4

1. F. de Saussure, *Course* . . . , p. 16.
2. De Saussure, *Les langages et le discours*, ch. I, p. 5.
3. Balázs, *Theory of the Film* (London, 1952), *passim.*, and more specifically ch. III (pp. 30–32, "A New Form-Language") and ch. VI (pp. 46–51, "The Creative Camera").
4. A. Malraux, "Esquisse d'une psychologie du cinéma," *Verve*, 2–8, 1940. (Separately published by Gallimard, Paris, 1946.) Essentially, this essay constitutes the chapter on "The Cinema" in *Musée imaginaire* (in *Psychologie de l'art*). Also published in Marcel L'Herbier's selection *L'Intelligence du cinéma* (Paris, 1945), pp. 372–84. Passage mentioned: pp. 375–76 of the last work.
5. E. Morin, *Le Cinéma ou L'homme imaginaire*, all of ch. III (pp. 55–90, "Metamorphose du cinématograph en cinéma.").
6. J. Mitry, *Esthétique et psychologie du cinema*, vol. I, *passim.*, and especially pp. 157–65 (paragraph 30, pp. 149–65, "Les Plans et les angles").
7. Malraux, "Esquisse d'une psychologie du cinéma."
8. D. W. Griffith, U.S.A., 1911.
9. Tchardynine, Russia, 1911.
10. E. Guazzoni, Italy, 1912.
11. Louis Feuillade, France, 1913.
12. Giovanni Pastrone, Italy, 1914.
13. Henrik Galeen, Germany, 1914.
14. Thomas Ince, U.S.A., 1914.
15. D. W. Griffith, U.S.A., 1915.
16. G. Sadoul, "Georges Méliès et la première élaboration du langage cinématographique," *Revue internationale de filmologie*, no. 1 (July-Aug. 1947), pp. 23–30.
17. In 1898, in *La Caverne maudite*, *Rêve d'artiste*, and *L'Atelier du peintre*.
18. Also in 1898, in *Les Quatres têtes embarrassantes* and *Dédoublement cabalistique*.
19. In 1898, also.
20. In 1899, in *Panorama de la Seine*.
21. J. Mitry, *Esthétique et psychologie du cinéma*, vol. 1, pp. 157–65 and 269–79.

22. See also F. de Saussure (*Course* . . . , p. 137): "Not all the facts of the syntagmatic class belong to syntax, but all the facts of syntax belong to the syntagmatic class."

23. In Louis Hjelmslev's sense: see all of the last part of *Prolegomena to a Theory of Language*.

24. In "The Cinema, Language or Language System?" (Chapter 3 of this book).

25. See for example Rudolf Arnheim, *Film als Kunst*, pp. 73–74; Jean Mitry, *Esthétique*. . . . vol. 1, pp. 337–46; Marcel Martin, *Le Langage cinématographique*, ch. VII (pp. 86–99, "Métaphores et symboles"), etc. It is the entire controversy about the "pure cinema" that should be mentioned here.

26. T. Sebeok, "Decoding a Text: Levels and Aspects in a Cheremis Sonnet," in *Style and Language*, pp. 221–35.

27. S. Levin, *Linguistic Structures in Poetry* (The Hague: Mouton and Co., 1962).

28. *L'Univers filmique* (Paris, 1953), a collective work under the direction of Étienne Souriau. For the concept of diegesis: Preface, p. 7. See also, by the same author, "La Structure de l'univers filmique et le vocabulaire de la filmologie," in *Revue internationale de filmologie*, no. 7–8, pp. 231–40.

29. M. Dufrenne, *Phénoménologie de l'expérience esthétique*, vol. I, pp. 240 ff.

30. R. Barthes, "Rhetorique de l'image," *Communications*, no. 4, Nov. 1964, pp. 40–51. Passage mentioned: p. 46.

31. André Martinet, *Elements of General Linguistics*. Passage referred to: 4.19, pp. 110–11 ("Lexemes and morphemes; modifiers"). Also Luis J. Prieto, *Principes de néologie* (London: Mouton and Co., 1964) (Janua Linguarum, minor series, XXXV). Passage referred to: 5.12, pp. 125–27 ("Oppositions grammaticales et oppositions lexicales").

32. R. F. Mikus, in *Lingua*, Aug. 1953, pp. 430–70. Passage referred to is section 18.

33. See Eric Buyssens, *Les Langages et le discours, op. cit.*, III B (pp. 22–30: "Distinction entre acte sémique et sème") and VIII C (pp. 74–82, "Modalité et substance du discours").

34. E. Souriau, "Les Grands caractères de l'univers filmique," in *L'univers filmique*, pp. 11–31. Passage referred to: pp. 30–31.

35. F. de Saussure always defined the linguistic signifier as an "acoustic image," not as a muscular or phonatory image. It is, therefore, a fact of hearing, and not of locution (*Course* . . . , pp. 13 and 66). The same idea is found among de Saussure's editors, Charles Bally and Albert Sechehaye, in their note on p. 66 of *Course* . . . , and, in greater detail, in Bally's *Le Langage et la vie*: It is by way of the listeners the individual innovations may become facts of idiom.

36. In vol. II of his *Esthétique* . . . , Jean Mitry develops the idea that what we call a filmic "metaphor" is always, fundamentally, a metonymy (see p. 447 of Mitry's book). Incidentally, I am not in entire agreement with this analysis: see "Problèmes actuels de théorie du cinéma" (not included in this book), in *Revue d'esthétique,* vol. XX, installment 2–3, April-Sept. 1967, special issue on the cinema, pp. 180–221; for the point under discussion see pp. 213–17.

37. De Saussure, *Course* . . . , part I, ch. II, pp. 71–78, "Immutability and Mutability of the Linguistic Sign."

38. Anne Souriau, "Succession et simultaneité dans le film," in *L'univers filmique,* pp. 59–73. Passage referred to: p. 68.

39. See for example Rudolf Arnheim, *Film as Art,* p. 96, or Marcel Martin, *Le Langage cinématographique,* pp. 148–49 (definition of "parallel montage").

40. E. Benveniste, "Structure des relations de personne dans le verbe," in *Bulletin de la Société de linguistique de Paris,* XLIII, 1946 (dated 1947), pp. 1–12; reprinted in *Problèmes de linguistique générale,* pp. 225–36. The "correlation of personality" distinguishes the third person (which is in fact a nonperson) from the first and second persons, which together constitute the marked term of the first correlation, within which the "correlation of subjectivity" (second correlation) distinguishes the first person (marked) from the second person (unmarked).

41. On the one hand in Chapters 3 and 5 in this book; on the other, in a number of texts not printed here: "Une étape dans la réflexion sur le cinéma" (a review of Jean Mitry's *Esthétique* . . . , vol. 1), in *Critique,* no. 214, March 1965, pp. 227–48 (for the point under consideration: pp. 228–34); also "Problèmes actuels de théorie du cinéma" (see ref. 36), pp. 213–21 for the point considered here.

42. See Albert Laffey, *Logique du cinéma*—the underlying idea of the book, and more specifically ch. III, pp. 51–90.

43. "Stratification in Language" *Word* X, pp. 163–88. Reprinted in *Essais linguistiques,* pp. 36–68. The taxeme: pp. 57 and 65.

44. L. Hjelmslev, *Elements of General Linguistics,* 3.12 ("Relevant features"), pp. 62–64.

5

1. See Chapter 3 of this book.

2. U. Eco, notably in his contribution to the round-table discussion on the theme of *Ideology and Language in the Cinema,* held in the framework of the Third Festival of the New Cinema (*Pesaro III,* Italy, June 1967). The substance of his discussion was reprinted in *Appunti per una semiologia delle communicazioni visivi* (Universita di Firenze, Bompiani Editore, 1967), pp. 139–152.

In his contribution to the discussion at Pesaro, Umberto Eco raised a number of objections to the concept of analogy presented here; in the paragraphs above I have taken into account my conversations with him at Pesaro, reminders of which one will also find in the Italian author's *Appunti* . . . , p. 141.

3. For references concerning Pasolini's theory of the *"im-segno,"* and for a resumé and discussion of his theory, see Chapter 6. The concept of the im-segno, despite my objections to it, is a very stimulating one and has helped me greatly to clarify my own thoughts about superposition of several distinct levels of organization at the heart of the "cinema" as a whole.

4. Greimas, *Sémantique structurale.*

5. B. Pottier, *Systematique des éléments de relation,* doctoral thesis, 1955; published in the same form in 1962 (Klincksieck, Paris). The concept of the seme, in the sense we are interested in here, is defined in Pottier's thesis, although the actual term occurs later, in *Recherches sur l'analyse sémantique en linguistique et en traduction mécanique* (Publications de la faculté des lettres de Nancy, 1963).

6. See Chapter 4.

7. The following passage is a repetition of the passage on p. 26.

8. In André Martinet's sense. See *Elements* . . . , p. 116.

9. P. Pasolini, "Le Cinéma de poésie," contribution to the First Festival of the New Cinema (*Pesaro I,* Italy, June 1965). Published in *Cahiers du cinéma,* no. 171, Oct. 1965, pp. 55–64. The passage referred to: pp. 55–56.

10. Mitry, *Esthétique* . . . , vol. 2, p. 381.

11. On this point, see Chapter 4.

12. See *Cinéma et langage* (doctoral thesis), in progress.

13. In "La Grande syntagmatique du film narratif," one of the three articles that were fused together to form this text.

14. "Considerations sur les éléments sémiologiques du film," a paper presented at the round-table discussion, *Per una nuova coscienza critica del linguaggio cinematografico* (*Pesaro II,* Italy, 1966). Minutes published in *Nuovi Argomenti* (Italy), new series, no. 2, April-June 1956. See pp. 46–66 for my contribution "Considerationi sugli elementi semiologici del film." (This text is not reproduced here; the first part presented an early version of my table of the large syntagmatic category.)

15. In "Un Problème de sémiologie du cinéma," one of the three articles this text is based on.

16. "Problèmes de denotation dans le film de fiction: Contribution à une sémiologie du cinéma" (the third of the initial articles).

17. In an analysis that constitutes Section III (originally texts 6 and 7) of the French edition of this book (see Author's Foreword).

18. On this point see "Le Cinéma, monde et récit," in *Critique,* no. 216, May 1965 (article not included here).
19. I have already spoken about description and its relationship to narration and to the image in another context, in Chapter 2 of this book.
20. Particularly A. Michotte van den Berck, *op. cit.,* pp. 249–61, and specifically pp. 252–54 ("l'effèt écran").
21. Mitry, *Esthétique* . . . , vol. II, pp. 9–61.
22. See my article "'Montage' et le discours dans le film. Un problème de sémiologie diachronique du cinéma" (not included in this book) in *Hommage à André Martinet,* 1968.
23. See Chapter 3. Also my article "Une Étape dans la réflexion sur le cinéma" (not included in this volume), *Critique,* no. 214, March 1965, pp. 227–48, and especially pp. 228–30.
24. See Chapter 4.
25. For the precise meaning of this term, see Chapter 3, second footnote p. 78.
26. By Souriau, in his study discussed in Chapter 4.
27. On this problem of filmic intellection, see Chapter 3.
28. "La Structure morphologique," a paper written for the 5th International Congress on Linguistics, 1939 (the congress was interrupted by the declaration of war, but the paper had been printed before the congress convened). Reprinted in *Essais linguistiques, op. cit.,* pp. 113–38. See especially pp. 123–28.
29. Gilbert Cohen-Séat's term (*Essai sur les principes* . . .).
30. On this question of the "encounter of the cinema and narrativity," and on its importance, see Chapters 3 and 4.
31. I took this point of view in Chapter 2 of this work.
32. See particularly C. Brémond, "Le Message narratif" (*Communications,* no. 4, 1964, special issue: "Recherches sémiologiques," pp. 4–32, and specifically pp. 31–32. Also "La Logique des possibles narratifs" (*Communications,* no. 8, 1966, special issue: "L'analyse structurale du récit," pp. 60–76).

8

1. "Qu'est-ce que le cinéma moderne? Tentative de réponse à quatre voix" (Pierre Billard, Rene Gilson, Michel Mardore, Marcel Martin), in *Cinéma 62,* Jan. 1962, no. 62, pp. 34–41 and 130–32. This debate produced no great revelations, but the ideas expressed in it correspond fairly well to the main interpretations commonly held at this time about the modern cinema.
2. *Ibid.,* p. 35.
3. *Ibid.,* p. 41.
4. *Ibid.,* pp. 37–38 (Mardore) and p. 38 (Billard).
5. *Ibid.,* p. 130.

6. *Ibid.,* p. 131.
7. *Ibid.,* p. 131.
8. *Ibid.,* p. 36. Also, especially: Marcel Martin, "Le Cinéma moderne, spectacle ou langage?", *Cinéma 62,* pp. 45–53 (portions of the conclusion of the new edition of *Le Langage cinématographique, op. cit.,* 1962). Martin's thesis is most clearly expressed on p. 49 of the article.
9. On the one hand: Interview with Bernardo Bertolucci and Jean-Louis Comolli in *Cahiers du cinéma,* no. 169, Aug. 1965, pp. 22–25 and 76–77. On the other hand: "Le Cinéma de poésie" (paper delivered, June 1965, at the First Festival of the New Cinema, Pesaro, Italy); published in *Cahiers du cinéma,* no. 171, Oct. 1965, pp. 56–64. The idea I am referring to is most clearly expressed on p. 24 of the interview.
10. J. Carta, "L'Humanisme commence au langage," *Esprit,* June 1960 (special issue: "Situation du cinéma français"), pp. 1113–32.
11. B. Balázs *Theory of Film,* (*op. cit.*), pp. 250–52. Distinction between the "epic" and the "dramatic"; the novel belongs to the epic category; the theater, and in some respects the cinema, to the dramatic category.
12. Interview with Michel Delahaye and Jacques Rivette, *Cahiers du cinéma,* no. 156, June 1964, pp. 19–29. Passage referred to: p. 20.
13. B. Pingaud, "Nouveau roman et nouveau cinéma," *Cahiers du cinéma,* no. 185, Dec. 1966 (special issue: "Film et roman: problèmes du récit"), pp. 27–41.
14. E. Souriau, "Les Grands caractères de l'univers filmique," in *L'univers filmique,* pp. 11–31. See p. 15.
15. P. Hadiquet, "En marge des festivals de courts métrages de Cracovie," *Image et son,* no. 187, Oct. 1965, pp. 33–36. Passage referred to: pp. 33–34.
16. Mitry, *Esthétique* . . . , vol. I, pp. 129–31, and *passim.*
17. M. Martin, "Notes sur la localisation et les déplacements du point de vue dans la description romanesque," *Revue des lettres modernes,* Summer 1958, no. 36–38 (special issue: "Cinema et roman"). This "subjectivism" by one of the leading upholders of the objective school has been carefully discussed by Bernard Dort ("Un Cinéma de la description," *Artsept,* no. 2, April-June 1963, pp. 125–30), and especially by Gerard Genette ("Vertige fixe," postscript to the 10/18 edition of *Dans le Labyrinthe,* 1964, pp. 273–306).
18. See Jean-Claude Bringuier, "Libres propos sur le cinéma-verité," *Cahiers du cinéma,* no. 145, July 1963, pp. 14–17, and specifically p. 15.
19. I have attempted to describe it to a great extent in Chapter 10, of this volume.
20. The reader will note that my category of the "ordered cinema" partly overlaps on that of the "real cinema" as defined by Raymond Bellour in "Un Cinéma réel," *Artsept,* no. 1, 1st quarter, 1963, pp. 5–27.

21. Previously mentioned debate (see ref. 1), p. 35.
22. See Eric Rohmer, "L'Ancien et le nouveau," Interview in *Cahiers du cinema*, no. 172, Nov. 1965, pp. 33–42 and 56–59. Passage referred to: p. 34.
23. Pingaud, in his article mentioned above (ref. 13).
24. Interview with Bernardo Bertolucci and J.-L. Comolli, p. 22. Also "Le Cinéma de poésie," p. 55.
25. See pp. 211–16, including footnote, p. 214.
26. Pasolini, "Le Cinéma de poésie," p. 60.
27. Mitry, *Esthétique . . .* , vol. I, pp. 359–62.
28. Previously mentioned interview, p. 22.
29. *Ibid.*, p. 22. "Le Cinéma de poésie," especially p. 63.
30. E. Rohmer, "L'Ancien et le nouveau," p. 33.
31. De Saussure, *Course . . .* , p. 137.
32. For this concept, see Chapter 3 of this volume.
33. For these concepts see Chapter 5.
34. Pasolini, "Le Cinéma de poésie," p. 55.
35. Interview (already mentioned), p. 22. "Le Cinéma de poésie," p. 55.
36. A. Laffay, *Logique du cinéma, passim.*, and especially p. 81.
37. Pasolini, "Le Cinéma de poésie," p. 56.
38. *Ibid.*, p. 56.

9

1. With regard to the cinema: Alain Virmaux, "Les limites d'une conquête," *Études cinématographiques*, no. 28–29, 4th quarter, 1963, pp. 31–39. For the term *"construction en abŷme,"* see p. 33.
2. *Ibid.*
3. *Ibid.*
4. R. Bellour, "La splendeur de soi-même," *Études cinématographiques*, pp. 27–30.
5. C. Jacotey, "Bilan critique," *Études cinématographiques*, pp. 62–68.
6. P. Kast, "Les petits potamogetons," *Cahiers du cinéma*, no. 145, July 1963, pp. 49–52.
7. Pierre Kast (p. 52), Alain Virmaux (p. 33), Raymond Bellour (p. 28): previously mentioned articles. Also Max Milner, "8½," *Etudes*, Sept. 1963.

10

1. G. Cohen-Séat, *Problèmes actuels du cinéma et de l'information visuelle*. Passage referred to: pp. 35–37 of vol. 2 (in the chapter "Le Contenu des films," pp. 35–43).
2. This idea was again expressed by Roger Leenhardt in a lecture delivered on Sept. 22, 1957, at Aix-en-Provence, for the *9e Congrès des*

sociétés de philosophie de la langue française. The title of the lecture was "Ambiguité du cinéma." It was published in *Cahiers du cinéma,* no. 100, Oct. 1959, pp. 27–38. Passage referred to: pp. 33–34.

3. Hjelmslev's lecture was delivered at the foundation anniversary of the University of Copenhagen, Nov. 26, 1963. Its title was "The Content Form of Language as a Social Factor." It is reprinted in *Essais linguistiques op. cit.,* pp. 85–95. Passage referred to (on the concept of ideology): p. 93.